MARIE DE FRANCE & THE POETICS of MEMORY

MARIE DE FRANCE & THE POETICS *of* MEMORY

LOGAN E. WHALEN

THE CATHOLIC UNIVERSITY
OF AMERICA PRESS
WASHINGTON, D.C.

Copyright © 2008
The Catholic University of America Press
All rights reserved

The paper used in this publication meets the minimum
requirements of American National Standards for Information
Science—Permanence of Paper for Printed Library Materials,
ANSI Z39.48-1984.

∞

LIBRARY OF CONGRESS CATALOGING-IN-PUBLICATION DATA
Whalen, Logan E.
Marie de France and the poetics of memory / Logan E. Whalen.
p. cm.
Includes bibliographical references and index.
ISBN 978-0-8132-1509-9 (cloth : alk. paper) 1. Marie, de France,
12th cent.—Criticism and interpretation. I. Title.
PQ1495.W43 2008
841'.1—dc22
2007015491

For Sandra

"Bele amie, si est de nus:
Ne vus sanz mei, ne jeo sanz vus."
Chievrefoil, 77–78

Contents

Acknowledgments ix

Introduction 1

1. Marie de France's Rhetorical Foundation 9
2. The Prologues and the Epilogues 35
3. The *Lais* 61
4. The *Fables* 103
5. The *Espurgatoire seint Patriz* and *La vie seinte Audree* 137

Conclusion 175

Appendix A. Priscian's *Institutiones grammaticae* and *Praeexercitamina* 181

Appendix B. Table of Extant Medieval Manuscripts of Marie de France's *Isopet* 184

Bibliography 187

Index 199

Acknowledgments

This book would not exist without the generous assistance of many people to whom I wish to express my deepest appreciation. First, I wish to thank Keith Busby, whose close reading of early drafts of the manuscript and whose many suggestions, especially concerning medieval manuscripts, were essential to the realization of this project. I owe the same debt of gratitude to Rupert T. Pickens, who taught me how to read Old French, gave me a passion for medieval studies, and, most important, introduced me to Marie de France. All of my research on her narratives, especially for this book, has been greatly informed by his vast knowledge of her works and his broad understanding of romance philology and medieval French literature in general.

I am extremely grateful to the staff at the Catholic University of America Press. The observations and suggestions of the anonymous outside readers significantly strengthened my argument and kept my analysis focused. In addition, Joan Tasker Grimbert graciously read my manuscript several times in the final stages of revision and made many helpful recommendations for clarifying my thoughts, especially on the *Espurgatoire seint Patriz* and *La vie seinte Audree*. I express my thanks to Suzanne Wolk and Theresa B. Walker for their patient and thorough copyediting, particularly to the former, whose attention to stylistic detail thwarted my efforts at times to complicate syntax. Their careful interventions greatly enhanced the final version. I also appreciate the assistance of Elizabeth A. Benevides in designing the cover. I especially thank the series editor, David J. McGonagle, for his professionalism in dealing with me from the very beginning of the project until its completion, a collaboration that began at a meeting during the

Acknowledgments

South Atlantic Modern Language Association Conference in Baltimore in 2002. His patience and understanding were essential to my completing the book.

I also thank George Economou and William Huseman for reading the first draft and making helpful suggestions on style and secondary sources. The fundamental ideas in this book grew from countless hours in coffee shops with my colleague and one of my closest friends, Pamela A. Genova, who advised me at every stage and often encouraged me to take another look. I have the good fortune of knowing and working with Dan Ransom, general editor of Variorum Chaucer at the University of Oklahoma. His editorial corrections and meticulous reading of my work at various stages often helped me avoid incoherence of expression.

My work on Marie de France draws upon the support of two colleagues and friends in particular. I thank Judith Rice Rothschild for her endless encouragement and for the many practical insights she has offered over the years. Her work on narrative technique in the *Lais* was the first book I read on Marie de France as a graduate student, and its timeless perspective continues to influence my thought. Likewise, June Hall McCash, one of the most important scholars of Marie de France, has been a constant source of inspiration, both personally and professionally. Her groundbreaking article in the July 2002 issue of *Speculum* provided solid evidence for attributing authorship of *La vie seinte Audree* to Marie de France and caused me to rethink the last chapter of this book. I also thank Judith Barban, who worked with McCash to produce a new edition, with English translation, of *La vie seinte Audree*. They were gracious enough to allow me to use their final draft in my discussion and citing of the text, even as it was going to press at the time of my own final revisions.

I express my most profound appreciation to several friends and colleagues whose encouragement and advice helped assure the completion of this book, especially to Norris J. Lacy, Elizabeth W. Poe, William W. Kibler, Matilda Tomaryn Bruckner, Kristin Burr, Mary E. Davis, Virginia Blanton, Douglas Kelly, and Helga

Acknowledgments

Madland. My very close friend and colleague, Michel Quereuil, and my dear sister, Autum Whalen, provided me with long periods of solitude in their homes, where I was able to work without distractions. I owe them much for the moral support that allowed me to make significant progress on the final version.

Research funding for this book was provided in the form of generous grants and travel support from several units at the University of Oklahoma to which I am extremely grateful: the Department of Modern Languages, Literatures, and Linguistics, the College of Arts and Sciences, the Research Council, and the International Programs Center.

In addition to the debt I owe to individuals, many institutions made this book possible. Chapter 4 represents a significant amount of manuscript consultation in several European libraries: Bibliothèque Nationale de France, Bibliothèque de l'Arsenal, Institut de Recherche et d'Histoire des Textes in Paris; Musée Condé in Chantilly; Bibliothèque Municipale de Lyon La Part-Dieu in Lyon; Bibliothèque Royale Albert Ier in Brussels; British Library in London; Bodleian Library and Merton College Library in Oxford; University Library, Parker Library, Fitzwilliam Museum, Gonville and Caius Library, and Trinity College Library in Cambridge; York Minster Archives in York; and Biblioteca Apostolica Vaticana in Rome. My thanks to the staff in the manuscript reading rooms of these institutions who assisted me during my consultation, especially to Christine Ruby at the IRHT and to Joe Maldonado and Michael J. Boggan at the British Library.

Some of the material in this book has previously appeared in articles and has been included here with the kind permission of the publishers. Chapter 1 is a reworking of my essay "Marie de France and the Ancients," in *"De sens rassis": Essays in Honor of Rupert T. Pickens,* ed. Keith Busby, Bernard Guidot, and Logan E. Whalen (Amsterdam: Rodopi, 2005), 719–28. Chapter 3 relies heavily on "A Medieval Book-Burning: *Objet d'art* as Narrative Device in the *lai* of *Guigemar,*" *Neophilologus* 80, no. 2 (1996): 205–11, and chapter 4 is based on "*Ex libris Mariae:* Courtly Book Ico-

Acknowledgments

nography in the Illuminated Manuscripts of Marie de France," which appeared in *Courtly Arts and the Art of Courtliness,* ed. Keith Busby and Christopher Kleinhenz (Woodbridge, U.K.: Boydell & Brewer, 2006), 745–53. Chapter 5 is a revised version of "A Knight in Hell: The Poetics of Memory for Clerical and Courtly Worlds in Marie de France's *Espurgatoire Saint Patrice,*" in *Courtly Literature and Clerical Culture,* ed. Christoph Huber and Henrike Lähnemann (Tübingen: Attempto, 2002), 19–27.

Most important, I thank my wife, Sandra. In addition to her moral support at every step of the way, she spent countless hours proofreading various parts of the manuscript. Finally, I thank my wonderful children, Reynolds, Jonathan, and Katherine, for their kind understanding during this project. Many hours that rightfully belonged to them were devoted to the pages of this book.

MARIE DE FRANCE & THE POETICS of MEMORY

Introduction

Marie de France wrote during an auspicious period in the history of French literature. Few literary texts in the vernacular appear before 1150; in the second half of the century works in French are abundant. Between the *Serments de Strasbourg* in 842 and the marriage of Eleanor of Aquitaine to Louis VII in 1137, one counts fewer than half a dozen major works in the *langue d'oïl*.[1] By 1152, when Eleanor married Henry Plantagenet, future king of England, a full-scale literary revival had been kindled, and the list of major literary works in the vernacular more than tripled before the beginning of the thirteenth century.

This sudden proliferation of texts that treated the *matière de Rome, matière de Bretagne,* and *matière de France* may be attributed to several factors, including, but not limited to, favorable royal patronage, a keen interest in the liberal arts, increasing attention to the disciplines of grammar and rhetoric from which the medieval arts of poetry and prose developed, and a desire on the part of medieval authors to ensure *translatio studii,* the transfer of knowledge from previous generations to future ones. Although the quality of the works that appeared during this time varies, they all betray the growing competence of authors in the art of literary composition.

The rhetoric of antiquity was available to medieval students through a broad selection of sources, but the surviving manuscripts from the period point to a privileged status for certain authorities, among them the works of Cicero, the *Rhetorica ad Herennium,* and Priscian, to name but a few. If authors of literature

---

1. See Peter France, *The New Oxford Companion to Literature in French* (Oxford: Clarendon Press, 1995), xxxviii–xxxix.

Introduction

in the Middle Ages were interested in keeping a textual tradition alive by assuring the transfer of material from a prior time to their own period, medieval compilers of the arts of poetry and prose were concerned with developing an instruction based on the classical divisions of rhetoric, while at the same time adapting it to fit the literary needs of their own students. What medieval authors gleaned from this instruction steeped in Roman tradition was an ability to gather material from existing sources, shape that material in their imaginations, combine it with other previously collected material in the storehouse of memory, and mesh the disparate parts into a new work that was suitable for their audience.

This process of medieval *inventio* found its fullest expression in the romances of Chrétien de Troyes, and specifically in the technique of *conjointure,* Chrétien's term for the art of combining source material in a way that reveals the *ingenium* of the author. This poetic craft is present from the beginning of Chrétien's literary career, in his first romance, *Erec et Enide*. But in this area he must share the stage with his contemporary, Marie de France, as she exhibits the same talent, though within the textual boundaries of a significantly shorter genre, the *lai*.

The *lai* of *Guigemar* is an assemblage of stories that revolve around the lovesick condition of the hero: the hunt for the stag, the episode where he discovers the lady enclosed in the castle by her jealous husband, and his separation from and eventual reunion with his new love. Reading between the couplets, as it were, one can imagine that these episodes may have existed somewhere in past works before they were discovered by Marie, tucked away in her memory, and later brought forth and adapted to satisfy the preferences of her courtly public. Much in the same way that Chrétien ties together different episodes of his romances in a symmetrical whole, Marie meshes the segments of her tale into a congruous textual unit. By all accounts of its structure and themes, the *lai* of *Guigemar* wants to be a romance; it is, for all intents and purposes, a romance waiting to happen, in need only of *amplificatio* to free it from the aesthetic confines of its genre.

Introduction

If Marie and Chrétien share an artistic ability to collect and reshape material, they also complement each other in their use of the art of *descriptio* to embellish the narrative fabric and to shift the action from one episode to the next. Their narrative expertise shows that they understood the usefulness of vivid descriptions that created lively images within the imaginations of the audience. These images could later be used by readers to re-create the story in their minds, the pictures that had been registered there serving as points of reference within the mental version of the narrative. This cognitive process was original neither to Chrétien nor to Marie; it is found earlier in monastic writings on meditation and prayer that were popular in the early Middle Ages, "in which a diagram-like 'picture' is created mentally which serves as the site for a meditational *collatio,* the 'gathering' into one 'place' of the various strands of a meditational composition."[2]

Marie's descriptions of objects, people, places, and events are not necessarily more detailed than some of Chrétien's. Chrétien's description of Erec's coronation robe, for example, is strikingly detailed.[3] Nor are they necessarily more elaborate than some of those of her predecessors in the *romans d'antiquité*.[4] Instead, her propensity to use this narrative device often and effectively within genres as short as the *lai* and the fable is the defining attribute of her literary talent, the touchstone that distinguishes her from other medieval authors.

---

2. Mary Carruthers, *The Book of Memory: A Study of Memory in Medieval Culture* (Cambridge: Cambridge University Press, 1990), 123.

3. Citing Macrobius as his source, Chrétien describes Erec's coronation robe in great detail, even down to the fur lining from exotic beasts. The most captivating feature of this garment is the illustrations on the exterior that depict the quadrivium, one division of the seven liberal arts that were an integral part of medieval learned society. The audience is told that four fairies represented in detail each aspect of the quadrivium: arithmetic, geometry, music, and astronomy. The other division of the seven liberal arts, the trivium, included grammar, rhetoric, and logic, and was not depicted on Erec's robe. See Chrétien de Troyes, *Erec und Enide,* ed. Wendelin Foerster (Halle: Niemeyer, 1934), lines 6713–809. All references are from this edition.

4. The *romans d'antiquité* were verse adaptations into Old French of epics from antiquity, like the *Eneas,* a medieval retelling of Virgil's *Aeneid*.

Introduction

In *Guigemar,* the description of the principal objects organizes the narrative and helps to compartmentalize the episodes in the *loci* of memory. These carefully related objects are associated with important episodes and serve as visual tags when we attempt to retrieve segments of the text from our memory, in much the same way that labels on file folders guide us to their contents. The marvelous description of the androgynous hind marks the episode where Guigemar is wounded and learns of his only recourse for healing; the elaborate representation of the mysterious ship ties together the previous scene with the one to follow; the painting on the castle wall tags the part of the narrative in which Guigemar's wound is healed; and, finally, the magic belt and knot label both the episode of the separation and the episode of the reunion of the two lovers.

As remarkable as Marie's talent is for using strategic descriptions to impart a visual dimension to the narrative, it is not her most original contribution to the developing vernacular literature of the late twelfth and early thirteenth centuries. Instead, her genius lies in the connection she makes between the representation of these visual descriptions and the faculty of memory. Repeatedly throughout her texts she unveils a desire to make the narrative suitable to be recorded in the minds of her audience. Vocabulary, narrative structure, descriptions, references to past authorities, and subject matter all work together in Marie's poetry to form an architecture of memory.

Marie's historical position with respect to the revival of the architectural mnemonic of antiquity that began in the thirteenth century is pivotal. Though she had no access to the *artes memorativae,* treatises devoted solely to the art of memory that were to develop in the centuries following her own, she nonetheless exemplifies some of the same techniques. Among the methods they supported are the creation of vivid images that are "extraordinary, wonderful, and intensely charged with emotion," and the storage of such images in compartments or *loci* of the imagination for future recall.[5]

5. Carruthers, *Book of Memory,* 133.

Introduction

Marie's understanding and implementation of this principle of memory is in some ways similar to the approach of Dante. Writing at the end of the thirteenth and beginning of the fourteenth century, and therefore with probable knowledge of the memory treatises, Dante demonstrates both aspects of this tenet, the former through his descriptions in the *Commedia* and the latter through the metaphor in his opening remarks to the *Vita nuova:* "In quella parte del libro de la mia memoria dinanzi a la quale poco si potrebbe leggere, si trova una rubrica la quale dice: *Incipit vita nova*" (In that part of the book of my memory before which there would be little to read is found a chapter heading which says: "Here begins a new life").[6] Marie does not explicitly evoke the compartmental structure of memory as Dante's metaphor of the chapter headings does. Nonetheless, the narrative arrangement of different episodes in her *Lais* implicitly reveals that she comprehended this method as a way to store source material in her own memory, and later to decompartmentalize it and rearrange it for the work at hand.

The obvious difference between Dante's understanding of these techniques and Marie's use of them a century earlier is that she was writing without benefit of the treatises on the art of memory that promoted such systematic design. In relation to the emphasis put on memory in later centuries, her early emphasis on this faculty raises the question of what led her to become a type of precursor of the mnemonic doctrine that pervades the later Middle Ages. One possible answer may be found in Mary Carruthers's assessment of the "medievalness" of the *artes memorativae*, which she believes is not "attributable to textual sources, such as some (unknown) non-Ciceronian body of rhetorical precepts," but rather "to manuscript painting conventions, the *Bestiary*, and various conventions of pictorial diagrams."[7]

While it may be difficult, if not impossible, to identify con-

---

6. Dante Alighieri, *Le opere di Dante,* ed. Michele Barbi (Florence: R. Bemporad et Figlio, 1921), see *Vita nuova,* I. All citations of Dante's works throughout this study are from this edition. The English translation here is from *Dante Alighieri: Vita Nuova,* trans. Mark Musa (Oxford: Oxford University Press, 1992), I.

7. Carruthers, *Book of Memory,* 123.

Introduction

clusively the precise sources from which Marie learned to create visual images in the mind and from which she drew her demonstrative concern for memory, studies such as Carruthers's *Book of Memory* and Douglas Kelly's *The Art of Medieval French Romance* provide clues to the influence of the medieval arts of poetry and prose and of the development of visual art in France and England through the end of the twelfth century. Leaning often on the valuable scholarship of these two authors, this book examines in detail Marie's mnemonic and rhetorical craft as author as expressed through various aspects of her descriptive narratives, and reveals a consciously developed poetics of memory.

To the best of my knowledge, no other author of medieval vernacular literature writing during Marie's period or before her stressed the importance of memory to the extent that she did. In all major prologues and epilogues to her works she explicitly focuses in some specific way on memory. Likewise, the exordial matter and/or closing comments of most of the twelve individual *lais* make direct reference to memory through the term "remembrance," or they invoke this faculty through other appropriate expressions. By contrast, Chrétien refers to memory only once in the prologues to his five romances: "Des or comancerai l'estoire / Qui toz jorz mes iert an memoire" (Now I will begin the story / That I have always remembered).[8] Furthermore, Marie's narratives are replete with vocabulary that is associated with the act of remembering. Yet surprisingly, as far as I have been able to determine, no previous scholarly work has presented a cohesive study of this construct of memory that opens and closes each of her extant narrative texts.

Marie looks forward to the memory treatises that appear after the close of the twelfth century, while at the same time she seems to be working partly in the knowledge on which these documents were based. It is as if she had her finger on the literary pulse of her time and could already sense the direction that narrative composi-

---

8. Chrétien de Troyes, *Erec und Enide,* lines 23–24. My translation.

Introduction

tion would later take under the influence of the *artes memorativae*. Her interest in memory and her desire that the audience be able to recall lessons from her texts can be seen partly through the way in which later medieval scribes and illuminators interpreted and then attempted to relate her *Fables* on the manuscript page.

Marie's poetics of memory are home to an intricate network of describing places, people, animals, events, and objects in her narrative texts. She embraces ideas like those found in Aristotle's *De memoria* even before they became available through Latin translation in the course of the thirteenth century. Carruthers reminds us of Aristotle's pronouncement on the subject: "Memory, even memory of objects of thought, is not without an image."[9] Marie's project of *inventio* makes judicious use of the art of *descriptio* as it creates mentally visual images that render her conception of the material memorable for her courtly public. Simply put, she wants her audience to use their imaginations, the same type of skill that she as author employs to collect material and deposit it in the appropriate part of memory.

Richard de Fournival, the author of *Li bestiaires d'amours* in the first half of the thirteenth century, recognized an intimate link between painting and literature. He believed that "images" in a text were not confined to the painted illuminations on a manuscript folio but were also mental images that the text itself "painted" in the mind of the audience to facilitate memory.[10] Marie de France was already well aware of this relationship and profited from it in order to give a visual dimension to her narratives. In much the same way that Tristan placed the hazel branch so that Iseut would recognize it and recall their previous times together, so too Marie strategically places vivid descriptions throughout her narratives so that we as audience may conceptualize her texts and thus retain them in the faculty of our memories, for rather than being simply a narrator of tales, she was an accomplished painter of narratives.

9. Carruthers, *Book of Memory*, 51.
10. Ibid., 223.

I

Marie de France's Rhetorical Foundation

Twelfth-century France witnessed an unprecedented production of literary texts written in the French vernacular. Like other major authors who wrote in French during this linguistically transitional epoch, such as Wace, Benoît de Sainte-Maure, and Chrétien de Troyes, the Anglo-Norman poet Marie de France developed a technique of literary composition steeped in the tradition of classical rhetoric. Douglas Kelly has pointed out that the classical influence on medieval poets came through their training in the arts of poetry and prose: "The medieval arts of poetry and prose draw on learned and scholastic traditions of ancient, and especially Roman, origin. These traditions linked poetics to one or more of the Liberal Arts, especially grammar and rhetoric."[1] Kelly has also argued convincingly that the significance of the medieval arts of poetry and prose to the development of medieval vernacular romance has been underestimated and deserves to be granted more attention in the study of medieval literary texts. He sees two fundamental reasons for contemporary scholarly neglect of these sources: "First, the instructional intent of the treatises distances them from the masterpieces. Like elementary grammars, they are propaedeutic to spoken or written fluency. Second, other sources not obviously related to poetics like medieval historiography, hagiography, and

---

1. Douglas Kelly, *The Art of Medieval French Romance* (Madison: University of Wisconsin Press, 1992), 32.

Rhetorical Foundation

oral traditions also contributed to the art of romance as it emerged and acquired integrity."[2] Given the apparently important role that training in the arts of poetry and prose played in the development of twelfth- and thirteenth-century vernacular literature, it follows that an understanding of such instruction could shed light on the poetics of medieval authors who learned to write through their study of the "ancients" as appropriated by medieval grammarians, rhetoricians, and glossators.

Furthermore, such an approach makes it possible to identify which parts of the grammatical or rhetorical paradigm a particular poet may have privileged over others, and the ways in which that aspect may have become essential to her or his own literary program. A brief analysis of the *artes poeticae* as they existed in antiquity and throughout the Middle Ages, and of the development of classical rhetoric and grammar and its eventual transmission into the treatises that codified the stages of medieval topical invention, will elucidate the argument presented in this book.[3]

Rhetoric and Grammar

The Ciceronian rhetoric of antiquity embodied five basic parts, as outlined in Cicero's *De inventione:* invention *(inventio),* arrangement *(dispositio),* style *(elocutio),* memory *(memoria),* and delivery *(pronuntiatio).*[4] All of these divisions are included a few years

---

2. Ibid., 7–8.

3. For a detailed study of the development of rhetoric from Greece, to Rome, to medieval Europe, and to the Renaissance, see James Murphy, *Rhetoric in the Middle Ages* (Berkeley and Los Angeles: University of California Press, 1974). Edmond Faral offers a thorough investigation of the arts of poetry and prose in the twelfth and thirteenth centuries in *Les arts poétiques du XIIe et du XIIIe siècle: Recherches et documents sur la technique littéraire du moyen âge* (Paris: Champion, 1924). For the most detailed analysis of the development of medieval French literary invention, stemming from the arts of poetry and prose as learned and implemented by medieval authors, see Kelly, *Art of Medieval French Romance.*

4. Cicero, *De inventione: De optimo genere oratorum; topica,* trans. H. M. Hubbell (Cambridge, Mass.: Harvard University Press, 1949): "Quare materia quidem nobis rhetoricae videtur artis ea quam Aristoteli visam esse diximus; partes autem eae quas

Rhetorical Foundation

later in the *Rhetorica ad Herennium*,[5] which James Murphy calls "one of the most influential books on speaking and writing ever produced in the Western world," adding that it can be regarded as "a complete textbook of rhetoric."[6] The *ad Herennium* also contains material not found in the *De inventione*, such as the complete listing of "figures" *(exornationes)* of speech and thought.[7] As Murphy notes, "the section on *memoria* is the oldest extant treatment of the subject."[8]

Memoria in the *De inventione,* though not first in the series of faculties listed, merits particular attention, since without it the speaker would not be capable of *pronuntiatio* of the other faculties *(inventio, dispositio,* and *elocutio)*: "memoria est firma animi rerum ac verborum perceptio" (1.7.9). Indeed, the author of the *ad Herenium* stresses the significance of memory to the entire rhetorical process, suggesting that all other parts of composition fall into its domain: "Nunc ad thesaurum inventorum atque *ad omnium partium rhetoricae custodem,* memoriam, transeamus" (Now let me turn to the treasure-house of the ideas supplied by Invention, to *the guard-*

---

plerique dixerunt, inventio, dispositio, elocutio, memoria, pronuncatio. Inventio est excogitatio rerum verarum aut veri similium quae causam probabilem reddant; dispositio est rerum inventarum in ordinem distributio; elocutio est indoneorum verborum ad inventionem accommodatio; *memoria est firma animi rerum ac verborum perceptio;* pronuncatio est ex rerum et verborum dignitate vocis et corporis moderatio" (1.7.9, emphasis added). All citations and English translations are from this edition.

5. Cicero, *Ad C. Herennium de ratione dicendi,* trans. Harry Caplan (Cambridge, Mass.: Harvard University Press, 1954): "Oportet igitur esse in oratore inventionem, dispositionem, elocutionem, memoriam, pronuntiationem. Inventio est excogitatio rerum verarum aut veri similium quae causam probabilem reddant. Dispositio est ordo et distributio rerum, quae demonstrat quid quibus locis sit conlocandum. Elocutio est idoneorum verborum et sententiarum ad inventionem adcommodatio. *Memoria est firma animi rerum et verborum et dispositionis perceptio.* Pronuntiatio est vocis, vultus, gestus moderatio cum venustate" (1.2.3, emphasis added). All citations and English translations are from this edition. See Murphy, *Rhetoric in the Middle Ages,* 19. He has pointed out that "the discussion of *inventio* [in the *Ad Herennium*] is essentially the same as Cicero's, a fact that may account for the widespread medieval belief that Cicero was the author."

6. Murphy, *Rhetoric in the Middle Ages,* 18–19.

7. For a useful chart listing these figures and tropes, see ibid., 21.

8. Ibid., 19.

Rhetorical Foundation

ian of all the parts of rhetoric, the memory) (3.16.28, emphasis added). The author's emphasis in this line, in a text that represents the oldest extant mnemonic system,[9] may help to explain the importance allocated to memory during the thirteenth century, when treatises on the subject began to appear in significant numbers.

In the *ad Herennium,* memory is divided into two facets, natural and artificial: "Sunt igitur duae memoriae: una naturalis, altera artificiosa. Naturalis est ea quae nostris animis insita est et simul cum cogitatione nata; artificiosa est ea quam confirmat inductio quaedam et ratio praeceptionis" (There are, then, two kinds of memory: one natural, and the other the product of art. The natural memory is that memory which is embedded in our minds, born simultaneously with thought. The artificial memory is that memory which is strengthened by a kind of training and system of discipline) (3.16.28). We are born with natural memory, while we create artificial memory through the use of figures and backgrounds. These backgrounds are mental grids in which images are arranged, much like placing them within the rooms of an imaginary building. The author explains that the two systems work together, natural memory being used to call forth from the storehouse of artificial memory the images or figures that have been created and placed there, and artificial memory, in its turn, sharpening the innate ability of the person to remember material through discipline and training in the invention and placement of such images. The image functions as a marker of the object we wish to remember and must be placed in a background that will facilitate its recall: "Imagines sunt formae quaedam et notae et simulacra eius rei quam meminisse volumus; quod genus equi, leonis, aquilae memoriam si volemus habere, imagines eorum locis certis conlocare oportebit" (An image is, as it were, a figure, mark, or portrait of the object we wish to remember; for example, if we wish to recall a horse, a lion, or an eagle, we must place its image in a definite background) (3.16.29).

---

9. See Cicero, *Ad C. Herennium,* 205n.

Rhetorical Foundation

In light of this type of mnemonic exercise, which is extolled in one of the best-known works of ancient rhetoric to come down to the Middle Ages, it is not surprising that medieval authors should be concerned with creating narratives that exploit the association of images, often in the nature of the *merveille*, with ideas or lessons that they wished their audiences to remember. The popularity of the *Rhetorica ad Herennium* and the *De inventione* during the twelfth century[10] makes it likely that an educated author like Marie de France, who was evidently well versed in the arts of poetry, as her works bear witness, had knowledge of them. Her implementation of the technique is signaled on many occasions throughout her narratives, such as in the case of the androgynous hind that utters a prophetic discourse to the wounded knight in *Guigemar*, discussed below.

Grammar, another division of the liberal arts that was ultimately important to the development of vernacular literature in the Middle Ages, appears first in the list of the Trivium, with rhetoric often appearing in second place. Just as memory was vital to the discipline of rhetoric, it played a crucial role in the teaching of grammar. Martin Irvine notices a common preface to grammatical commentaries, showing that memory was indeed one of the keys of wisdom.[11] He notes the significance of *grammatica* to the preservation of a written tradition from antiquity through the medieval period, showing that it functioned as "the only point of access to all of the orders of textual knowledge," and that it had an essentially constitutive function, making a certain kind of literacy and literary culture possible per se: "Both the textual objects defined or constructed through grammatical discourse and the social relations enacted and replicated through the institutional

---

10. See Murphy, *Rhetoric in the Middle Ages*, 109. He notes their appearance in medieval library catalogues during the twelfth century: thirteen times for the *Rhetorica ad Herennium* and thirty-two times for Cicero's *De inventione*.

11. Martin Irvine, *The Making of Textual Culture: "Grammatica" and Literary Theory, 350–1100* (Cambridge: Cambridge University Press, 1994), 461: "Quot sunt claves sapientie? V. Que? Assiduitas legendi, *memoria retinendi*, sedulitas interrogandi, contemptus diviciarum, honor magistri" (emphasis added).

Rhetorical Foundation

practice of the discipline are inscribed everywhere in medieval culture."[12] In its classical and then later medieval contexts it is not solely the study of language, as in the university classroom of our day; rather, "it is first of all the science of speaking and writing correctly *(recte loquendi),* and then the art of interpreting the poets *(enarratio poetarum).*"[13]

During the transitional period between late antiquity and the early Middle Ages, the study of grammar began to enjoy privileged expression as a tradition of its own, separate from that of rhetoric, beginning with the *Ars poetica* of Horace between 23 and 13 B.C., and then with the *Barbarismus* of Donatus around A.D. 350.[14] This tradition reached its apogee in the sixth century with Priscian's *Institutiones grammaticae,* of which there are more than one thousand extant manuscripts, and Murphy underscores the importance of this movement in relation to the epoch in which Marie composed her narratives: "Donatus, Priscian, and their imitators, copyists, and commentators dominate grammatical instruction during the period up to A.D. 1200."[15] It is no coincidence, then, that Marie de France mentions Priscian by name in her prologue, a subject treated in chapter 2.

The debt that medieval theories of grammar and rhetoric owe to the classical tradition is significant. The preceding brief account demonstrates the manner in which certain precepts within these first two branches of the Trivium made their way into the medieval practice of vernacular literary composition. Classical *artes poeticae* in general were adapted by, and found expression

---

12. Ibid., xiv. For the development and divisions of *grammatica,* c. 350–c. 1150, see the chart on p. 6.

13. Murphy, *Rhetoric in the Middle Ages,* 24–25. He uses the term *loquendi* to refer to both reading and writing because Quintilian explains that the two are connected: "Nam et scribendi ratio coniuncta cum loquendo est . . ." (1.4.3). Quintilian's *Institutio oratoria* makes this distinction in A.D. 92: "Haec igitur professio, cum brevissime in duas partes dividatur, recte loquendi scientiam et poetarum enarrationem" (1.4.2). Murphy discusses and cites Quintilian at pp. 22–26.

14. Ibid., 42–88. Murphy discusses in detail the transition of rhetoric and grammar from their classical expressions to their medieval manifestations.

15. Ibid., 139.

Rhetorical Foundation

through, medieval grammarians and rhetoricians to accommodate the needs and usage of their contemporary literary practitioners, and certain aspects of classical grammar and rhetoric eventually became codified *mutatis mutandis* as medieval literary theory. The resulting Ciceronian theory, as expounded in various treatises, was the foundation of instruction for poets in the twelfth century, such as Marie de France and Chrétien de Troyes, who not only perfected its implementation in toto but also advanced certain elements of composition over others, developing a personal style of *inventio* that would be imitated in the following centuries.

Medieval Literary Topical Invention

Although the medieval rhetorical and grammatical paradigm of literary composition that developed from the epideictic art of the "ancients" represents a rather complex and somewhat diverse body of writing, the art of literary topical invention *(inventio)* as it was expressed in the Middle Ages can best be summed up by what Kelly has recognized as three primary stages: "First, the author has an idea or mental conception of a subject. Second, material is sought and identified through which the initial conception may find appropriate statement and elaboration. Third, the mental conception and the *materia* are meshed as the subject matter of the work."[16]

Memoria was an integral part of *inventio* as it was understood and practiced in the Middle Ages, since the second stage of this process, the search for subject matter, depended heavily on the author's storehouse of memory. Moreover, when quoting Alcuin's dialogue with Charlemagne, Carruthers notes, "*Memoria* is a storehouse, custodian of invention and cogitation, of 'things' and 'words,' and without it, even the most eminent of the speaker's other talents will come to nothing."[17] Accordingly, the author of the *ad Herennium* begins his discussion of memory with

---

16. Kelly, *Art of Medieval French Romance*, 38.
17. Carruthers, *Book of Memory*, 144.

Rhetorical Foundation

an encomium similar to the one quoted above. One example of Marie's dependence on memory is her constant reference to the stories she remembers from the Bretons and in turn draws upon in composing her own work: the *Lais*.

In essence, then, training in the medieval arts of poetry, and ipso facto in classical grammar and rhetoric, provided a model of literary composition through which authors expressed themselves in a way that revealed their own *ingenium,* that is to say, an "inborn or natural talent, the capacity, intelligence, and insight necessary to invent a work; it governed the cognitive faculty called imagination, or the invention of identifiable images."[18] Marie and other poets of the twelfth-century Renaissance implemented different rhetorical figures and tropes—known as *exornationes* in the *ad Herennium*—to "mesh" the existing *materia* into their own conception of the work. Kelly emphasizes the relevance of these techniques to the process of *inventio,* pointing out that medieval treatises on poetics stressed their importance: "They constitute the form or mode of expression of the work's *qualitas.* They give access to the formal and conceptual intentions of the author, like God's designs discovered in the world's *ornatus.*"[19] Such devices are indispensable to the process of literary invention, and when certain ones are employed frequently and explicitly enough in a given text, they expose the author's penchant for promoting that particular aspect of rhetoric over others that are available to her or him.

When a medieval author enlists with consistency particular dimensions of rhetoric over others to carry out a narrative plan, it may be viewed as the medieval equivalent of contemporary authorial originality, in other words, how a particular author represents a preexisting literary model. Kelly defines this idea as the work's *figura,* "the stamp of auctorial conception on the work's *materia.* It is mirrored in every step of composition. The entire opus is accordingly the image of the *figura* originally conceived in

---

18. Kelly, *Art of Medieval French Romance,* 34.
19. Ibid., 58–59.

Rhetorical Foundation

the artist's mind. *Figura* not only forms, it combines into configuration."[20] Certain literary texts from the twelfth century, particularly those of Marie and Chrétien, suggest that authors were fully cognizant of their rhetorical talent, and they indeed succeeded in treating the material at hand in a manner that exposed such intelligence, as they left their authorial mark on the text. In fact, stylistic features figure prominently among methods of investigation modern scholars use to attribute works to authors.

Ingenium and Marie de France's Narrative Design

Within the context of the preceding remarks, it comes as no surprise that the prologue to Marie's *Lais* begins with an encomium of the act of literary composition and a *captatio benevolentiae* that justifies her own poetic endeavor and places her squarely in the company of those who share this gift of *ingenium*:

> Ki Deus ad duné escïence
> E de parler bone eloquence
> Ne s'en deit taisir ne celer,
> Ainz se deit voluntiers mustrer.
> Quant uns granz biens est mult oïz,
> Dunc a primes est il fluriz,
> E quant loëz est de plusurs,
> Dunc ad espandues ses flurs.
> (Pr 1–8)[21]

Anyone who has received from God the gift of knowledge and true eloquence has a duty not to remain silent: rather should one be happy to reveal such talents. When a truly beneficial thing is heard by many people, it then enjoys its first blossom, but if it is widely praised its flowers are in full bloom.

---

20. Ibid., 61–62.
21. Unless otherwise noted, all references to the *Lais* are from Jean Rychner's edition of the *Lais*, *Les Lais de Marie de France,* Classiques Français du Moyen Age 93

Rhetorical Foundation

Marie's own awareness of the arts of medieval poetry is evidenced by the juxtaposing of two of the most fundamental qualities of medieval literary invention as outlined earlier: the acquisition of material from acquired knowledge ("escïence"), and the capacity to organize it and communicate it to an audience ("de parler bone eloquence").

The significance of lines 1–2 from the prologue of the *Lais,* most likely the earliest extant work composed by Marie de France, cannot be overemphasized as it relates to the entire corpus of the poet. Not only do these lines recall the process of literary invention in general, but they also invoke what I believe are two of the most salient aspects of her own poetics: memory and description. The reference to "escïence" points to *memoria,* for Marie clearly and consistently demonstrates that it is from her storehouse of memory that she has gained the knowledge necessary to create her own version of the tales that she assembles. Likewise, her works reveal a concern for creating images that will be easily retained in the imagination of her audience. The phrase "de parler bone eloquence" refers not only to the technique of literary *inventio* as a whole but, in Marie's case, also and especially to the art of *descriptio,* the rhetorical device that will permeate her narratives to follow. In essence, memory and description, two elements of medieval topical invention inherited from classical rhetoric by means of medieval training in the arts of poetry, are the hallmark of Marie de France's style.

(Paris: Champion, 1983). I adopt Rychner's abbreviations and his spelling for the titles of the General Prologue and the individual *lais:* Pr (General Prologue), *G (Guigemar), Eq (Equitan), F (Fresne), B (Bisclavret), Lv (Lanval), DA (Deus Amanz), Y (Yonec), La (Laüstic), M (Milun), Cht (Chaitivel), Chv (Chievrefoil),* and *El (Eliduc).* Translations are from *The Lais of Marie de France,* 2d ed., trans. Glyn S. Burgess and Keith Busby (London: Penguin, 1999). Burgess and Busby offer an accurate translation in fluid English prose, although they rely on a different edition of the Old French text from the one used in this book, namely, Alfred Ewert, *Marie de France: Lais* (Oxford: Blackwell, 1944). I use Burgess and Busby's translation unless otherwise noted.

Rhetorical Foundation

Memory

Memory has long played an important role in organized society, whether to celebrate past events, to remember important people, to recall significant moral lessons, or to gain mental access to recorded stories or history. In the Pentateuch, for example, two passages from the book of Deuteronomy instruct the Israelites to remember the statutes and commandments of God by writing them down, wearing them on their hands and foreheads, and posting them on their doors.[22] They were first admonished to commit requisite passages of Hebrew scripture to memory, after which time the written reminder was displayed in a conspicuous location and functioned as a mnemonic device that helped them recall the precepts contained therein; the sight of the physical object brought forth the words of their law from the storehouse of memory. This model of memory, used to preserve a tradition of the past, is quite impressive given that this custom is still observed today, more than three thousand years later, by traditional Jews: a *mezuzah,* a small box containing an inscription of the aforementioned passage from Deuteronomy, is attached to the doorpost, and *tefillin,* or phylacteries, small leather pouches holding quotations from the scriptures, are worn on the forehead and on the left arm.[23]

Of course, this Jewish custom is only one among countless instances where memory works to preserve the past and to assure the transmission of knowledge from one generation to the next. In the same manner, memory has always been vital to the survival of literature during periods of history in which there were varying degrees of oral and written media, or in which cultures privileged the oral performance of texts over the written.[24] This faculty was especially useful during the early Middle Ages

---

22. Dt 6:6–9 and 11:18–20.
23. I thank Norman A. Stillman in the Department of History at the University of Oklahoma for explaining this tradition to me.
24. For a study of the oral performance of texts during the Middles Ages, see

Rhetorical Foundation

in western Europe, when few, other than clerics, could read the language of their society. Carruthers highlights the role of *memoria* in the transmission of knowledge: "From antiquity on, *memoria* was fully institutionalized in education, and like all institutions it was adapted to circumstances of history. *Memoria* unites written with oral transmission, eye with ear, and helps to account for the highly 'mixed' oral-literate nature of medieval cultures that many historians of the subject have remarked."[25] One testimony to the performative aspect of literature during this time, and to the need for the faculty of memory to recall and reproduce it, is the recurrence of "formulae" and *laisses similaires* in the *chanson de geste,* a genre that begins to take shape as early as the eleventh century in France.

Scholarly controversy still abounds over the extent to which orality played the decisive role in the development of the epic.[26] At the end of the nineteenth century the prevailing "traditionalist" view, marshaled by Gaston Paris, was that the *chansons de geste* developed from oral poems, or *cantilènes,* at the time of, or immediately following, the events they portrayed.[27] This view was challenged by an "individualist" theory championed by Joseph Bédier in the first part of the twentieth century with an argument that the poems did not develop from an oral tradition at the time of the events of the narrative but were first written down beginning in the twelfth century, each by an "individual" poet who drew upon Latin sources that had chronicled the history of the Carolingian empire.[28]

---

the collection of essays in Evelyn Birge Vitz, Nancy Freeman Regalado, and Marilyn Lawrence, eds., *Performing Medieval Narrative* (Cambridge: D. S. Brewer, 2005).

25. Carruthers, *Book of Memory,* 122.

26. See William W. Kibler's entry "Chanson de geste," in William W. Kibler and Grover A. Zinn, eds., *Medieval France: An Encyclopedia* (New York: Garland, 1995), 195–97.

27. Gaston Paris, *Histoire poétique de Charlemagne* (Paris: A. Lainé & J. Harvard, 1865; reprint, Geneva: Slatkine Reprints, 1974).

28. Joseph Bédier, *Les légendes épiques,* 3d ed., 4 vols. (Paris: Champion, 1926–29).

Rhetorical Foundation

It was in the middle of the twentieth century that Jean Rychner proposed a "neotraditionalist" view that placed an emphasis squarely on the role of memory in the transmission of the *chanson de geste*.[29] As William Kibler has noted, "Rychner showed how a poet could memorize motifs, themes, and formulae and skillfully recombine them for oral presentation, recomposing the poem each time he sang it, using his own stock of formulae."[30] Rychner's view demonstrates the importance of memory in the literary development of the twelfth century, as this formulaic literature reflects the need of *jongleurs* to repeat hemistiches at regular intervals, or to describe similar episodes in different *laisses*, in order to follow a linear development of the story line and maintain a point of reference in texts that were often thousands of lines in length.

As the Middle Ages progressed, so too did the craft of memory. It became more than just a rhetorical device with which to recall material from the past, whether for the purpose of monastic meditation, as during the transitional period from antiquity into the Middle Ages,[31] or for rhetorical purposes in the act of literary composition as taught during the early medieval era, when vernacular literature, especially poetry, began to flourish.[32] From the early thirteenth century onward, memory was no longer simply

---

29. Jean Rychner, *La chanson de geste: Essai sur l'art épique des jongleurs* (Geneva: Droz, 1955).

30. Kibler, "Chanson de geste," 196.

31. See Mary Carruthers, "Boncompagno at the Cutting-edge of Rhetoric: Rhetorical *Memoria* and the Craft of Memory," *Journal of Medieval Latin* 6 (1996): 44–64. She argues that memory as an "art" or "craft" in and of itself before the thirteenth century was known "from meditational practices developed for monastic prayer and for the 'memory' of Scripture" (44–45). See also her article, "The Poet as Master Builder: Composition and Locational Memory in the Middle Ages," *New Literary History* 24, no. 4 (1993): 881–904. She does not suggest that memory as a "division" of rhetoric was absent from twelfth-century training in the liberal arts, merely that when it did reappear as an "art," as put forth by the "ancients" like Cicero, "it did so within the context of these long-standing monastic practices" (882).

32. My discussion throughout the rest of this section owes much to Frances A. Yates, *The Art of Memory* (Chicago: University of Chicago Press, 1966), and to Carruthers, *Book of Memory*.

Rhetorical Foundation

a part of rhetoric; instead, the study of memory began to emerge as an "art" of its own and was codified by treatises devoted either in large part or solely to its commentary, such as those by John of Garland, Albertus Magnus, and ultimately Thomas Bradwardine, who produced a bona fide *ars memorativa*.[33] Carruthers shows that in the thirteenth century the study of memory begins to depart from its previously held association with rhetoric and to move toward an alliance with logic and philosophy, largely owing to the translation into Latin of Aristotle's *De anima* and *De memoria,* and to the subsequent commentary on these texts by Albertus Magnus and Thomas Aquinas. She also identifies a "medievalness" in this new direction of the "arts of memory" that she attributes to "manuscript painting conventions, the *Bestiary,* and various conventions of pictorial diagrams."[34]

This paradigmatic shift also revives the classical aspect of memory that emphasizes the "architectural mnemonic" (Carruthers's term; Yates refers to it as the "Ciceronian mnemonic"), or the "places and images" design of artificial memory that has its roots in Aristotle and the *ad Herennium*. In this line of thought, images are put into various *loci,* such as in the rooms of a mentally constructed architecture, so that they can later be called forth from the faculty of memory by revisiting the locations in which they were deposited.[35] It is clear, then, that memory is diverse at different periods of the Middle Ages: on the one hand, because of the classical influence of "ancients" like Cicero, the *ad Herennium,* and Aristotle, which led to its revival as an "art" form, and on the other,

---

33. For a thorough discussion of the complexity of the arts of memory as they eventually developed into a body of writing during the Middle Ages and into the Renaissance, see Yates, *Art of Memory,* 50–128, and Carruthers, *Book of Memory,* 122–55.

34. Carruthers, *Book of Memory,* 123.

35. In order to prevent a possible confusion of terms, unless otherwise noted I use the expression "architecture of memory" to refer specifically to Marie de France's general narrative plan and the way in which she enlists this dimension of *inventio* as set forth in my argument. This is not to suggest that she was unaware of the potential of artificial memory in the context of an "architectural mnemonic" that was soon to develop in the thirteenth century, and she may indeed have had such a plan in mind when she describes the wall painting in *Guigemar,* discussed in chapter 3.

Rhetorical Foundation

owing to the necessity of religious orders to develop a mnemonic program that would preserve their faith through the memorization of Holy Writ. As Carruthers remarks, "more than one sort of art of memory was known during the Middle Ages, and we must keep this in mind when we talk about revivals and developments within the arts (I stress the plural) of memory."[36]

Since Marie de France wrote toward the end of the twelfth century, before the appearance of the medieval *artes memorativae,* one may assume that she drew upon training in the classical art of rhetoric to develop memory as a literary technique. She composes her narratives in such a way that they express a special concern with memory, not simply because it secures for posterity her role as author and prevents her works from being attributed to another, certainly a stated *desideratum* in the prologue and epilogue of some of her works, but mainly because it ensures that her stories, and the moral lessons they contain, will be transmitted to her audience in a manner that will facilitate their recall.

Memory is apparent in her texts on two levels. First, it is a tool that she herself implements in her capacity as poet to gather source material for her invention. This process may be evident in her narrative as she cites her sources, or it may be intimated through unspecified intertextual references to preexisting *materia*. Second, it is a construct that she hopes to situate in the minds of her audience by marking certain events with an extraordinary image. As a poet trained in the art of literary invention, she understands the value of a rich storehouse of memory to the creative process. By extension, one of her chief preoccupations as author is to generate narratives that are favorable to memory from the perspective of her audience. In other words, a close study of her texts points to Marie's plan to create a type of visual image in the mind's eye of her audience that will help them retain significant events or lessons of the story in the faculty of their memory.

To this end she enlists different techniques, such as repetition

---

36. Carruthers, "Boncompagno at the Cutting-edge of Rhetoric," 45.

Rhetorical Foundation

and anaphora, to effect retention on the part of her auditors and/or readers. This is the case in the *lai* of *Deus Amanz,* where at the beginning of the text, in order to be certain that her listeners or readers will correctly situate the geographical location of the story, she repeats the name of the town, or a form of the name, four times within seven lines. Likewise, in the *lai* of *Lanval* she uses anaphora to enunciate the benevolent qualities of the hero, and in Karl Warnke's edition of this text the name Lanval appears eight times within only nine octosyllabic lines (209–17). As effective as these two techniques prove to be, however, it is most surely by her more widely used technique of intricate descriptions that she leaves her mark on the literary world of the twelfth century. Indeed, it is possible to speak of an "art of description" at work in Marie's poetics, and even to postulate that the technique of *descriptio* lies at the very heart of her program of invention and her network of memory.

The Art of Description

Descriptio, as the Latin word implies on a fundamental level, is a trope of classical rhetoric devoted to the description of people, animals, places, inanimate objects, and events in the *materia.* But *descriptio,* in the context of topical invention, implies more than mere description of persons and objects. As Kelly suggests, "It is more precisely 'elucidation.' ... The author considers the *materia,* the persons, things, and actions contained in it, then models them according to his or her conception of the work. The technique was widespread in the Middle Ages."[37] It is tempting to see the twelfth-century proliferation of literature as the genesis of the widespread use of *descriptio,* especially when one considers the inchoate nature of the trope as it is implemented in the paucity of vernacular literature prior to this period, and given the increasingly frequent adoption of it as a fully developed literary tech-

---

37. Kelly, *Art of Medieval French Romance,* 49–50.

Rhetorical Foundation

nique, culminating with its privileged status in the works of Marie de France and Chrétien de Troyes by century's end.

Generally speaking, medieval poets of the twelfth century often relied on the use of narrative description as part of their literary craft. The technique is fairly common in the *romans d'antiquité*, one example being the lengthy description of Carthage in the *Roman d'Eneas*, a twelfth-century French *translatio* of Virgil's *Aeneid*.[38] Furthermore, descriptions are ubiquitous in Chrétien's romances. His descriptive talents are evidenced in several ways: by the descriptions of physical attributes, such as the beauty of Cligès or the ugliness of the hideous peasant in *Yvain*; by the descriptions of events like that of the knights' appearance in the "gaste forest" at the beginning of *Perceval*; and by the descriptions of objects such as Erec's coronation robe at the end of *Erec et Enide*.[39]

But the salient feature of description in Marie's narrative design that distinguishes her from such predecessors as the authors of the *romans d'antiquité*, and from contemporaries like Chrétien, is the amount of textual space allocated to its use in proportion to the rest of the narrative. Though she wrote in two of the shortest genres of the twelfth century, the *lai* and the fable, she nonetheless devoted significant segments of her texts to detailed descriptions. These detailed descriptions do not remain mere aesthetic adornments or textual embellishments but rather become a crucial part of Marie's poetic *ingenium*, as she deliberately uses the art of *descriptio* to construct a narrative architecture of memory that will facilitate the future recollection of important moral and didactic lessons.

In this manner, *inventio* and memory are intricately linked in

---

38. See *Le roman d'Eneas*, ed. J.-J. Salverda De Grave, Classiques Français du Moyen Age 44, 62 (Paris: Champion, 1925–29), vv. 407–508.

39. Chrétien de Troyes, *Cligès*, ed. Claude Luttrell and Stewart Gregory (Cambridge: D. S. Brewer, 1993), beginning at line 2741; *Yvain: Le chevalier au lion*, ed. Wendelin Foerster (Manchester: Manchester University Press, 1942), lines 288–326; *Le roman de Perceval ou le conte du Graal*, ed. Keith Busby (Tübingen: Niemeyer, 1993), beginning at line 69; and *Erec und Enide*, lines 6713–809.

Rhetorical Foundation

her literary plan, and her developed descriptions are strategically intended to give substance to her thoughts, to create a visual representation no less significant than that of the written word. This creative process is in keeping with the accepted medieval attitude toward memory, and Carruthers suggests that "objects conceived through thought alone, 'can be most easily retained in the mind if they are also conveyed to our minds by the mediation of the eyes.' Of course, many things or events are of a nature that we either have not seen or cannot see what we wish to remember. In these cases, we should make them visible [to the mind] by marking them with a sort of image or figure *(quasi et imago et figura).*"[40] With this observation in mind, one may suppose Marie to have understood that, through carefully assembled descriptions, she could create a type of mentally visual image, an *imago* or *figura,* as it were, that would help her as poet retain the *materia* in the faculty of her memory, and that would also ultimately help those who received her works to "see" the narrative in their own minds and therefore recall its significant moments. The implications here are broad and significant: the process applies not only to her courtly audience in general but also to the scribe who read or heard her works and then recorded them in written form, and to the eventual illuminator as well, who in turn took the image that the story created in his mind and translated it into an actual painted picture on the manuscript page.

Despite the many descriptions of people, places, events, and animals throughout her works, Marie's expertise is most apparent when she describes inanimate objects. These descriptions acquire a visual dimension that she often reinforces with terms relating to the act of writing, reading, seeing, and drawing. They work together to build and support an architecture of mnemonic narrative that will burn the image into the minds of her audience and facilitate future recollection of that image. As Rupert T. Pickens has observed in his study on the poetics of Marie de

---

40. Carruthers, *Book of Memory,* 22.

Rhetorical Foundation

France, specifically when discussing embedded discourse within the *Lais*, these objects may be either "verbaux," "quasi-verbaux," or "non-verbaux" in nature.[41] For the purpose of the discussion in the chapters that follow, I use the term "verbal object" to mean any object or textile that contains an explicit, identifiable, written text, such as the hazel stick on which Tristan writes his name in *Chievrefoil*, or the fragment of embroidered samite in *Laüstic* that conveys the sad fate of the bird and the adventures of the lady to her lover. On the other hand, a "quasi-verbal object" refers to a written text of which the exact contents are not registered within the narrative itself, as with the book of Ovid that is alluded to, but not specifically identified, in the description of the painting of Venus in the *lai* of *Guigemar*, or the unknown inscription on the inside of the ring in *Fresne* that in the end helps to reveal the true identity of the twin. And, finally, a "nonverbal" object carries no written text at all, as is the case with the mysterious yet elaborately described ship in *Guigemar*.

Marie de France's Extant Works

Three different narrative texts from the second half of the twelfth century have been confidently attributed to Marie de France over the years—the *Lais*, the *Fables (Isopet)*, and the *Espurgatoire seint Patriz*—while a fourth narrative text, *La vie seinte Audree*, has become the object of recent critical attention. Some scholars, including myself, now place it in Marie's corpus.[42] The-

---

41. Rupert T. Pickens, "Poétique et sexualité chez Marie de France: L'exemple de *Fresne*," in *Et c'est la fin pour quoy sommes ensemble: Hommage à Jean Dufournet*, ed. J.-C. Aubailly et al., 3 vols. (Paris: Champion, 1993), 3:1120–21.

42. Although it has not been possible to date with certainty the extant works generally attributed to Marie de France, it is commonly accepted scholarly opinion that they were all composed during the last half of the twelfth century in the following order: *Lais, Fables,* and *Espurgatoire seint Patriz; La vie seinte Audree* was most probably composed after the *Espurgatoire*. The dating of these texts is discussed in their respective chapters. I discuss the question of authorship and dating of the *Audree* in chapter 5. Meanwhile, I proceed with my analysis throughout the first four chapters while treating this text as one of Marie de France's works.

Rhetorical Foundation

ses works are preserved in a total of twenty-nine manuscripts and one fragment of fifteen lines, all dating from the early thirteenth to the end of the fifteenth century.[43] The texts vary in length, from the collection of short fables in the Aesopic tradition, to the assembly of longer, but still brief, narrative *lais,* to the longest text, the *La vie seinte Audree* (4,625 lines). In one way or another, all of these texts reveal Marie's preoccupation with her project of *inventio* and memory-oriented narratives. In order to demonstrate how her plan of literary invention comes to fruition in the context of an individual work, each chapter that follows examines a separate text, except the last chapter, which examines the two hagiographic texts together: the prologues and epilogues, the *Lais,* the *Fables,* and the *Espurgatoire seint Patriz* and *La vie seinte Audree.*

Of all Marie's works, the *Lais* exhibit the most judicious use of *descriptio* as a rhetorical device. Her memory-oriented project is brought to the foreground by a remarkable parade of detailed descriptions in which people, animals, places, events, and an assortment of inanimate objects are assigned special status. Every *lai,* from the shortest *(Chievrefoil)* to the longest *(Eliduc),* accommodates the type of stylized descriptions that impart a sense of energy to the narrative register and inform the global program of memory throughout the collection.

Marie's attention to *descriptio* in the *Lais* promotes an imaginative *locus* that is conducive to *memoria.* She enlists a vocabulary that reinforces the act of remembering, and all the individual *lais,* in one way or another, convey to the audience her concern with memory. Her detailed description of the painting in the *lai* of *Guigemar,* for example, shows how she gives mentally visual form to objects in her written narrative texts so that they will later be easily remembered.

Like the *Lais,* the *Fables* also bear witness to the rhetoric of *descriptio,* but within such a context of narrative economy—individual fables are often fewer than fifty lines and sometimes fewer

---

43. For the manuscript tradition of each work, see the respective chapters below.

Rhetorical Foundation

than twenty—elaborate, lengthy, and fully developed descriptions are prohibited. Consequently, description, while it is still germane to the overall structure of the collection, plays a smaller role than it does in the *Lais*. Instead, the engaging aspect of Marie's *Fables* as they relate to the art of memory abides in the reception of these exemplary tales by future generations who were responsible for the *mise-en-page*.[44]

An analysis of the manuscript tradition indicates how scribes and illuminators in the first centuries after the composition of her *Fables* interpreted them scripturally and iconographically. In the prologue and epilogue to the *Fables* the poet makes direct reference to memory, both for posterity's sake (she identifies herself by name), and for the purpose of recollection, in her exhortations to the reader to remember important moral lessons posited in the narratives. The ideas that these recorded statements evoke take physical shape on the manuscript page in the form of miniatures that depict the literary activity of the author, and in the form of mnemonic markers that highlight the "moralité" of each fable. In this way the manuscript tradition of Marie's *Fables* clearly exposes an interest on the part of those responsible for the written and aesthetic reproduction of the stories in conceptualizing her literary program of memory-oriented narrative, thus ensuring that future readers or copiers of the book will have those concepts available to their mind's eye.

Whereas the *Lais* and the *Fables* are assemblages of brief narratives, each collection originating from more than one source, the *Espurgatoire seint Patriz* is a single text that draws exclusively on the *De purgatorio Sancti Patricii* composed by a monk from Saltrey. Though Marie's work is a translation of the twelfth-century Latin composition, she nonetheless, on certain occasions, embel-

---

44. In modern times the *Lais* have eclipsed the *Fables* in popularity and have generated substantially more scholarly activity. The reverse was true in the Middle Ages. Contemporary scholarship, though, suggests that the *Fables* are enjoying a revival in popularity of late, evidenced by the significant number of recent translations, books, and articles on the subject.

Rhetorical Foundation

lishes the narrative with her own descriptive design. The very architecture of Saint Patrick's Purgatory is a background conducive to her own poetic architecture of memory, and the *descriptio* of geography in the work supports that construction.

Marie uses both "remembrance" and "memoire" in the same line in the prologue to the *Espurgatoire:* "vueil en Romanz metre en escrit, / si cum li livre le nus dit, / en remembrance e en memoire, / 'Des Peines de l'Espurgatoire'" (I wish to put into writing in French, / The Pains of Purgatory, / Just as the book tells us about them, / As a recollection and record) (4–6).[45] Though her syntactical juxtaposition of two synonyms is common practice in Old French narrative,[46] her use of the technique in the opening lines of the prologue serves to call attention, from the very beginning of the text, to the importance of memory. Marie's poetic corpus as a whole suggests that she understood two different interpretations for the act of memory; on the one hand, it was intended to represent posterity of authorship, while on the other it related to the retention of moral lessons and subject matter. As for the specific meanings of "remembrance" and "memoire" in Old French, Tobler and Lommatzsch ascribe "Gedächtnis" to both definitions but differentiate between the two by associating the entry for "remembrance" with "Erinnerung," the meaning that it has in modern English, that is remembrance, memory, recollection, recall; whereas in the entry for "memoire," in addition to being rendered by the word "Gedächtnis," the meaning is also defined by "Erinnerungsvermögen," or the ability, capacity, or power of memory, that is to say, the faculty of memory.[47]

45. All references to the *Espurgatoire seint Patriz* and to the *De purgatorio Sancti Patricii* are from *Das Buch vom Espurgatoire S. Patrice der Marie de France und seine Quelle,* ed. Karl Warnke (Halle: Niemeyer, 1938). Unless otherwise noted, all English translations of the *Espurgatoire* are from *Saint Patrick's Purgatory: A Poem by Marie de France, Translated with an Introduction and Notes,* trans. Michael J. Curley (New York: Center for Medieval and Early Renaissance Texts and Studies, 1993).

46. See Peter F. Dembowski, "Vocabulary of Old French Courtly Lyrics—Difficulties and Hidden Meanings," *Critical Inquiry* 2, no. 4 (1976): 763–79. Dembowski discusses binomial constructions in the context of Old French courtly lyric poetry.

47. Adolf Tobler and Erhard Lommatzsch, eds., *Altfranzösisches Wörterbuch,* 11 vols. (Wiesbaden: F. Steiner, 1956–1973).

Rhetorical Foundation

This subtle difference in the use and meaning of these terms that relate to the process of memory is also supported by the absence of the word "memoire" among the synonyms for "so(u)venir" listed by Arnulf Stefenelli in *Der Synonymenreichtum der altfranzösischen Dichtersprache*. Under the rubric "sich erinnern" he treats several Old French synonyms that express the ability of recollection: *souvenir, membrer, remembrer,* and *recorder.* Stefenelli stresses the meaning of these terms by citing textual examples of their juxtaposition with corresponding antonyms, such as lines 1805–6 from the *Roman de Brut:* "Leïr nen *out* mie *oblié,* / Ainz *out bien sovent remembré*" (Leir was not forgotten, / but was often remembered), where he remarks that *remembrer* is an antonym of *oblier,* as are the verbs *membrer* and *recorder.*[48] It is tempting to view his omission of the word "memoire" in the list above as a decision based on grammatical function—these terms are all infinitives and "memoire" is a noun—but Stefenelli has the opportunity to refer to the noun "memoire" through verbal expressions such as Marie's use of it in the aforementioned line from the epilogue to the *Espurgatoire:* "metre en memoire." He does in fact mention a verbal construction with the noun "remembrance" in reference to a line from the *Roman de Troie.*[49]

One cannot determine, based solely on the evidence posited in his study, whether Stefenelli believes that the use of "memoire" in Old French signifies something slightly different from "remembrance," the former for the faculty or storehouse of memory in general, the latter for purposes of immediate recall or for posterity. It is difficult to imagine, however, that its omission from his list of synonyms results from simple oversight. Tobler and Lommatzsch cite the use of the term "memoire" in works as early as Geoffrey of Monmouth and Wace.

In addition to the *Espurgatoire,* chapter 5 analyzes *La vie seinte Audree,* a late twelfth- or early thirteenth-century text that represents a translation of the Latin hagiographic account of the life of

---

48. Arnulf Stefenelli, *Der Synonymenreichtum der altfranzösischen Dichtersprache* (Vienna: Hermann Böhlau, 1967), 219. See also note 44 for the Latin verb *recordor.*
49. Ibid., 217.

Rhetorical Foundation

Saint Etheldreda. A vocabulary rich in terms that evoke the art of memory and the mnemonic narrative order of this text support the theory that the poet we refer to as Marie de France is most probably the author of both the *Espurgatoire* and the *Audree*. My comparison of the rhetorical designs in both works calls for a reconsideration of the *Audree* and its inclusion in her corpus.

Critical Approach

The critical approach of this book adheres closely to the texts under discussion, and to their manuscript tradition. This adherence does not exclude contemporary literary theory, which at times serves the needs of this text-based investigation. Comparative analysis also plays a crucial role in this book, for the works of Marie's predecessors, contemporaries, and successors are sometimes instrumental in situating and clarifying her own poetic view.

To support the plan presented in the chapters that follow I have consulted the extant manuscripts of Marie de France's works, as well as some texts that share an affinity with her own, particularly to the fable genre.[50] These include certain manuscripts of the *lais anonymes,* various Old French *Isopets,* and some Latin and Old French bestiaries. Consequently, my assessments of the texts in question are sometimes empirical in nature, especially concerning the manuscript tradition and the iconographical program of the *Fables.*

The classical influence of grammar and rhetoric in the Middle Ages serves as the background against which I analyze Marie's own literary program, and my discussion owes much to the work of James Murphy. My comments on the art of medieval literary composition, especially as it relates to topical invention and narra-

---

50. I have consulted all of the manuscripts in question, with the exception of the fifteen-line Nottingham fragment and Cologny, Bodmer 113, a fifteenth-century manuscript that is a nearly exact copy of both the text and the illuminations in Paris, Bibliothèque Nationale, fr. 2173.

Rhetorical Foundation

tive description, reflect the critical mode of the works of Douglas Kelly and his many valuable contributions in these domains. His understanding of the medieval process of literary invention informs much of the discussion that follows.

In the area of gender and cultural criticism, I have turned to the work of such Marie de France scholars as Sahar Amer, Karen Jambeck, and Harriet Spiegel, whose insights provide an understanding of the poet's works in their cultural context. My analysis of *La vie seinte Audree* draws much from the recently published study by June Hall McCash and from the work of Rupert T. Pickens, and follows their arguments that Marie de France wrote this work as well as the other three that have traditionally been attributed to her. Finally, in the area of memory in medieval culture, the works of Frances Yates and Mary Carruthers, especially the latter, allow me to elucidate the important dimension of memory in the poetics of the first woman to compose in the French vernacular.

2

The Prologues and the Epilogues

To avoid possible confusion, the fifty-six-line prologue that precedes Marie de France's *Lais* in the Harley 978 manuscript of the British Library is often referred to in contemporary critical discourse as the "General Prologue," which distinguishes it from the exordia of individual *lais,* especially the prologue of *Guigemar* that immediately follows it in this same manuscript.[1] Of the five extant manuscripts that preserve at least one or more of the *lais,* Harley 978 is unique in that it is the only manuscript to record the General Prologue, and is also the only manuscript that assembles all twelve *lais* ("assembler," as Marie says in the General Prologue).

Whether Marie wrote the General Prologue before, during, or after the composition of the *lais* that follow in Harley 978 may still be open to debate, but its relevance to her literary plan as a

---

1. See Rychner's edition of the *Lais,* 239. He has suggested that the first eighteen lines of *Guigemar* were originally intended as the prologue to the *Lais:* "Il est possible que nous ayons dans les v. 1–18 [de *Guigemar*] un petit prologue plus ou moins indépendant que Marie avait peut-être placé dès l'abord en tête de son ouvrage et qu'elle ne supprima pas lorsqu'elle composa son prologue-dédicace [des *Lais*]; c'est que notamment elle y avait signé son œuvre." Pickens elaborates on Rychner's distinction between the prologue to *Guigemar* and the General Prologue to the *Lais,* suggesting that we view the former as the first and the latter as the second. See his "La poétique de Marie de France d'après les prologues des *Lais,*" *Lettres Romanes* 32 (1978): 367–84.

whole is clear.[2] I share the view of Pickens, who sees the General Prologue as representing a synopsis of her literary motivations more than displaying the beginnings of her literary career, "le résultat de sa plus grande maturité créatrice" (the result of her greatest creative maturity).[3] While all her narrative texts testify in one way or another to her competence in the art of rhetoric, the fifty-six octosyllabic rhymed couplets of this exordial text have a value of their own. They spell out the poet's *causa scribendi* and function as a microcosm and brief apology of the process of literary invention in general that will permeate all her projects. The exordial matter in these lines has received a great deal of scholarly attention as a type of authorial manifesto in which she expounds her views on literary *translatio* and the poet's role in the elucidation and transmission of knowledge from one generation to the next.

Remembrance and *Captatio Benevolentiae*

The opening lines of this prologue, quoted in chapter 1, extol the virtues of literary composition and they function as a *captatio benevolentiae* that justifies Marie's decision to write. This opening passage no doubt is meant to remind the audience of the parable of the talents, from Matthew 25:14–30.[4] Marie's attempt in these

---

2. See Richard Baum, *Recherches sur les œuvres attribuées à Marie de France* (Heidelberg: Carl Winter, 1968), 32–41. Baum argues here, I think unconvincingly, that all the *lais* in the collection cannot be attributed with certainty to Marie de France. He cites several reasons for his position, including the repetition of material in the prologue of *Guigemar* that is found in the General Prologue immediately preceding it, the lack of an epilogue as found in the *Fables* and the *Espurgatoire*, and his belief that not all of the texts in the collection conform to our understanding of the *lai* as a genre. I believe that most of the evidence offered in critical analysis over the years, both cultural and linguistic, suggests otherwise.

3. Pickens, "Poétique d'après les prologues," 368. Unless otherwise noted, all English translations of secondary sources are mine.

4. For studies on Marie's allusion to the parable of the talents, see Brewster Fitz, "The Prologue to the *Lais* of Marie de France and the *Parable of the Talents:* Gloss and Monetary Metaphor," *Modern Language Notes* 90, no. 4 (1995): 558–64; Alexandre

Prologues and Epilogues

lines to acquire the goodwill of her audience by showing that it is an author's duty to use the talent that has been bestowed upon her or him—"Ne s'en deit taisir ne celer, / Ainz se deit voluntiers mustrer" (a duty not to remain silent: rather should one be happy to reveal such talents)—is more than a mere rhetorical device. Indeed, when one considers that she counts herself among the elite group of authors who possess "escïence," and to whom are given the "bone eloquence" of speaking, it becomes apparent that her assertion is audacious and courageous, coming from a woman who was writing in the exclusively male literary milieu of the period.

Marie's entry into the literary domain of her time emphasizes the role and responsibility of the author in the transmission of knowledge. She chooses to begin her text with the object pronoun "Ki," which assumes a privileged syntactical position as the first word of the first line of the General Prologue. In this way, the author takes center stage at the very beginning of her literary works, in her prefatory remarks, as she establishes the importance of continuing the tradition of *translatio studii,* the transfer of knowledge from one generation or culture to the next.

Furthermore, the first eight lines of this prologue reflect a partial paradigm of the art of medieval *inventio* and the poetics of literary rhetoric as outlined in chapter 1. The noun "escïence" means knowledge or intelligence, and by extension evokes the craft of memory, since memory is the storehouse of all knowledge.[5] Memory, as we have already seen, is an important step in the process of *inventio.* Marie's observation that this "escïence" is a gift from God recalls the distinction between natural and artifi-

---

Leupin, "The Impossible Task of Manifesting 'Literature': On Marie de France's Obscurity," *Exemplaria* 3, no. 1 (1991): 241–42; Andrew Cowell, "Deadly Letters: '*Deus Amans,*' Marie's 'Prologue' to the *Lais,* and the Dangerous Nature of the Gloss," *Romanic Review* 88, no. 3 (1997): 337–56; and Herman Braet, "Marie de France et l'obscurité des anciens," *Neuphilologische Mitteilungen* 79, no. 2 (1978): 180–84. Braet proposes that Marie's invocation of this parable is intended to invite future readers to gloss her text.

5. See Tobler and Lommatzsch, *Altfranzösisches Wörterbuch,* s.v. "escïence."

Prologues and Epilogues

cial memory made by the author of the *ad Herennium,* discussed in chapter 1. Whether an innate gift, for the writer of pagan antiquity, or a God-given talent, for the writer of Christianized medieval Europe it is likely that "escïence," in the General Prologue, encompasses both the memory that is part of our natural cognition and the memory that is trained through study and discipline. Medieval authors had a natural ability for recall, just as all fully cognizant people do, but as part of their specialized training in the arts of poetry they also developed and perfected techniques to safeguard in the library of their minds the works that they had previously heard or seen.

The General Prologue is significant to an understanding of Marie's narrative design because the stages of literary invention to which she alludes expose her concern for memory and her competence in the arts of poetry. As we shall see, the prologue offers evidence that she is conscious of the process through which authors commit preexisting works to their memories, works they will later call forth and tailor for their own purposes and audience according to the stages of *inventio.* Kelly, in reference to Marie, has commented on this process and has shown the important role that memory plays in its production:

> A source may be either material or mental (*status sensilis* or *status archetypus* [= actual and archetypal states]). This differentiates between the source as an antecedent version of the work the author proposes to write, and a conception of the work that springs from the *ingenium,* a mental construct or imagination, drawn up in and visible, as it were, to the mind's eye. The source of such imaginations is the memory. Memory is both the faculty for mental recall and the record of past thoughts and actions. Both of these senses are implied in Marie de France's allusions to Breton lais and the adventures they relate.[6]

---

6. Douglas Kelly, "Obscurity and Memory: Sources for Invention in Medieval French Literature," in *Vernacular Poetics in the Middle Ages,* ed. Lois Ebin (Kalamazoo: Western Michigan University, Medieval Institute, 1984), 34.

Prologues and Epilogues

Marie recognizes the relevance of this type of memory to her own success as poet and would like her audience to reap the benefits of such a process as well. Consequently, her texts are laden with carefully constructed, detailed descriptions, in the hope that the audience will be able to "see" the narrative in their mind's eye and have a mental record of the precepts they contain.

Likewise, the verb "parler" in "de parler bone eloquence" of the second line signifies more than a speech act. As the prologue continues to show, this expression is also designed to suggest the process of literary *inventio* in general and to include the act of writing as well. One must keep in mind that within the study of grammar the distinction between preparation for oral discourse and preparation for written discourse *(recte loquendi)* did not exist in the Middle Ages.[7] More specifically, it is the ability of an author to arrange the matter at hand and present it to an audience in such a manner that allows the work to take on new life. In Marie's case, specifically throughout all the narrative texts that follow the General Prologue, "de parler bone eloquence" showcases among other literary talents a special concern for narrative description.

The Flower of Memory

If Marie is especially concerned with memory, then her choice of a floral metaphor in the beginning of the General Prologue is certainly not fortuitous:

> Quant uns granz biens est mult oïz,
> Dunc a primes est il fluriz,
> E quant loëz est de plusurs,
> Dunc ad espandues ses flurs.
> (Pr 5–8)

When a truly beneficial thing is heard by many people, it then enjoys its first blossom, but if it is widely praised its flowers are in full bloom.

---

7. See chapter 1, note 13. Written texts, especially poetry in the vernacular, were meant to be read aloud in the Middle Ages.

Prologues and Epilogues

"Fluriz" and "flurs" recall the *début printanier* that was quite common in medieval French romance and lyric. Moreover, Carruthers has likened the honeycomb and beehive motif to the flower trope: "It seems to me that this association of bee-cells and honey, with books whose wisdom is to be packed into the compartments, *cellae* or *loci* of an ordered memory, carries over also to the metaphors that liken books and memory to fields and meadows *(campi* and *prata)* full of flowers, which the reader must cull and digest in order to store the *cella* of his memory."[8] By associating the act of composing poetry with the multiplying of flowers, Marie highlights the significance of the role of memory in the process of *inventio*. In fact, the etymology of "florilegium" (from Latin *flori,* flowers, plus *legere,* to gather), a word that describes a volume of collected writings in late antiquity and the Middle Ages, reflects the idea of gathering a variety of material into a single, specific *locus,* in this case a book with leaves *(folii)*.

Carruthers attributes to Seneca the figure of the beehive or honeycomb that is often employed in medieval writings to represent memory and book collecting as part of the process of literary composition, and she quotes from his letters in the twelfth-century curriculum of rhetoric, the *ars dictaminis:* "We ought to imitate bees, as they say, which fly about and gather [from] flowers suitable for making honey, and then arrange and sort into their cells whatever nectars they have collected."[9] Marie, like other poets of her time such as Béroul, Chrétien, and Thomas d'Angleterre, is analogous to the bee, as she uses the faculty of memory to store material that has been gathered from various sources. Just as the bee uses pollen that has been collected from different flowers in the field to produce honey, so too medieval poets chose different parts of previously acquired literary material from memory, and combined them with other parts to produce a work that in some ways resembled the sources from which it was taken but in reality represented something new. Properly speaking, *inventio,* or

---

8. Carruthers, *Book of Memory,* 38.
9. Ibid., 191–92.

Prologues and Epilogues

"finding," was not the visitation of flowers, but the discovery of relationships among the gathered bits of "pollen," the making of honey.

Priscian and Memory

In the next thirteen lines of the General Prologue, Marie continues to justify, and lend credibility to, her own literary undertakings by enlisting the common rhetorical *topos* of *auctoritas:*

> Custume fu as ancïens,
> Ceo testimoine Precïens,
> Es livres ke jadis feseient,
> Assez oscurement diseient
> Pur ceus ki a venir esteient
> E ki aprendre les deveient,
> K'i peüssent gloser la lettre
> E de lur sen le surplus mettre.
> Li philosophe le saveient,
> Par eus meïsmes entendeient,
> Cum plus trespassereit li tens,
> Plus serreient sutil de sens
> E plus se savreient garder
> De ceo k'i ert a trespasser.
> (Pr 9–22)

It was customary for the ancients, in the books which they wrote (Priscian testifies to this), to express themselves very obscurely so that those in later generations, who had to learn them, could provide a gloss for the text and put the finishing touches to their meaning. Men of learning were aware of this and their experience had taught them that the more time they spent studying texts the more subtle would be their understanding of them and they would be better able to avoid future mistakes.

Among all the other implications of these lines, including the justification for taking preexisting material and adapting it to the concerns at hand, the fact that she mentions Priscian by name is of particular significance, for nowhere else in the works that have been attributed to her does she specifically name a grammarian or rhetorician. This historical reference is different from her mention of the Bretons in the *Lais,* or the book of King Alfred in the *Fables,* both alleged sources of material for her stories. Instead, this is an explicit revelation of at least one of the authorities from whom she learned to write, as is evidenced by her understanding of the grammarian's "testimony," or rather what he himself had to say about the art of literary composition. Her belief that Priscian "testifies" to the veracity of her comments on textual transmission shows her familiarity with the views of at least one of the authors of the arts of rhetoric and grammar who represented part of her curriculum in literary training.

Perhaps no other lines from Marie de France have prompted more critical exchange than lines 9–22, and while the scope of the current investigation does not allow for an intricate account of all opinions expressed on this passage over the years, a basic understanding of certain divergent critical perspectives will nonetheless be beneficial in establishing the importance of this authorial reference to her overall narrative plan of description and memory.

The principal debate over Marie's meaning in these lines has centered on her reference to Priscian and the authorial intention of earlier authors. Scholars have traditionally associated lines 9–22 from Marie's text with Priscian's opening paragraph of the *Institutiones grammaticae,* one of the most influential treatises on grammar and widely used for instruction during the Middle Ages.[10] This assumption appears to be based on the general acceptance, since the end of the nineteenth century, of Warnke's association of Marie's comments with Priscian's *Institutiones,* which is, as far as I know, the earliest suggestion of such a relationship.[11]

---

10. See Appendix A for this text. See also the article by Tony Hunt, "Glossing Marie de France," *Romanische Forschungen* 86, nos. 3–4 (1974): 396–418. He notes that more than "500 manuscripts of the *Institutiones* survive, of which 347 are dated to before the end of the twelfth century" (403).

11. *Die Lais der Marie de France,* ed. Karl Warnke, 3d ed. (Halle: Niemeyer, 1925), 259–60 (p. 225 in the first edition of 1885).

Prologues and Epilogues

Most attention given to this passage has focused on the meaning of lines 12–16, in which Marie comments on the intention of the ancients:

> Assez oscurement diseient
> Pur ceus ki a venir esteient,
> E ki aprendre les deveient,
> K'i peüssent gloser la lettre
> E de lur sen le surplus mettre.

> To express themselves very obscurely so that those in later generations, who had to learn them, could provide a gloss for the text and put the finishing touches to their meaning.

The question arises whether she had in mind a commentary more from the perspective of the ancients or more from that of the moderns.[12] In other words, did those authors who preceded her expressly leave their texts obscure so that contemporary authors like herself could extract their hidden meanings and elucidate them through their own interpretation? Or did she mean to say that the ancients naturally wrote obscurely because they did not possess the knowledge that later authors would acquire? Does she therefore expect the future readers of her text to make their own glosses?

Although these questions may never be answered with certainty, they have nonetheless generated much textual analysis of Marie's General Prologue and several hypotheses for Marie's motive in citing Priscian. One problem has been that Marie's mention of the obscurity of the ancients cannot be supported directly by Priscian's comments in the opening sentences of his *Institutiones,* for his concern is with older grammarians, while Marie refers to preceding authors of literary texts. In assessing the critical dialogue that has developed over this reference, Mary-Louise Zanoni summarizes the different approaches in this way: "the definition of Marie's poetic principles by internal analysis of the prologue itself; the comparison of Marie's literary craft to the methods of

---

12. See my article "Marie de France and the Ancients," in *"De sens rassis": Essays in Honor of Rupert T. Pickens,* ed. Keith Busby, Bernard Guidot, and Logan E. Whalen (Amsterdam: Rodopi, 2005), 719–28.

Prologues and Epilogues

scriptural exegesis and the concomitant assertion that the *Lais* have a hidden Christian significance; and the examination of how Marie's contemporaries understood Priscian's statements on the relationships of ancient authors and later interpreters."[13] Among the many studies to which Zanoni alludes, of those that have attempted to outline Marie's poetics through an internal analysis of the General Prologue, Pickens offers a detailed and original reading, showing how each of the five sections that he examines relates to Marie's corpus in general. His analysis of the relationships linking these sections reconciles a "poetics of writing" with a "poetics of *mouvance*." Each *lai* individually and all the *lais* collectively are products of a process of *mouvance*. Marie's writing hers down is a moment in the history of this process; and, in their continued reception, Marie's *lais* are themselves subject to the process.[14] Memory plays a significant role in this paradigm, as Pickens notes in reference to section 1: "Tout se passe selon l'intention créatrice du poète, qui *fait* un poème *pur remembrance* (cf. Pr 35), *pur remembrer* quelque chose (cf. *El* 1183, *Cht* 2 et 111)—c'est-à-dire, simultanément l'œuvre rappelle à l'auditeur ce qu'elle commémore et se soumet à ses activités mnémoniques et interpréta-

---

13. Mary-Louise Zanoni, "'Ceo Testimoine Precïens': Priscian and the Prologue to the *Lais* of Marie de France," *Traditio: Studies in Ancient and Medieval History, Thought, and Religion* 36 (1980): 408.

14. Pickens, "Poétique d'après les prologues," 367–70. His five sections are: (1) 1–8 ("Lieux communs d'exorde" [florescence]), (2) 9–22 (reference to Priscian), (3) 23–32 ("lieux communs d'exorde" [*causa scribendi* and the process of writing]), (4) 33–42 (history of Marie's *lais*), and (5) 43–56 (dedication). He works from a Zumthorian model of *mouvance*, or the mobility of a text during its transmission; see Paul Zumthor, *Essai de poétique médiévale* (Paris: Seuil, 1972). Other informative studies include Sally L. Burch, "The Prologue to Marie's *Lais*: Back to the *Littera*," *AUMLA: Journal of the Australian Universities Language and Literature Association* 89 (May 1998): 15–42; Jean-Claude Delclos, "Encore le prologue des *Lais* de Marie de France," *Le Moyen Âge* 90, no. 2 (1984): 223–32; and Alfred Foulet and Karl D. Uitti, "The Prologue to the *Lais* of Marie de France: A Reconsideration," *Romance Philology* 35, no. 1 (1981–82): 242–49. Delclos argues for coherence in the General Prologue and sees the opening lines as reconciling Marie's literary task with that of her predecessors. Foulet and Uitti examine the *topoi* of *auctoritas* and *translatio studii* and offer detailed commentary on line 16, "E de lur sen le surplus mettre," and lines 21–22, "E plus se savreient garder / De ceo k'i ert a trespasser."

Prologues and Epilogues

tives, et l'auditeur à la fois souffre une stimulation intellectuelle et se met à scruter le poème" (Everything takes place according to the creative vision of the poet, who *creates* a poem *to be remembered* [cf. Pr 35], '*to recall* something' [cf. *El* 1183, *Cht* 2 and 111]—that is to say, the work simultaneously reminds the listener of what it commemorates and becomes subject to his or her mnemonic and interpretive activities, and the listener at the same time undergoes an intellectual stimulation and begins to scrutinize the poem).[15]

As for a hidden Christian significance in the *Lais*, Leo Spitzer was the first to suggest that Marie's reference to Priscian was designed to support an approach of biblical exegesis to her text, and his view was soon afterward championed by D. W. Robertson.[16] Approximately ten years later Mortimer Donovan steered attention away from the religious reading of this passage, embracing the belief that the ancients may have been obscure, but not intentionally so; he cites references to Priscian by other twelfth-century authors to support his claims.[17] Ultimately, the approach of scriptural exegesis was firmly rejected by Tony Hunt, who saw in Marie's reference to Priscian an association with the humanism of her own time.[18] Moreover, Kelly argues convincingly that Donovan's

---

15. Pickens, "Poétique d'après les prologues," 374–75.

16. Leo Spitzer, "The Prologue to the *Lais* of Marie de France and Medieval Poetics," *Modern Philology* 41, no. 2 (1943–44): 96–102; D. W. Robertson Jr., "Marie de France, *Lais*, Prologue, 13–16," *Modern Language Notes* 64, no. 5 (1949): 336–38.

17. Mortimer Donovan, "Priscian and the Obscurity of the Ancients," *Speculum* 36, no. 1 (1961): 75–80. See also Ana-María Holzbacher, "El Prólogo de los *Lais*: No se ha dicho aún la última palabra," *Boletín de la Real Academia de Buenas Letras de Barcelona* 41 (1987–88): 227–57. In reference to the twelfth-century glossators that Donovan cites, she writes, "Por nuestra parte, nos parece que de estas citas podemos deducir: que la frase de Prisciano mencionada por otros autores no va en ellos ligada a la idea de oscuridad voluntaria; que Prisciano es dado como ejemplo de autor oscuro comentado por los glosadores, y, por último, que la frase de Prisciano aparece asociada a la idea de progresión y está apoyada por el ejemplo de los profetas" (246). Holzbacher's article is basically a recapitulation of all the scholarly discussion to date on these lines of Marie.

18. Hunt, "Glossing Marie de France," 407. He notes, "It emerges from such evidence [references to twelfth-century glossators of Priscian] that, in her prologue, Marie probably refers not to the procedures of Scriptural exegesis but to the wide-

view that the ancients were not intentionally obscure was inconsistent with textual evidence, noting that "Marie's words suggest that the Ancients did know what they were obscuring, both by the intentionality expressed in the preposition of purpose *Pur* in v. 13, and by the sense of vv. 21–22, not considered by Donovan."[19]

While all of these points of view have a certain merit in their own context, and have done much to further our understanding of Marie's poetics, they have nonetheless stopped short of broadening the scope of her reference to Priscian, namely, by failing to consider the possibility that she may have had in mind another work from this sixth-century grammarian. In fact, to the best of my knowledge, Zanoni is the only scholar to date who has suggested that Priscian's *Praeexercitamina* are also a viable candidate for Marie's citation.

The *Praeexercitamina* were Latin translations of the *Progymnasmata* of the second-century rhetorician Hermogenes of Tarsus.[20] Kelly reminds us that these preparatory school exercises included "practice in invention" and "amplification of words and actions in description."[21] These exercises were significant because, "as a supplement to his [Priscian's] grammar, they brought the Latin Middle Ages the elements of Greek rhetorical theory, and did so with the omission of everything which was pertinent only to political and judicial oratory."[22]

The availability of the *Praeexercitamina* throughout the Middle Ages is well attested. Zanoni shows that they were often appended to manuscripts of the *Institutiones* and that they "were nearly, if not equally, as popular as the *Institutiones*."[23] One must also keep

---

spread concept of progress which characterized the centres of humanism in her day and which often attracted the tag from Priscian as an illustrative *sententia*."

19. Kelly, "Obscurity and Memory," 35.

20. Murphy, *Rhetoric in the Middle Ages,* 72.

21. Douglas Kelly, *The Medieval Imagination: Rhetoric and the Poetry of Courtly Love* (Madison: University of Wisconsin Press, 1978), 34.

22. Ernst Robert Curtius, *European Literature and the Latin Middle Ages,* trans. Willard R. Trask (Princeton: Princeton University Press, 1953), 442.

23. Zanoni, "'Ceo Testimoine Preciens,'" 410n.

Prologues and Epilogues

in mind that Marie's literary training was no doubt completed before the appearance of popular treatises devoted solely to the arts of poetry and prose, such as Matthew of Vendôme's *Ars versificatoria* (ca. 1175) and Geoffrey of Vinsauf's *Poetria nova* (ca. 1210), and consequently depended on the more rhetorically oriented treatises that formed the base of medieval instruction, including the one currently under discussion. Zanoni notes that "Marie was, in short, a child of the older, more rhetorical school of poetic apprenticeship, and may well have been set the task of composing pieces in accordance with the recommendations of Priscian's *Praeexercitamina* at some point in her schooling." In her observations of possible texts available to Marie, in addition to Priscian's *Institutiones* and *Praeexercitamina*, she specifically names Cicero's *De inventione* and the pseudo-Ciceronian *Rhetorica ad Herrenium*.[24]

When one considers Marie's narrative design of consciously crafted description that calls to memory material from the past and ensures its survival for posterity, the case for inclusion of the *Praeexercitamina* becomes even more appealing. That is to say, this collection contains divisions that treat parts of composition vital to literary invention. In particular, the division *De descriptione* opens by discussing the various types of properties that can be described and by showing the importance of creating images that are visual to our imagination: "Descriptio est oratio colligens et praesentans oculis quod demonstrat" (Description is speech that brings forth and makes present before the eyes the thing that it designates).[25] The verb *colligo* is related to memory, and the expression *colligo animo*, as used by Cicero, can be translated as "to bring to mind, to recall to memory."[26]

---

24. Ibid., 411.
25. My translation. See Heinrich Keil, ed., *Grammatici Latini,* 8 vols. (Leipzig, 1855–80; reprint, Hildesheim: Georg Olms, 1961). In the *Praeexercitamina*, 3:430–40, the divisions, in order, are as follows: *De fabula, De narratione, De usu, De sententia, De refutatione (quam Graeci* ΑΝΑΣΚΕΥΗΝ *vocant), De loco communi, De laude, De comparatione, De allocutione, De descriptione, De positione,* and *De legis latione.* See Appendix A for *De laude* and *De descriptione*.
26. See Charlton T. Lewis and Charles Short, eds., *A Latin Dictionary* (1879;

Prologues and Epilogues

In fact, I propose that Priscian's opening sentence in this section on description reflects Marie's principal concern throughout all her works, especially throughout the *Lais* that are contained in the same manuscript as the General Prologue, in which the reference to the Latin grammarian is found. This declaration could serve as a motto for the whole of her literary career, as she repeatedly demonstrates her ability to gather material from the past and bring it to life so that it takes on a visual dimension to the mind's eye. This principle looks forward to the words of Richard de Fournival in his thirteenth-century text *Li bestiaires d'amours:* "Car quant on voit painte une estoire, ou de Troies ou d'autre, on voit les fais des preudommes ki cha en ariere furent, ausi com s'il fussent present. Et tout ensi est il de parole. Car quant on ot .i. romans lire, on entent les aventures, ausi com on les veïst en present" (For when one sees a story painted of Troy or somewhere else, one sees the deeds of noblemen who lived back then as if they were present. The same is true of speech. For when one hears a romance read aloud, one understands the adventures just as if one could see them before one's eyes).[27] Marie, drawing on her knowledge of learned grammarians like Priscian, understood the commemorative power of vivid descriptions decades before Fournival praised their qualities in his own text. As Kelly has commented, "Marie de France learned from him [Priscian] how to pierce the obscurity of her sources and bring back past memory in language meaningful to her contemporaries. Hence, the Prologue to the *Lais* expresses a historical consciousness and the art which made it practicable in vernacular literature."[28]

Priscian's *Praeexercitamina* cannot be overemphasized as it relates

---

reprint Cambridge: Clarendon Press, 1962), *colligo* 1. They quote Cicero: "cum et nostrae rei publicae detrimenta considero, et maximarum civitatum veteres animo calamitates colligo." *Colligo* 1 is *colligo, colligere,* and means basically to collect; *colligo* 2 is *colligo, colligare,* which means to bind together. I thank Rupert T. Pickens for pointing out *colligo animo* to me and for providing me with the reference.

27. My translation. See Richard de Fournival, *Li bestiaires d'amour,* ed. Cesare Segré (Milan: Riccardi, 1957), 5.

28. Kelly, "Obscurity and Memory," 50–51.

Prologues and Epilogues

to instruction in the description of objects. Edmond Faral noted that the popular treatises on the arts of poetry that were starting to develop during and after the time in which Marie wrote are silent on this subject, with the sole exception of Matthew of Vendôme's text: "En fait de descriptions de choses, on ne trouve dans les arts poétiques que celle des saisons de l'année et d'un jardin par Matthieu de Vendôme (II, 107, 108 et 111)" (As for descriptions of things, one finds in the Arts of Poetry only those of the seasons and of a garden in Matthew of Vendôme).[29] As mentioned earlier, the date of the *Ars versificatoria* (ca. 1175) makes it unlikely that Marie drew her inspiration for detailed descriptions from it, since her works are for the most part contemporaneous with it.

It is more certain that the influence on Marie's style of literary composition came from a text of rhetoric and grammar more classical in nature, probably the *Praeexercitamina* itself. Priscian's text has much to offer in the area of describing objects, especially in the division *De laude*.[30] As Faral notes, this section reflects the various types of description to be found throughout vernacular literature of the late twelfth and early thirteenth centuries in France and England, including descriptions of all sorts of animals, weapons and armor, clothing, etc.: "Il est certain que ces descriptions ont fait, au moins à l'origine, l'objet d'un enseignement, et on en a comme indice, entre d'autres, le rapport qu'elles présentent avec ce passage-ci des *Praeexercitamina* de Priscien" (It is certain that these descriptions, at least in the beginning, were a topic of instruction, and we have as one indication, among others, the relationship that they demonstrate with this passage from Priscian's *Praeexercitamina*).[31] As will be discussed below, it is this kind of attention that Marie gives to the task of describing objects within her narratives.

---

29. Faral, *Arts poétiques du XIIe et du XIIIe siècle,* 81.
30. See Appendix A.
31. See Faral, *Arts poétiques du XIIe et du XIIIe siècle,* 82. Faral cites *De laude* in his discussion on the description of objects, but from a different edition of Priscian's texts (Halm).

Prologues and Epilogues

In light of the content in Priscian's Latin translation of these Greek exercises in style, we may need to reconsider Marie's reference to him in lines 9–22 of the General Prologue. In fact, her intentions in citing Priscian go far beyond a desire to call to mind only the opening paragraph of the *Institutiones,* as scholarship has traditionally held, though I do not exclude that particular text from those she may have had in mind. It seems to me, in view of the preceding discussion, that her reference is intended to include his writings in general, whether the *Institutiones* or the *Praeexercitamina,* and above all else to align herself with his venerable reputation.[32] By calling forth the authority of such an important figure in the history of medieval training in the arts of rhetoric and grammar, she not only justifies the process of topical invention that she undertakes, but also empowers her own literary milieu—the Anglo-Angevin court for which she wrote—through the *topos* of *translatio studii* implicit in her reference to Priscian. Knowledge passes from the Greek world of Hermogenes to the Roman world of Priscian, and then to Marie's medieval England and France.

Furthermore, her reference to Priscian, in so far as it singles out one of her mentors in literary training, may also have been intended to give her audience a clue to understanding the meaning of her texts. If the audience understands that she is following the doctrine of Priscian, there is a better chance that they will be capable of esteeming her descriptive narratives. As Kelly reminds us, "If Marie de France learned to write by studying Priscian, what she learned was the ability to digress from the *matiere* at hand in

---

32. See Zanoni, "'Ceo Testimoine Precïens,'" 411. Zanoni also concludes that Marie is referring to both of the Priscian texts instead of merely to the *Institutiones:* "Rather, the close thematic correspondence between the *Praeexercitamina* and Marie's Prologue would argue in favor of an interpretation that Marie, when she asserts that 'Ceo testimoine Precïens,' is accurately and fully revealing the sources of her literary discussion. Those sources are both the opening discourse of the *Institutiones* and also its companion piece, the *Praeexercitamina;* for both these works by Priscian were probably very well known to Marie as the school texts from which she had received her early training in the sister arts of Latin grammar and rhetoric."

Prologues and Epilogues

order to discover—to invent—a *san* which descriptions, among other amplificatory subjects, can enunciate, schematically, systematically, and satisfactorily for the proposed audience."[33] It seems reasonable, given the substantial use of descriptions throughout all of her narratives, that she singles out Priscian because his emphasis on *descriptio* as part of the paradigm for medieval topical invention best suits her own technique.

Remembrance and *Memoire* in the Prologues and Epilogues

Later in the General Prologue, Marie announces the role that memory plays in the preservation of material from the past and in the transmission of that material to the present culture. As lines 1–22 establish an important part of her poetic design, lines 33–42 also represent her goal of writing:

> Des lais pensai, k'oïz aveie.
> Ne dutai pas, bien le saveie,
> Ke pur remambrance les firent
> Des aventures k'il oïrent
> Cil ki primes les comencierent
> E ki avant les enveierent.
> Plusurs en ai oï conter,
> Nes voil laissier ne oblier.
> Rimé en ai e fait ditié,
> Soventes fiez en ai veillié!
> (Pr 33–42)

So I thought of lays which I had heard and did not doubt, for I knew it full well, that they were composed, by those who first began them and put them into circulation, to perpetuate the memory of adventures they had heard. I myself have heard a number of them and do not wish to overlook or ne-

---

33. Douglas Kelly, "The Art of Description," in *The Legacy of Chrétien de Troyes*, ed. Norris J. Lacy, Douglas Kelly, and Keith Busby, 2 vols. (Amsterdam: Rodopi, 1987), 1:196.

Prologues and Epilogues

glect them. I have put them into verse, made poems from them and worked on them late into the night.

These lines recall the same theme from the beginning of the prologue, namely, the way in which Marie will draw on source material to create stories that are uniquely fashioned after her own poetic perspective; as Kelly notes, "Her evaluation amounts to the archeological reconstruction of past monuments from extant remains."[34] The way in which she "invents" these stories, that is to say, the way in which she reconstructs them to fit her own literary plan, depends upon the faculty of her memory, since her "sources are at one and the same time 'material' and 'mental'—simply summed up in her phrase: 'Des lais pensai, k'oïz aveie.'"[35]

That Marie is occupied with memory is apparent from her comments in line 35 of the General Prologue, where she asserts that the authors of the *lais* that she has heard originally made them in order to perpetuate the memory of the stories from which they were composed: "Ke pur remambrance les firent." Likewise, Marie, in her turn, is interested in preserving these stories for posterity, and she proclaims, "Nes voil laissier ne oblier" (I do not wish to neglect or forget them) (Pr 40).[36] She has worked hard—"Soventes fiez en ai veillié" (I have worked on them late into the night) (Pr 42)—to ensure that this material will be remembered in the future. Part of this labor has involved the attention to descriptions that she learned from Priscian.[37]

"Remembrer" and any of its forms, including "remembrance,"

---

34. Kelly, "Obscurity and Memory," 36.
35. Ibid., 36.
36. My translation differs from Burgess and Busby here by insisting on the sense of "not to forget them," i.e., "to remember them," for the verb "nes ... oblier." Even though in my translation I maintain their choice of the expression "not to neglect them," I nonetheless understand "nes ... laissier" to carry more of a sense of "not to leave them behind," i.e., "not to forget them," or "to remember them."
37. While Marie may have learned her art of description from a variety of classical and medieval sources through her training in literary composition, Priscian is nonetheless the only authority she cites by name, and his strategies of description are the ones that seem to come through most clearly in her works.

Prologues and Epilogues

are not serendipitous vocabulary choices for Marie. Nor is it by chance that the word "remembrance" appears in the General Prologue, where Marie uses it to demonstrate the significance of memory to the process of topical invention. Terms that evoke the process of memory are always strategically placed throughout her texts to give significance to the surrounding textual elements. Of the occasions on which Marie's name appears in a prologue or epilogue—once in the prologue to *Guigemar* in the *Lais,* once in the epilogue to the *Fables,* once in the epilogue to the *Espurgatoire,* and once in the epilogue to the *Audree*—it does so in the context of memory, by employing the nouns "remembrance" and "memoire."

In lines 3 and 4 of the famous epilogue to the *Fables* she chooses "remembrance" for rhyming the couplet "me numerai pur remembrance: / Marie ai num, si sui de France" (I shall name myself for posterity: Marie is my name, and I am from France).[38] Although Marie's *Espurgatoire* is a translation of H. of Saltrey's *De Purgatorio Sancti Patricii,* her comments in the prologue and epilogue of the work are original.[39] Though H. mentions memory in prefatory comments to his *Purgatorio,* his actual prologue is silent on the matter. However, Marie's prologue is explicit about the subject, and in lines 2297–98 she places her name on the same textual level as the word "memoire": "Jo, *Marie,* ai mis, en memoire, / le livre de l'Espurgatoire." (I, Marie, have put / the Book of Purgatory into French, / as a record).[40] Interestingly, *La vie seinte*

---

38. References to Marie de France's *Fables* are from *Die Fabeln der Marie de France,* ed. Karl Warnke (Halle: Niemeyer, 1898). Unless otherwise noted, all English translations of the *Fables* are from *The Fables of Marie de France: An English Translation,* trans. Mary-Lou Martin (Birmingham, Ala.: Summa Publications, 1982).

39. Many writers have conventionally expanded the "H." in H. of Saltrey, as it appears in the manuscript, to "Henry." Yolande de Pontfarcy shows that there is really no scholarly basis for this choice, and she points out that the name "Henry" is not found in the Latin source, *De Purgatorio Sancti Patrcii.* See her edition of the text, *Marie de France, L'Espurgatoire Seint Patriz: Nouvelle édition critique accompagnée du De Purgatorio Sancti Patricii (éd. de Warnke), d'une introduction, d'une traduction, de notes et d'un glossaire* (Louvain: Peeters, 1995), 5n11.

40. Curley's translation here of "have put . . . as a record" for "ai mis, en mem-

Prologues and Epilogues

Audree follows a similar design in lines 4624–25 of the epilogue, strengthening the case that both of these hagiographic texts were composed by Marie de France: "Ici ecris mon non Marie / Pur ce ke soie remembree" (Here I write my name "Marie" so that I may be remembered).[41]

Furthermore, the use of terms that relate to memory are so ubiquitous in the *Lais* that Denise McClelland has referred to "un vocabulaire mémoriel" in reference to Marie. This verbal network is "une consolidation des souvenirs (*remembrance, remembrer, recorder en sun queor,* pléonasme poétique) en particulier par l'œuvre artistique et littéraire, le lai, qui perpétuera la mémoire des aventures extraordinaires" (a consolidation of memories [*remembrance, remembrer, recorder en sun queor,* poetic pleonism] in particular by the artistic and literary work, the lay, that will perpetuate the memory of extraordinary adventures).[42] Terms and expressions that evoke memory can be found throughout the *Lais,* to be sure, but their occurrence in the General Prologue that precedes the collection of *Lais,* and in the exordial matter that precedes many individual *lais* themselves, gives them privileged status. These terms are also occasionally grouped at the end of *lais* in the last few lines, at which point Marie is usually recalling the generation of texts. In these positions, either before or after the diagesis of the text, they are associated with the creative process of *inventio,* because the audience is consistently reminded that the purpose of putting the story into the vernacular is to preserve it in memory.

Guigemar, the first *lai* after the General Prologue in Harley 978, opens with a prologue that has some of the same *topoi* as

---

oire," is accurate, since the Latin verb *recordor,* "to record," is etymologically linked to memory (to recollect, to remember, to recall). See note 42 below.

41. All references to and English translations of *La vie seinte Audree* are from *The Life of Saint Audrey: A Text by Marie de France,* ed. and trans. June Hall McCash and Judith Clark Barban (Jefferson, N.C.: McFarland & Co., 2006).

42. Denise McClelland, *Le vocabulaire dans les Lais de Marie de France* (Ottawa: Éditions de l'Université d'Ottawa, 1977), 54.

Prologues and Epilogues

the larger prologue that precedes it, especially *captatio benevolentiae* and *translatio*. Possibly intended as the original prologue to the entire collection of *lais*,[43] it begins with an appeal to the faculty of memory: "Oëz, seignurs, ke dit Marie, / Ki en sun tens pas ne s'oblie" (Hear, my lords, what Marie has to say, who was not forgotten in her own time) (G 3–4).[44] In addition to the aforementioned autorevelation of Marie from the *Fables,* the *Espurgatoire,* and the *Audree,* her name is once again associated here with the cognitive process of memory.

The prologue to *Equitan* is even more direct in its evocation of memory:

> Jadis suleient par pruësce,
> Par curteisie et par noblesce,
> Des aventures qu'il oeient,
> Ki a plusurs genz aveneient,
> Fere les lais pur remembrance,
> Qu'um nes meïst en ubliance.
> Un ent firent, k'oï cunter,
> Ki ne fet mie a ublier.
>
> (*Eq* 3–10)

In days gone by these valiant, courtly and noble men [the Bretons] composed lays for posterity and thus preserved them from oblivion. These lays were based on adventures they had heard and which had befallen many a person. One of them, which I have heard recited, should not be forgotten.

Faced with the potential threat of oblivion of the adventures in question, the Bretons composed a *lai* to assure their preservation. This is also the case for the opening of *Bisclavret,* where Marie wants to guard against a loss of memory: "Quant des lais faire m'entremet, / Ne voil ublier *Bisclavret*" (In my effort to compose lays I do not wish to forget *Bisclavret*") (B 1–2).[45] In fact, Marie's

---

43. See note 1 above.   44. My translation. See note 36.
45. I substitute "forget" where Burgess and Busby have "omit" for the verb "ublier." See note 36.

Prologues and Epilogues

fear of this *lai* being forgotten and its veracity disbelieved, is apparently so strong that she reminds the audience in the last few lines of the text that *Bisclavret* was made to be remembered:

> L'aventure k'avez oïe
> Veraie fu, n'en dutez mie.
> De Bisclavret fu fez li lais
> Pur remembrance a tuz dis mais.
> (*B* 315–18)

> The adventure you have heard actually took place, do not doubt it. The lay was composed about Bisclavret to be remembered for ever more.

Thus *Bisclavret* begins and ends by invoking the act of memory, just as the entire collection of *lais* opens and closes with reminders of this faculty.

That Marie desires to remember her sources and the story she creates from them is also attested by her opening couplet to *Chaitivel:* "Talent me prist de remembrer / Un lai dunt jo oï parler" (I am minded to recall a lay of which I have heard) (*Cht* 1–2). This desire to remember is also shared at times by the characters within the *lais* themselves, as is the case with Tristan, who wishes to compose a *lai* so that his adventures with Iseut are not forgotten: "Pur les paroles remembrer, / Tristram, ki bien saveit harper, / En aveit fet un nuvel lai" (Tristram, a skilful harpist, in order to record his words [as the queen had said he should], used them to create a new lay) (*Chv* 111–13). Finally, just as the *Lais* begin with a statement of the significance of memory to the literary process of *inventio*, "Ke pur remambrance les firent" (they [the lays] were composed … to perpetuate the memory) (*Pr* 35), so too does the collection end with a reminder that is almost verbatim:

> De l'aventure de ces treis
> Li auncïen Bretun curteis
> Firent le lai pur remembrer,
> Qu'um nel deüst pas oblier.
> (*El* 1181–84)

Prologues and Epilogues

> From the story of these three the ancient courtly Bretons composed a lay to be remembered, so that it should not be forgotten.

One might say that memory has the first and last words in the *Lais* in general, just as it does within the individual *lai* of *Bisclavret*.

Marie's collection of fables in the Aesopic tradition was probably composed sometime between the *Lais* and the *Espurgatoire seint Patriz*.[46] Like the *Lais*, her *Fables* open with a prologue, but whereas the *Lais* lack organized closing remarks for the whole work, the *Fables* end with an epilogue that summarizes Marie's *causa scribendi* of the brief narrative tales that precede it. These opening and closing passages are significant to Marie's poetics because they take up again the theme of memory that was prevalent in the General Prologue to the *Lais* and in the prefatory and postliminary commentaries of many of the individual *lais*.

At first glance, it may appear that Marie's main justification for writing is found toward the end of the prologue to the *Fables* in the form of a dedication:

> A mei, ki la rime en dei faire,
> n'avenist nïent a retraire
> plusurs paroles ki i sunt;
> mes nepuruec cil m'en sumunt,
> ki flurs est de chevalerie,
> d'enseignement, de curteisie;
> e quant tels huem m'en a requise,
> ne vueil laissier en nule guise
> que n'i mete travail e peine,
> ki que m'en tienge pur vileine;
> mult dei faire pur sa preiere.
>
> (27–37)

It was not at all becoming to me, whose task it was to compose the verse, to repeat several words which are found here, but nevertheless he who is the flower of chivalry, of learning,

---

46. For dating her *Fables*, see chapter 4.

Prologues and Epilogues

and of courtliness commissioned me, and when such a man has commanded me, in no way do I want to neglect being diligent and thorough about it, no matter who may take me for uncourtly. I must do my best on account of his request.

In the epilogue, we learn that the person referred to in line 31, "ki flurs est de chevalerie," is a certain Count William:

> Pur amur le cunte Willalme,
> le plus vaillant de cest reialme,
> m'entremis de cest livre faire
> e de l'Engleis en Romanz traire.
> (Epilogue 9–12)

For the love of Count William, the most valiant of this realm, I undertook to write this book and to translate it from English into French.

It may never be possible to determine the true identity of this William, but numerous attempts have been made over the past century to ascertain exactly who commissioned Marie to write this collection of fables and to whom she dedicates her work.[47]

While one cannot deny that royal patronage appears to have been one reason for Marie's recording her own version of Aesopic fables, as the preceding reference shows, an additional literary agenda is revealed in the opening lines of the prologue:

> Cil, ki sevent de letreüre,
> devreient bien metre lur cure
> es bons livres e es escriz
> e es essamples e es diz,
> que li philosophe troverent
> e escristrent e remembrerent.
> Par moralité escriveient
> les bons proverbes qu'il oeient,

---

47. See, in particular, the introduction to the English prose translation of the *Lais* by Burgess and Busby. For other discussions, see the articles listed in Glyn S. Burgess, *Marie de France: An Analytical Bibliography* (London: Grant and Cutler, 1977).

Prologues and Epilogues

> que cil amender s'en poïssent
> ki lur entente en bien meïssent.
> (1–10)

All the good books, writings, fables, and proverbs that thinkers have composed, written, and transcribed should truly be heeded by well-read people, for the ancients who wrote down these good proverbs that they heard did so for the purpose of moral edification, in order that those who set their mind upon the good might improve themselves.

The appeal not to neglect a literary talent found in the first two lines, as well as the references to the "bons livres e es escriz" of line 3 and the "philosophe" of line 5, clearly recall the opening to the General Prologue discussed above. Furthermore, the verb "remembrer" in line 6 evokes the theme of memory that Marie followed in her first work.[48]

When reflecting on the frequency with which she makes reference to the act of memory, it is indeed surprising that in the myriad scholarly writings devoted to Marie de France over the past century no one has yet attempted a synthesis of this theme as it relates to her works in general. On every occasion that she identifies herself in her writings, she associates her name syntactically with "remembrance" or "memoire." Moreover, she almost never addresses her audience directly in the form of commentary in any of her works, with the exception of the morals at the end of individual fables, without in some way invoking the faculty of memory. This narrative penchant is most clearly evident in her prologues and epilogues to the works under consideration, but it is also present in many of her opening and closing commentaries to individual *lais*.

The prologues and epilogues of any literary work are impor-

---

48. Here Martin translates "remembrerent" as "transcribed." While that translation is valid, and while her prose translation of the *Fables* as a whole represents an accurate and superbly fluid reading in English, I would give "remembrerent" in this context its rhetorical significance of "memory" within the paradigm of *inventio*, as

Prologues and Epilogues

tant, but for the works of Marie de France their significance cannot be stressed enough. They are the blueprint with which she constructs the mnemonic architecture of her narratives. From the very beginning of her endeavors, the *topoi* of *captatio benevolentiae, causa scribendi, translatio studii,* and *auctoritas* show that she recognizes the power of memory within the creative process of medieval literary *inventio.* As she attests her association with the works of Priscian, she ensures the respect of her audience and cues them to her capability in the domain of grammar and rhetoric. In the texts that follow her exordial comments, she will reveal her literary talents, particularly in the art of description.

---

discussed in chapter 1. This reading is reinforced by "troverent," a word that also belongs to the process of medieval topical invention.

3

The *Lais*

As noted in chapter 2, Harley 978 in the British Library, London, is the only manuscript containing all twelve of Marie de France's *lais*.[1] *Guigemar*'s position as the first *lai* in the collection, preceded only by the General Prologue, strategically emphasizes the significance of Marie's descriptive style and architecture of memory.[2] The earlier discussion of the prologues and epilogues demonstrated how the General Prologue functions as a type of poetic manifesto in which Marie evokes the process of literary *inventio* and focuses on the act of remembering. *Guigemar*, in turn, is the most descriptive of all her *lais*, and also opens with a prologue that highlights memory. Thus Marie demonstrates her program of narrative description.

Marie may have chosen the *lai* as a genre in which to compose her first narrative work because it perfectly accommodates

---

1. London, BL, Harley 978, fols. 118–60, has the General Prologue, then all the *lais*, in the following order: *Guigemar, Equitan, Le Fresne, Bisclavret, Lanval, Deus Amanz, Yonec, Laüstic, Milun, Chaitivel, Chievrefoil*, and *Eliduc*. Other manuscripts with one or more *lais* include BL, Cott.Vesp. B.XIV, fols. 1–8 *(Lanval)*; Paris, BNF, nouv. acq. fr. 1104, fols. 1a–45vb *(Guigemar, Lanval, Yonec, Chievrefoil, Deus Amanz* [fragmentary], *Bisclavret* [fragmentary], *Milun, Le Fresne,* and *Equitan)*; BNF, fr. 2168, fols. 47a–58b *(Yonec* [fragmentary], *Guigemar,* and *Lanval)*; and BNF, fr. 24432, fols. 241b–245a *(Yonec)*.

2. For a detailed analysis of the possible order in which the *lais* that appear in Harley 978 were actually composed, see chapter 1, "The Problem of Internal Chronology," in Glyn S. Burgess, *The Lais of Marie de France: Text and Context* (Athens: University of Georgia Press, 1987). This chapter is an expanded version of Burgess's article "The Problem of Internal Chronology in the *Lais* of Marie de France," *Zeitschrift für französische Sprache und Literatur* 91, no. 2 (1981): 133–55.

The *Lais*

her literary plan of vivid textual descriptions. The modest plot structure and the economical length of these tales make detailed descriptions stand out more than they would in a longer genre such as romance. In other words, the less complicated and the shorter the narration, the more likely it is that the audience will take note of her descriptive amplifications and retain the images described in their memories.

Exactly how to define the *lai* as a genre has been the subject of some controversy for many years.[3] Prudence Mary O'Hara Tobin has noted that "ces compositions commémoraient un événement, une légende, une *aventure* dont elles s'inspiraient" (these texts commemorated an event, a legend, an *adventure* from which they draw their inspiration).[4] These tales were notably and consistently short. Marie's *lais,* for example, range from 118 lines *(Chievrefoil)* to 1,184 lines *(Eliduc)*. The *lais* often take up aspects of the *merveilleux,* and at times intrusions from the fairy world. They are sometimes set in a courtly context, twice in an Arthurian setting, and for the most part the stories take place in the Celtic world, more precisely within the geography of England and Ireland *(Bretagne majeur),* and Brittany *(Bretagne mineur)*. These texts almost always contain the element of *aventure* that is at the heart of medieval French romance, though it is presented in a more abbreviated form and generally with less emphasis on intentionally seeking the adventure. In the case of Arthurian *lais,* Beate Schmolke-Hasselmann has recognized that they differ from verse romance in that they are confined to one central adventure, are more concise, and contain no subplots.[5] She also shows that Arthurian verse romance and the Arthurian *lai* developed simul-

---

3. For a full discussion on the definition of the *lai* as a genre, see the part of Frappier's study titled "Remarques sur la structure du lai, essai de définition et de classement" (23–29), in his edited collection *La littérature narrative de l'imagination, des genres littéraires aux techniques de l'expression,* Colloque de Strasbourg, 23–25 avril 1959 (Paris: Presses Universitaires de France, 1961).

4. Prudence Mary O'Hara Tobin, ed., *Les lais anonymes des XIIe et XIIIe siècles,* Publications Romanes et Françaises 143 (Geneva: Droz, 1976), 9.

5. Beate Schmolke-Hasselmann, *Der arthurische Versroman von Chrestien bis Froissart* (Tübingen: Niemeyer, 1980), 7n.

The *Lais*

taneously, but that the *lai* eventually became integrated into verse romance by the technique of *conjointure,* as practiced by romance authors like Chrétien.[6] *Conjointure,* it may be added, is the tying together of various material in a manner that reflects the process of literary *inventio.*[7] In so far as we can judge, Marie de France was the first to present the genre of the *lai* in narrative form, and she makes it known on several occasions that she "heard" these stories from Breton sources, sometimes in the form of song. Marie's narrative version of these oral stories gave rise to the anonymous *lais* that began to develop at the beginning of the thirteenth century.

The *Lais* and the Pictorial Arts of the Twelfth Century

Marie's *Lais* were composed well before the appearance of treatises in the thirteenth century that deal primarily with memory as an art in itself,[8] or for that matter even before most medieval texts devoted solely to the arts of poetry and prose. Since Marie employs techniques that are to be elaborated later in these various treatises, two questions arise: Where, outside the framework of her training in rhetoric and grammar, does Marie find the impetus for creating a narrative architecture that is concerned with memory, as evidenced by her insistence on the terms *remembrance* and *memoire* (discussed in the previous chapter); and what, if any, are the influences that lead her to create mentally visual images through her narrative descriptions as if she were actually painting on a canvas?

The resurrection of the architectural mnemonic of antiquity

---

6. Ibid., 14. See also her chart on p. 10 and the discussion on pp. 15–19.

7. Kelly treats the topic of *conjointure* in his works cited in this book. For further reading on his treatment of the subject, see his *Sens and Conjointure in the Chevalier de la Charrette* (The Hague: Mouton, 1966).

8. Matilda Tomaryn Bruckner has given a satisfactory window of composition for the *Lais,* taking into consideration the probable date of the *Roman d'Eneas* (1160), which is undoubtedly a source of influence on Marie's *Guigemar,* and the fact that there is no conclusive evidence that Marie had knowledge of Chrétien's romances: the *Lais* could have been composed between 1160 and 1170. See Bruckner's entry on Marie de France in Kibler and Zinn, *Medieval France,* 589–91.

The *Lais*

that developed in the course of the thirteenth century had its roots, to a certain extent, in the rediscovery of the works of Aristotle, particularly the *De anima,* but Marie did not have access to these texts in the second half of the twelfth century. Yet the *Lais* are very mnemonic, both in the use of vocabulary that reinforces association with the acts of seeing, reading, and writing, and by their descriptive representations of people, places, events, and objects in such a fashion that the visual image created recalls the theme or themes of the particular text in which it is found.

The answers to these questions, focusing on sources for the interrelationship of memory and mentally visual objects in Marie's works, are elusive, and research thus far has not taken a direction that would seek out possible inspirations. A theory in this area would have to take into account not only Marie's literary talent but also that of other poets of the mid- to late twelfth century, such as the authors of the *Roman de Thèbes* and the *Roman d'Eneas,* and Chrétien de Troyes, to name a few, who also incorporated mentally visual elements in their narratives. There appears to be a nascent literary movement in the latter part of this century toward representing verbal concepts as if they were works of art, or at least pictorial images. Though I have uncovered no conclusive evidence that would settle the issue, several possibilities must be considered.

One area that needs to be explored is the pictorial narrative program of illumination that was beginning to emerge in England during the twelfth century. This system of illumination was able to narrate a story in linear progression solely through the use of images, the scene from each individual miniature recounting a particular episode of the story in question without the use of written text. Most notably, this type of representation took the form of prefatory cycles of miniatures that introduced the biblical text of the Psalms in Psalters that were used for recitation during the divine hours.[9] Robert Calkins has shown that this "tradition of plac-

---

9. For a history of the illumination program of the Psalter in the Middle Ages, see Robert Calkins, *Illuminated Books of the Middle Ages* (Ithaca: Cornell University Press, 1983), 212–25.

The *Lais*

ing a group of full-page frontispieces or cycles of miniatures before the Psalms may have begun in England circa 1050."[10] Perhaps the most celebrated twelfth-century example of this program of illumination is found in the St. Albans Psalter that was produced in England between 1119 and 1123 and that contains forty full-page miniatures, most of which are New Testament scenes.[11]

One should not underestimate the impression that visual art left on its viewers in the Middle Ages. Visual representation of narrative accounts left open the possibility of personal interpretation of the message they portrayed, and it could encourage the memory of certain elements of the story with which it was associated over other elements. Such a potential influence was recognized by the Church, which essentially tried to prohibit pictorial narrative in religious art prior to the twelfth century. Otto Pächt has remarked that "the ban on pictorial narrative in religious art—for this is what it amounted to—lasted until about 1120 when simultaneously, in the North and South of England, fully fledged picture cycles suddenly made their appearance."[12] Not only could visual art influence the general audience, it could also have a profound impact within its own medium. As an example, the St. Albans Psalter greatly affected future iconography by breaking with previous tradition in its representation of the deposition to such an extent that the representation of this same scene in Psalters from the following centuries imitated its theme.[13]

---

10. Ibid., 212. Calkins notes that the oldest surviving example is the Cotton Psalter (London, BL, Cotton Tiberias C.VI), which has full-page scenes of the Life of David and the Life of Christ. In addition to encouraging an exegetical reading of the New Testament, Calkins has signaled an implicit connection of lineage, Christ descending from the house of David. I would argue that, in addition to other possible functions, these illuminated images provided the reader with a visually mnemonic reminder of the importance of the whole of the biblical message, the fulfillment of the Old Testament by the New, as he or she prepared to recite the texts that followed them.

11. Ibid., 214.

12. Otto Pächt, *The Rise of Pictorial Narrative in Twelfth-Century England* (Oxford: Clarendon Press, 1962), 13.

13. Ibid., 30–31. St. Albans Descent from the Cross is important because it breaks

The *Lais*

The most obvious question raised by the proliferation of pictorial narrative in the form of prefatory cycles in Psalters during the decades preceding Marie de France is whether or not she had direct access to the manuscripts that contained these images, and it is hard to imagine that she would not have, especially those manuscripts produced in the areas of England near the locations in which she may have been living and writing. It is entirely reasonable to suppose that a writer who was associated with Henry II's court, as Marie was, would have had these sources at hand. We do know from her own intertextual references that she had access to works of Ovid, Priscian, and H. of Saltrey, as well as to the sources for the Life of Saint Etheldreda, and possibly to a book of fables by King Alfred. While it may be difficult to establish with any degree of certainty that she had indeed seen the St. Albans Psalter in particular, or any other illuminated Psalter for that matter, it is probable that she knew this program of narrative art, given her familiarity with both secular and religious texts. Calkins has shown that, "in the early Middle Ages the psalter was the most commonly used book for private devotions, and it remained so until the fourteenth century, when it was supplanted by the Book of Hours."[14] The supposition that Marie frequently read religious texts is even more plausible if one accepts the theory that she was an abbess herself, a hypothesis that has been put forth by some scholars.[15]

The possible influence of painting and other visual arts on Marie's narrative technique is further supported by her generous use of colors throughout the *Lais*. Antoinette Knapton has identified six different colors that appear in several of the texts:

---

with the tradition of simply representing this scene as an intermediary between the Crucifixion and the Entombment, and makes of it an important scene of passion on its own merits. Before the appearance of this scene in St. Albans, iconography depicts the action with one arm still nailed to the cross and one arm taken down. In this scene, and in the pictorial representation throughout the following centuries, both arms are already taken down, and the narrative of the Passion is stressed.

14. Calkins, *Illuminated Books of the Middle Ages*, 207.

15. See the discussion of Marie's identity in the introduction to Burgess and Busby's translation of the *Lais*.

The *Lais*

"Marie emploie six couleurs: or, Pourpre (ici deux nuances, une sombre, une vive), vermeil, vert, blanc et bis. L'or domine: objets de ce métal éclatant sont mentionés seize fois; puis vient le blanc, dix fois; la pourpre, cinq—six, si l'on tient compte d'un encensoir d'améthyste dans *Yonec* (506); la couleur vermeille, quatre; la bise, trois; la verte, deux" (Marie uses six colors: gold, purple [two shades here, one dark, one brilliant], bright red, green, and grayish brown. Gold dominates: objects made of this bright metal are mentioned sixteen times; then comes white, ten times; purple, five, or six if one includes an amethyst censer in *Yonec* (506); the color bright red, four; grayish brown, three; green, two).[16] Four of these colors—*or, vermeil, vert,* and *bis*—are commonly used in the illumination of Romanesque manuscripts during the twelfth century and in the Gothic manuscripts that began to appear around the end of the twelfth and beginning of the thirteenth century, especially in religious books. Knapton points out that these four colors were the same ones predominantly used by the Catholic Church at that time, and sees Marie's use of them as further evidence that she was either an abbess or intricately involved in some way in ecclesiastical matters.[17] She also notes the absence of other colors that would have been available to her at the time, such as orange, yellow, blue, and black.[18] Marie may have chosen her particular colors over the others available to her because they render a more vivid picture than do the ones just mentioned. Gold has an especially striking quality and, as Knapton notes, Marie employs it the most among her colors, sixteen times.

Besides illuminated manuscripts, Marie would have had other visually oriented media available to her.[19] One wonders, for ex-

---

16. Antoinette Knapton, "La poésie enluminée de Marie de France," *Romance Philology* 30, no. 1 (1976–77): 178.
17. Ibid., 182.
18. Knapton does, however, suggest that the color orange may be evoked in line 131 of *Fresne* by the hyacinth stone that is set in the ring to accompany the baby (178–79). I agree with Burgess and Busby, who translate the stone as ruby, which would have more of a red quality.
19. For two thorough studies on the visual perception of narrative art during

The *Lais*

ample, whether she had seen the Bayeux Tapestry. Indeed, it is possible that she would at least have had knowledge of it and its subject matter, given her close chronological proximity to its execution and the probability that she was writing for the Anglo-Angevin court. One must keep in mind that Marie's *Lais* date from approximately only a hundred years after the Battle of Hastings depicted in the tapestry. The events portrayed in this textile were therefore still relatively pertinent to the life of an Anglo-Norman. The history surrounding the Bayeux Tapestry's production and subsequent public exhibition is uncertain. It was possibly displayed in cathedrals or even in more secular venues such as castles. One engaging aspect of the Bayeux Tapestry is that it tells a story in which the images assume a narrative role at times superior to that of the written text.[20]

While it is true that the various scenes throughout this embroidered account of the invasion of England are accompanied by brief commentaries in Latin, often the visual image is nonetheless privileged over the written word. Moreover, three different pictorial narratives run simultaneously: the main scenes of the Norman Conquest occupy the center and largest portion of the tapestry, and two different border scenes, one running along the top, the other along the bottom, depict fables and episodes from everyday life, usually unrelated to the main story.[21] It is difficult to forget such images as a group of Englishmen pointing to the sky (top

---

Marie de France's period, see the two essays in Madeleine H. Caviness, *Art in the Medieval West and Its Audience* (Aldershot: Ashgate, 2001): "Images of the Divine Order and the Third Mode of Seeing," II, 1–22, and "'The Simple Perception of Matter' and the Representation of Narrative, ca. 1180–1280," III, 1–17. In the former, Caviness discusses the fourfold theory of Richard of St. Victor, the first mode of which focuses on the "exterior and visible world," a mode that "would give rise to narrative illustration restricted to the actual appearances of figures, things, and actions" (9).

20. For general studies on the Bayeux Tapestry, see Shirley Ann Brown, *The Bayeux Tapestry: History and Bibliography* (Woodbridge, U.K.: Boydell & Brewer, 1988).

21. For studies on the peripheral narratives, see both sections of the article by Hélène Chefneux, "Les fables dans la tapisserie de Bayeux," *Romania* 60, no. 237 (1934): 1–35; and 60, no. 238, 153–94. Chefneux argues that the source for the fables depicted in the margins of the Bayeux Tapestry is similar to the source used by Marie de France in her *Isopet* collection.

The *Lais*

border of the tapestry), where one follows their gaze to both a depiction of Halley's comet and the words "Isti mirant stellam." The capacity of this representation to recall certain parts of the pictorial narrative and to situate one's place within the entire story is a testimony to the mnemonic value of the simultaneous use of written word and visual image.

An artistic medium that Marie de France was probably familiar with is one that she uses in her own art to convey a fundamental theme in the *lai* of *Guigemar*, namely, a wall painting.[22] The painting of Venus that adorns the castle walls in *Guigemar* is, in my view, one of the most memorable narrative moments in all of Marie's texts and will be discussed at length below. Like illuminated manuscripts that contained pictorial narratives and narrative textiles such as the Bayeux Tapestry, frescoes were an integral component of the Romanesque art that was flourishing during the century in which Marie de France wrote. Stacy Boldrick has remarked that, "other than illuminated manuscripts, wall paintings were the dominant and most accessible form of painting in romanesque France."[23] If Marie had spent any time in her native France, and if she were in some way involved in ecclesiastical affairs, she would probably have been exposed to this medium of visual representation.

Also prevalent during Marie's time, iconography in sculptures on churches around the capitals of columns, on portals, and on façades in general displayed narrative sequences that served as visual reminders to a largely illiterate culture.[24] The same is true, of

---

22. See Maylis Baylé, "La Tapisserie de Bayeux et l'ornementation dans l'Europe du nord-œust," in *La Tapisserie de Bayeux: L'art de broder l'Histoire*, ed. Pierre Bouet, Brian Levy, and François Neveux (Caen: Presses Universitaires de Caen, 2004), 303–25. See especially pp. 323–24 for a discussion of the relationship between wall paintings in England and the Bayeux Tapestry. For a general study on wall paintings in England, see the essays in Sharon Cather, David Park, and Paul Williamson, eds., *Early Medieval Wall Painting and Painted Sculpture in England* (Oxford: BAR, 1990).

23. See Stacy L. Boldrick, "Romanesque Art," in Kibler and Zinn, *Medieval France*, 816–19.

24. For an overview of Romanesque sculpture, see Jean M. French, "Romanesque Sculpture," in Kibler and Zinn, *Medieval France*, 819–21. French describes the

course, of stained glass windows, and although the medium was not as prominent in the twelfth century as it was in the thirteenth, there were nonetheless several important programs in cathedrals like York and Canterbury.[25] The vivid depictions of the subjects recounted popular biblical stories that were intended to preserve certain key scenes in the public memory, such as the account of creation, the fall of humankind, and redemption though the Passion of Christ. At times, even secular representation made its way into these primarily religious media, although its placement there was generally for didactic reasons, either to show the consequences of sin or to exploit the religious aspect of a secular narrative. Two examples among many are scenes inspired by events from the *Chanson de Roland* represented in the Charlemagne Window of the cathedral in Chartres and in sculptures on the façade of the cathedral in Angoulême. In these cases, the secular representations were probably included to celebrate the triumph of Christians over pagans.[26]

---

earliest examples of façade sculpture as "an art of power, of energy in tension, imaginative, expressive, with a love of variation and decorative effect and of geometric, stylized, and even fantastic forms" (819). For a more thorough discussion, see George Zarnecki, *English Romanesque Sculpture: 1066–1140* (London: Alec Tiranti, 1951), and Deborah Kahn, *Canterbury Cathedral and Its Romanesque Sculpture* (Austin: University of Texas Press, 1991).

25. See Madeleine H. Caviness, *Stained Glass Windows* (Turnhout: Brepols, 1996), 41. Caviness outlines the rebuilding of the Canterbury Cathedral in the last quarter of the twelfth century, after the fire of 1174, and shows that some of the windows were completed by 1177. For these and other dates concerning Canterbury's program of glazing, see Caviness, *The Early Stained Glass of Canterbury Cathedral: Circa 1175–1220* (Princeton: Princeton University Press, 1977), 23–35. For further details on early stained glass in England, see June Osborne, *Stained Glass in England* (London: Frederick Muller, 1981), 20–29. For further discussion on early stained glass, and for reproductions of some of the iconography, see Madeleine H. Caviness, *The Windows of Christ Church Cathedral Canterbury* (Oxford: Oxford University Press, 1981); Caviness, *Paintings on Glass: Studies in Romanesque and Gothic Monumental Art* (Aldershot: Ashgate, 1997); and Louis Grodecki, *Le vitrail roman* (Fribourg: Office du Livre, 1977), 198–214.

26. For the Charlemagne Window, see the Digital Resources Library of the University of Pittsburgh, where Alison Stones has organized a comprehensive visual guide and descriptions of the stained glass program in the Chartres Cathedral: http://images.library.pitt.edu/cgi_bin/i/image/image_idx.

The *Lais*

Visual art of the twelfth century struggled to break free of its static dimensions and move toward a dynamic interpretation of the subject. Pächt summarizes the situation of art during this period as follows: "Representations of dialogues are nothing new in medieval art. They are part of that vast medieval repertory of nonvisual subject matter with which Christian art had to accommodate itself. Hence also its constant concern with a 'language' of gestures as a substitute for audible language."[27] In the end, one could say that the challenge in art of this period was to create an image that could be read as a narrative, whereas Marie's goal at the end of the twelfth century was to create a narrative that could be seen as an image in the mind's eye. Her task may have been facilitated by the visual culture in which she found herself, a culture in which she could easily draw upon the examples of pictorial narratives in the media of manuscript illuminations, textiles, decorative wall paintings, and church iconography.

Memory and Language in the *Lais*

Throughout the *Lais,* Marie de France makes frequent use of vocabulary that supports a narrative program designed to call attention to certain textual elements. On at least two occasions this vocabulary is mnemonic by its mere repetition; there are several occurrences of a single word or its derivative within the space of only a few lines. This is the case in the *lai* of *Deus Amanz,* where the location of the story that is about to unfold is repeated several times within only twenty lines:

> Jadis avint en Normendie
> Une aventure mut oïe
> De deus enfanz ki s'entreamerent;
> Par amur ambedui finerent.
> Un lai en firent li Bretun:
> De *Deus Amanz* reçuit le nun.

---

27. Pächt, *Rise of Pictorial Narrative,* 54.

The *Lais*

> Veritez est ke en Neustrie,
> Que nus apelum Normendie,
> Ad un haut munt merveilles grant:
> Lasus gisent li dui enfant.
>
> (*DA* 1–10)

> There once took place in Normandy a now celebrated adventure of two young people who loved each other and who met their end because of love. The Bretons made a lay about them which was given the title *The Two Lovers*. The truth is that in Neustria, which we call Normandy, there is a marvellously high mountain where the two young people lie.

In these lines, Marie singles out not only the geographical location but also the subject and title of the *lai* itself when she evokes the image of the two lovers. In fact, the lovers as a couple are mentioned three times in these ten lines: "De deus enfanz," "De Deus Amanz," and "li dui enfant." Marie seems to be especially intent on the audience's recognizing and later recalling the theme of this particular story.[28]

Marie is also concerned that her audience take note of the location of the events in this tale, and three times she names the region in which they take place, employing "Normandie" twice and "Neustrie" once. Even more impressive are the following lines, which specify the exact location within the broader region:

> Pres de cel munt a une part,
> Par grant cunseil e par esgart,
> Une cité fist faire uns reis,
> Ki esteit sire des Pistreis;
> Des Pistreis la fist il numer
> E Pistre la fist apeler.
> Tuz jurs ad puis duré li nuns;

---

28. For a thorough study of the narrative technique in this *lai*, see Judith Rice Rothschild, *Narrative Technique in the Lais of Marie de France: Themes and Variations*, vol 1. (Chapel Hill: North Carolina Studies in the Romance Languages and Literatures, 1974), 139–67.

The *Lais*

> Uncore i ad vile e maisuns.
> Nus savum bien de la contree
> Que li Vals de Pistre est nomee.
> (*DA* 11–20)

Near this mountain, on one side, a king, who was lord of the Pistrians, wisely and carefully had a city built which he named after the inhabitants and called Pitres. The name has survived to this day and there is still a town and houses there. We know the area well, for it is called the Valley of Pitres.[29]

The name of the town, "Pistre," is used twice, and the name of its inhabitants, the "Pistreis," is mentioned twice as well, all within ten lines. Thus the geography is specifically named seven times within the first twenty lines of text, not including the two uses of the word "munt," which refers to the mountain the lovers are to ascend. While we cannot be certain of her reasons for this geographical emphasis, one possibility may be a desire to develop an identifiable location within the minds of her audience. The audience may have already been familiar with this geography, and their reconstruction of this particular location within the imagination would serve as a concrete background against which she could paint the action of the narrative.

A significant detail of this particular *lai* is that the legend of the two lovers still survives in contemporary Normandy near the town of Pitres, where an oral version of the tale has been documented in recent years.[30] Whether or not the survival of this story in modern culture perpetuates the memory of Marie's *lai* or draws its inspiration from an oral version that precedes Marie's text, possibly the same source she herself drew upon, is impossible to say. It is clear, though, that Marie wanted her immediate audi-

---

29. The name "Pistre" is evoked four times in the original Old French passage, not three as in the translation by Burgess and Busby.

30. See Rychner's edition of the *Lais*, 261–62. He notes that Gustave Cohen actually heard an oral version of the story recounted by a local resident in the area. For more on the survival of the story in contemporary Normandy, see Cohen, "Marie de France, le lai des *Deux Amants*," *Mercure de France* 265 (1936): 61–68.

ence to remember her story, as is evidenced by the repetitive nature of lines 1–20. In addition to the technique of repetition that opens the *lai,* she closes the story with a metaphor that reflects her desire for the recall of her text by future generations:

> Ele le pleint a mut haut cri,
> Puis ad geté e espaundu
> Le veissel u li beivre fu.
> Li muns en fu bien arusez;
> Mut en ad esté amendez
> Tuz li païs e la cuntree:
> Meinte bone herbe i unt trovee
> Ki del beivrë orent racine.
> (*DA* 222–29)

She lamented him loudly and then threw away the vessel containing the potion, scattering its contents so that the mountain was well sprinkled with it, and the land and surrounding area much improved. Many good plants were found there which took root because of the potion.

Symbolizing the regeneration of Marie's text for a future audience, the vial of potion that is scattered upon the mountain assures the growth of plants whose roots are well established.[31]

A similar concern with repetition is found in the *lai* of *Lanval*. In this case, Marie uses anaphora to establish the name of the hero in the minds of her audience:

> Lanval donout les riches duns,
> Lanval aquitout les prisuns,
> Lanval vesteit les jugleürs,
> Lanval faiseit les granz honurs,
> Lanval despendeit largement,

---

31. See Domenico Fasciano, "La mythologie du lai *Les Deux Amants,*" *Rivista di Cultura Classica e Medievale* 16, no. 1 (1974): 79–85. Fasciano sees the *lai* of *Deus Amanz* as a reminder of classical myth and has noticed that this scene at the end of the tale, in which the potion is scattered on the ground, causing grass to spring up, ties this text to previous legends of regeneration.

The *Lais*

> Lanval donout or e argent:
> n'i ot estrange ne privé
> a qui Lanval n'eüst doné.
> Mult ot Lanval joie e deduit:
> u seit par jur u seit par nuit,
> s'amie puet veeir sovent,
> tut est a sun comandement.
>
> (*Lv* 209–20)

Lanval gave costly gifts, Lanval freed prisoners, Lanval clothed the jongleurs, Lanval performed many honourable acts [Lanval disbursed generously, Lanval gave gold and silver]. There was no one, stranger or friend, to whom he would not have given gifts. He experienced great joy and pleasure, for day or night he could see his beloved often and she was entirely at his command.[32]

The repetitious sonority helps the audience recall this particular passage, in which Lanval's benevolent qualities are given after his name in each line.[33] The recollection of these lines provides perspective at later points in the story, when his character is called into question by the queen. In all, Lanval's name is used a total of thirty-nine times in 644 octosyllabic lines, eight of which appear in lines 209–20; by contrast, the name of Guigemar occurs only twenty-two times in the 886 lines of the eponymous *lai*.[34]

The arrangement of vocabulary terms in such a manner as to

---

32. These lines are from Warnke, not from Rychner, because his edition includes the additional two lines in the anaphora. Busby and Burgess translate Ewert's edition, also containing only four lines in the anaphora, so I have inserted between brackets my own translation of the additional lines, 213–14.

33. For a thorough discussion of the descriptive narrative elements in *Lanval*, see Judith Rice Rothschild, "Description and Visualizable Movement in Marie de France's *Lais*," in *L'imaginaire courtois et son double: Actes du VIe Congrès Triennal de la Société Internationale de Littérature Courtoise (ICLS), Fisciano (Salerno), 24–28 juillet 1989*, ed. Giovanna Angeli and Luciano Formisano (Naples: Edizione Scientifiche Italiane, 1991), 409–19.

34. Hélène Naïs, *Index des Lais de Marie de France*, Cahiers du CRAL, 1ère série, no. 34 (Nancy: Centre de Recherches et d'Applications Linguistiques de l'Université de Nancy II, 1979).

The *Lais*

facilitate recall of the text in question demonstrates Marie's concern with the auditory aspect of description and its effectiveness in helping the audience to recall key points of her tales. Moreover, words associated with seeing and perceiving are used with great frequency throughout the twelve *lais,* whether relating to action on the part of the subject or to the visual nature of the object being perceived;[35] vocabulary that evokes the aural and oral faculties is also strongly represented.[36] The universality of this vocabulary in the *Lais,* in conjunction with terms that explicitly refer to the act of remembering, is in keeping with the poet's focus on memory.[37] Cognitive recall is strengthened if we are able to hear (or read) a text at the same time we see it in our minds through the help of vivid descriptions that cause its aesthetic qualities to take form.

Descriptio: Verbal, Nonverbal, and Quasi-Verbal Objects

Descriptions in Marie de France's *Lais* that are at times quite detailed in nature may be seen as the center around which she structures her entire narrative design. The *lais anonymes* that appear in the thirteenth century have been said to be influenced by Marie's texts, and Lucien Foulet goes as far as to identify them as imitations, or in some cases even plagiarisms, of Marie's work.[38] However, as Tobin has noted, it is the element of description that truly sets Marie's *lais* apart from the thirteenth-century texts in the same genre, with one exception: "Les descriptions sont, en général stylisées et sommaires, quoique *Graelent* contienne des de-

---

35. Ibid.: aparceveir (26 times), escrire (5), escrit (6), escriture (1), lettré (1), lettre (8), lire (3), lis (1), peindre (1), peinture (1), regard (2), regarder (4), veeir (135), and veie (4).

36. Ibid.: dire (199 times), dis (1), dit (1), ditié (1), entendre (21), entente (4), escrier (5), numer (30), oïr (110), parler (94), parole (14), recunter (6).

37. Ibid.: membrer (2 times), oblier (4), recorder (2), remembrance (3), remembrer (8), souvenir (1), ublier (6), and ubliance (1).

38. See especially pp. 36 and 56 in Lucien Foulet, "Marie de France et les lais bretons," *Zeitschrift für romanische Philologie* 29, no. 1 (1905): 19–56, 293–322.

The *Lais*

scriptions très vivantes" (The descriptions are, in general, stylized and cursory, although *Graelent* contains vivid descriptions).[39] In particular, she explains that the characters of the *lais anonymes* are "moins nettement dessinés et moins vivants que ceux de Marie" (not as clearly constructed and less lively than those of Marie).[40]

Though Marie exhibits competence in describing people—for example, the encomium of Lanval's courtly characteristics—and places, like the location of the castle that houses the imprisoned lady in *Guigemar,* or even events, as the example of the tournament in *Chaitivel* shows, her true genius lies in the textual energy that she is able to impart to the objects she describes. These objects are more often than not the key to retention of the themes of the *lai* that contains them, and they frequently constitute a synecdoche for the entire *lai*.[41] In other words, to memorize and remember the object and its attributes is to memorize and recall the *lai* as a whole.

In chapter 1, I gave and defined Pickens's identification of three types of objects prevalent throughout Marie de France's *Lais:* "verbaux," "quasi-verbaux," and "non-verbaux." One striking example of a verbal object is found in the *lai* of *Chievrefoil.* Composed of only 118 lines, it is the shortest of Marie's *Lais,* but, as Keith Busby remarks, it "derives its poetic intensity precisely from the fact that its content and its language are largely connotative and not denotative."[42] Indeed, it is through "connotation" in the form of description of a verbal object that Marie is able to evoke in the minds of her audience the entire Tristan legend as they knew it, but within a narrative economy that recounts only a single episode of this legend:

39. Tobin, *Lais anonymes,* 77.
40. Ibid., 80.
41. As shown below, Kelly has already suggested that the message written on the stick in *Chievrefoil* is a synecdoche for the whole Tristan legend (*Art of Medieval French Romance,* 177). I propose here that many of the objects that Marie describes in her narrative take on a similar function as they relate to the *lai* in which they are found.
42. Keith Busby, "'Ceo fu la summe de l'escrit' (*Chevrefoil,* line 61), Again," *Philological Quarterly* 74, no. 1 (1995): 2.

The *Lais*

> Le jur que li reis fu meüz,
> Tristram est el bois revenuz.
> Sur le chemin que il saveit
> Que la rute passer deveit,
> Une codre trencha par mi,
> Tute quarreie la fendi.
> Quant il ad paré le bastun,
> De sun cutel escrit sun nun.
> Se la reïne s'aparceit,
> Ki mut grant garde s'en perneit—
> Autre feiz li fu avenu
> Que si l'aveit aparceü—
> De sun ami bien conustra
> Le bastun, quant el le verra.
> *(Chv 47–60)*

On the day the king set out, Tristram entered the wood along the road he knew the procession would have to take. He cut a hazel branch in half and squared it. When he had whittled the stick he wrote his name on it with a knife. If the queen, who would be on the look-out, spotted it (on an earlier occasion she had successfully observed it in this way), she would recognize her beloved's stick when she saw it.

Marie's text clearly indicates that Iseut had previously registered this sign in the faculty of her memory, and when she saw it again she knew exactly what it signified, as is later reiterated in lines 81–82: "Le bastun vit, bien l'aparceut, / Tutes les lettres i conut" ([she] saw the piece of wood and realized what it was. She recognized all the letters). This object has a polyvalent function on two semantic levels. Within the episode itself, Iseut is able to recall the past events that are evoked by the sight of the stick. Likewise, within the broader context of the *lai* of *Chievrefoil,* the audience is reminded of the Tristan story in general, as these extradiagetic encounters between Tristan and Iseut are evoked by the latter's previous, similar experiences with the hazel stick.

In addition to his name, it is possible that Tristan also wrote other words on the hazel branch:

The *Lais*

> Ceo fu la summe de l'escrit
> Qu'il li aveit mandé e dit
> Que lunges ot ilec esté
> E atendu e surjurné
> Pur espïer e pur saveir
> Coment il la peüst veeir,
> Kar ne poeit vivre sanz li.
>   (*Chv* 61–67)

> That was all he wrote, because he had sent her word that he had been there a long time, waiting patiently and watching out for an opportunity to see her, for he could not possibly live without her.

Line 61 has generated much debate among scholars as to exactly what else, if anything, Tristan actually carved on the stick with his knife.[43] Some claim that it was the entire contents of lines 61–78, especially given the beautiful image of the honeysuckle vine and hazel tree that Marie describes in the last part of this passage:

> D'euls deus fu li tut autresi
> Cume del chievrefoil esteit
> Ki a la codre se perneit:
> Quant il s'i est laciez e pris
> E tut entur le fust s'est mis,
> Ensemble poënt bien durer,
> Mes ki puis les voelt desevrer,
> Li codres muert hastivement
> E li chievrefoilz ensement.
> "Bele amie, si est de nus:
> Ne vus sanz mei, ne jeo sanz vus."
>   (*Chv* 68–78)

> The two of them resembled the honeysuckle which clings to the hazel branch: when it has wound itself round and attached itself to the hazel, the two can survive together: but

---

43. The studies that treat this episode are too numerous to cite, but many can be found in Burgess, *Analytical Bibliography*, 121–22; Supplement no. 1, 68; Supplement no. 2, 158–59.

The *Lais*

if anyone should then attempt to separate them, the hazel quickly dies, as does the honeysuckle. "Sweet love, so it is with us: without me you cannot survive, nor I without you."

Just as the vine and the tree would die if they were separated, so too would Tristan and Iseut perish if they were unable to remain together. One fascinating aspect of Marie's image of the hazel tree and honeysuckle lies in her presentation of these objects as parasitic, while they in fact have a symbiotic relationship in the botanical world. I have found nothing to suggest that medieval perception at this time would have classified this tree and plant as inseparable, and can only assume that she created the metaphor in this manner, contrary to botanical knowledge, in order to bring energy to the image and impress it in the minds of her audience to make it easier for them to remember.[44] Kelly has suggested that "this single episode, a synecdoche, stands for the whole Tristan legend, as its botanic marvel is a metaphor for the union of Tristan and Iseut."[45]

That an object such as a hazel stick could have contained the entire text of lines 61–78 has been given credibility by two possible theories. First, it has been suggested that the message could have been recorded in the ogam alphabet, which uses notches for vowels and lines for consonants.[46] Also, Busby has raised the possibility that the message could have called to mind a tally stick, like the ones used at the end of the twelfth century as receipts for business transactions. The tally stick was split in half after the transaction was recorded so that the information was incomplete unless the two halves were held together. As Busby points out, this is a perfect reflection of the message in lines 77–78: "Bele amie, si est de nus: / Ne vus sanz mei, ne jeo sanz vus."[47]

Whether Tristan wrote only his name, his name and lines 77–

---

44. I express my appreciation to Norris J. Lacy for suggesting the botanical details concerning the relationship of the hazel tree and the honeysuckle.

45. Kelly, *Art of Medieval French Romance*, 177.

46. See Maurice Cagnon, "*Chievrefeuil* and the Ogamic Tradition," *Romania* 91, no. 362 (1970): 238–55.

47. See Busby, "'Ceo fu la summe,'" 1–15, esp. 11–12.

The *Lais*

78, or his name and the entire contents of lines 61–78 is perhaps impossible to determine with certainty from the available evidence, and in the end is not crucial to the comprehension of the story. Indeed, since the text clearly tells us that Tristan and Iseut had used this method of communication before, they could just as easily have used a stick entirely void of written text to signal their tryst. In other words, Marie as author may have deliberately chosen to include writing on the stick in her story, whether simply Tristan's name or a great deal more, for the benefit of her audience. In this case, the writing would not be for Iseut's benefit but for that of the audience, who would have the image and scene impressed that much more deeply on their minds. It is evident, then, regardless of what the actual script recorded, that this verbal object has a cognitively mnemonic value and is in keeping with the general plan throughout the *Lais*, as Busby has remarked: "The commemorative function of the *lai* is an essential part of Marie's aesthetic program as it can de distilled from the poems in the Harley manuscript."[48]

What the author's words "connote" is just as important as what they actually say. Marie's description of this object creates a type of medieval "objective correlative" as proposed by T. S. Eliot, an image placed in the mind's eye of her audience that helps them identify the theme of inseparable love. In the same manner that Iseut saw the hazel branch and then remembered previous encounters with her lover, the audience, after having heard or read the *lai* of *Chievrefoil*, would thereafter recall, each time they were able to bring forth this image from the faculty of their memory, not only the whole of the Tristan story but also Marie's unique contribution to the legend in the form of the hazel branch inscribed with at least Tristan's name, as well as in the image of the honeysuckle vine that entwines the hazel tree.

In the last few lines of the poem, Marie tells us that Tristan makes a new *lai* in order to preserve the joy that he and Iseut have shared together:

48. Ibid., 3.

The *Lais*

> Pur la joie qu'il ot eüe
> De s'amie qu'il ot veüe
> E pur ceo k'il aveit escrit
> Si cum la reïne l'ot dit,
> Pur les paroles remembrer,
> Tristram, ki bien saveit harper,
> En aveit fet un nuvel lai.
>
> (*Chv* 109–13)

On account of the joy he had experienced from the sight of his beloved and because of what he had written, Tristram, a skilful harpist, in order to record his words (as the queen had said he should), used them to create a new lay.

Concerning Tristan's creative endeavors, Busby reminds us that "the act of writing also functions as a commemoration—a *mise en memoire* or a *mise en remembrance*—of certain deeds and events."[49] Tristan creates a *lai* to help him remember his amorous encounters with Iseut, but in the end, as June Hall McCash writes, "It is not a *lai* that will preserve their *joie,* for even as we are told of its creation, the event is already in the past, as the verb tenses emphasize, but merely the *memory* of that joy."[50]

A verbal object is also at the heart of the *lai* of *Milun* in the form of letters that are paired with other objects in the narrative—a ring and a swan—to serve as a means of communication between Milun, the lady he loves, and other characters in the story. The letters contain important information and announce feelings of love, reveal the identity of Milun's child, and bring the news of the death of the lady's husband to Milun.

In the beginning of the text, we are told that the sister of the lady will recognize their child from the description contained in the letter:

---

49. Ibid., 9.
50. June Hall McCash, "'Ensemble poënt bien durer': Time and Timelessness in the *Chevrefoil* of Marie de France," *Arthuriana* 9, no. 4 (1999): 34–35.

The *Lais*

> Vostre anel al col li pendrai
> E un brief li enveierai;
> Escriz i ert li nuns sun pere
> E l'aventure de sa mere.
>   (*M* 77–80)

I shall hang your ring round its neck and send her a letter. In it will be its father's name, and the story of its mother's misfortune.

Clearly, both the verbal letter and the nonverbal ring are responsible for the revelation of the identity of the child. Furthermore, the description that surrounds the letter and ring after the child is born and when it is placed in the crib with these objects is even more elaborately embellished:

> Al col li pendirent l'anel
> E une aumoniere de seie
> Avoec le brief, que nuls nel veie;
> Puis le cuchent en un bercel,
> Envolupé d'un blanc lincel.
> Dedesuz la teste a l'enfant
> Mistrent un oreiller vaillant
> E desus lui un covertur
> Urlé de martre tut entur.
>   (*M* 96–104)

They hung around the child's neck the ring, a silk purse, and then the letter, making sure that it could be seen. Then they laid the child in a cradle, covered in a white linen sheet. Beneath its head they placed an expensive pillow and over the child a coverlet with a hem of martin skin.

The letter, and by extension the revelatory discourse it contains, is associated with a description that becomes progressively enhanced in the text. That is to say, it is not so much the letter itself as the care with which it is attached that is striking. Thus Marie makes certain that we will not forget its significance later in the *lai*, or better still, that our remembering the use of the various

The *Lais*

letters throughout this text will help us to recall the emotional and psychologically charged story of Milun in general.

Rings appear on several occasions in the *Lais*. In addition to *Milun*, a ring is also used in the *lai* of *Yonec* as a magical device that prevents the *malmariée*'s husband from remembering certain details of his encounter with his wife's lover:[51]

> Li chevaliers l'aseüra:
> Un anelet li ad baillé,
> Si li ad dit e enseigné,
> Ja tant cum el le gardera,
> A sun seignur n'en membera
> De nule rien ki fete seit,
> Ne ne l'en tendrat en destreit.
>
> (*Y* 414–20)

The knight reassured her, gave her a ring, and told her that as long as she kept it her husband would remember nothing that had happened and would not keep her in custody.

In this case, the ring is a nonverbal object since it is not inscribed with any explicit written text, and its narrative function stands in contrast to the previously discussed episode from *Milun,* where the ring is used as a device that reveals information rather than concealing it.

In the *lai* of *Fresne,* the use of a ring is similar to its use in *Milun*. The ring is not only an object that unveils hidden meaning, it also serves to spark the memory of past events. Rings are traditionally understood as symbolic representations of eternity.[52] For Marie this object serves to connect the past to the present, a symbol of narrative continuity. The memory of Fresne's birth and her future identity as royalty are assured by three different ob-

---

51. For a detailed study on the ring in medieval narrative literature, see Alain Corbellari, "Les jeux de l'anneau: Fonctions et trajets d'un objet dans la littérature narrative médiévale," in Busby, Guidot, and Whalen, *"De sens rassis,"* 157–67. See p. 160 as it relates to the *lai* of *Yonec.*

52. See J. E. Cirlot, *A Dictionary of Symbols,* trans. Jack Sage, 2d ed. (New York: Philosophical Library, 1971), s.v. "ring."

The *Lais*

jects: a linen wrapping, a piece of fine brocade that her father had brought back from Constantinople, and a ring of pure gold.[53]

> En un chief de mut bon chesil
> Envolupent l'enfant gentil,
> E desus un paile roé;
> Ses sires li ot aporté
> De Costentinoble, u il fu:
> Unques si bon n'orent veü!
> A une piece d'un suen laz
> Un gros anel li lie al braz;
> De fin or i aveit une unce,
> El chestun out une jagunce,
> La verge entur esteit lettree:
> La u la meshine ert trovee,
> Bien sachent tuit vereiement
> Qu'ele est nee de bone gent.
> (F 121–34)

They wrapped the noble child in a cloth of fine linen and then placed over her the finest piece of striped brocade which her husband had brought from Constantinople, where he had been. With a piece of her ribbon, the lady attached to the child's arm a large ring made from an ounce of pure gold, with a ruby set in it and lettering on the band. Wherever she was found, people would then truly know that she was of noble birth.

---

53. See Rupert T. Pickens, "Marie de France and the Body Poetic," in *Gender and Text in the Later Middle Ages*, ed. Jane Chance (Gainesville: University Press of Florida, 1996), 135–71. Pickens discusses the rapport of this episode with similar ones in *Laüstic, Yonec,* and *Milun,* especially in terms of a written text accompanied by an oral explanation. See also Grace Morgan Armstrong, "Engendering the Text: Marie de France and Dhouda," in *Translatio Studii: Essays by His Students in Honor of Karl D. Uitti for His Sixty-Fifth Birthday,* ed. Renate Blumenfeld-Kosinski et al., Faux Titre 179 (Amsterdam: Rodopi, 2000), 27–49. Armstrong notes that, "unlike Milun's son and the nightingale *[Laüstic],* which this richly swaddled baby also recalls, she is accompanied by no explanatory written message which would individualize her story" (31). For an analysis of message exchange in twelfth-century texts, see the book by Jacques Merceron, *Le message et sa fiction: La communication par messager dans la littérature française des XIIe et XIIIe siècles* (Berkeley and Los Angeles: University of California Press, 1998).

The *Lais*

Although the text written on the inside of the ring is not specified, it may be safe to assume that the inscription was in some way an indication of the royal lineage of Fresne's family because of the luxurious nature of this object, which weighs an ounce in pure gold and is set with a ruby. Similarly, the oriental silk tissue from Constantinople reveals aristocratic affiliation.

Apart from recalling an earlier episode in the narrative, these two objects in particular, the verbal object of the ring and the nonverbal object of the brocade, also have a discursive function of generating stories from different characters throughout the text: the mother, the chambermaid, the porter of the abbey, the abbess, the father, and Gurun. Each of these persons takes a role in the transmission of Fresne's origin, and their discourse usually centers on the mention of the two objects in question.

The generous repetition of these objects within a relatively short *lai* of 518 lines is notable. They are mentioned by name no fewer than sixteen times within approximately four hundred lines of text, and on one occasion they are named five times within only nineteen lines (413–32). It is apparent that Marie did not want her audience to lose sight of these objects, for they most certainly had the power of spurring memory, as the text explicitly states:

> La palie esgarde sur le lit,
> Que unke mes si bon ne vit
> Fors sul celui qu'ele dona
> Od sa fille k'ele cela.
> Idunc li remembra de li:
> Tuz li curages li fremi.
> (F 413–18)

She saw the brocade on the bed, the like of which she had never seen, save for the one she had given away with the daughter she had concealed. Then she remembered her and trembled in her heart.

In the end, it is these objects, and the memory of past events they recall, that enable the mother to identify the adult Fresne as her child from years ago:

The *Lais*

> "—Bele, pois jeo veeir l'anel?
> —Oïl, dame, ceo m'est mut bel!"
> L'anel li ad dunc aporté
> E ele l'ad mut esgardé.
> Ele l'ad bien reconeü,
> E le palie k'ele ad veü.
> Ne dute mes, bien seit e creit,
> Qu'el meïsmes sa fille esteit.
> Oiant tuz dist, nel ceile mie:
> "Tu es ma fille, bele amie!"
> (*F* 441–50)

"Fair one, may I see the ring?" "Yes, my lady, with pleasure." She brought her the ring and the lady looked at it carefully, easily recognizing it and the brocade. She had no doubt, for she now knew for sure that this was indeed her daughter, and, for all to hear, she said openly: "You are my daughter, fair friend!"

For the characters within the *lai* of *Fresne*, the description of these objects ensures the transmission of the story of Fresne's birth and the ultimate revelation of her previously hidden identity. For the audience of Marie's text they have a similar function, in that they will help call forth from the storehouse of memory at a later date the entire contents of her own tale.

Birds also figure prominently in the *Lais*. They serve several purposes, from recording past episodes, as in *Laüstic*, to communicating written messages, as the swan does in *Milun*, to transforming lovers into zoomorphic form, and consequently making amorous encounters possible, such as the hawk does in *Yonec*. Birds have long been associated with memory; they were discussed in medieval *artes memorativae*, and medieval manuscripts made frequent use of them in their iconography.[54] While it is not possible to argue that Marie uses them solely for mnemonic purposes, one cannot dismiss the role of the nightingale in preserving the memory of the *aventure* in the *lai* of *Laüstic*.

---

54. See Carruthers, *Book of Memory*, 33, 35–37, and 246–47.

The *Lais*

Under guise of rising to hear the song of the bird at night, the lady is able to slip away from her sleeping husband and speak through the window with a knight whose house is just next door. After her husband discovers her reason for rising from bed so often, he captures the bird and kills it in front of his wife, thereby effectively eliminating the possibility of future encounters. At the end of *Laüstic,* the corpse of the nightingale becomes a verbal object that is used as a message from the lady to her lover.

Fearing that her lover will believe he has been abandoned, since she no longer has an excuse to go to the window at night, she conceives of a means through which she can communicate to him what has transpired:

> "Une chose sai jeo de veeir:
> Il quidera ke jeo me feigne;
> De ceo m'estuet que cunseil preigne.
> Le laüstic li trametrai,
> L'aventure li manderai."
> (*La* 129–34)

"I know one thing for certain. He will think I am fainthearted, so I must take action. I shall send him the nightingale and let him know what has happened."

As an object in and of itself, the dead nightingale will henceforth be a sign that their relationship, at least as they have known it, is now dead as well. However, in addition to the symbolic quality of the object itself, the lady takes further steps to ensure that the dead bird will transmit her message:

> En une piece de samit
> A or brusdé e tut escrit
> Ad l'oiselet envolupé;
> Un suen vaslet ad apelé,
> Sun message li ad chargié,
> A sun ami l'ad enveié.
> (*La* 135–40)

The *Lais*

> She wrapped the little bird in a piece of samite, embroidered in gold and covered in designs. She called one of her servants, entrusted him with her message and sent him to her beloved.

We are not told exactly what she embroidered on the piece of samite in which she wrapped the bird. It may have been a text that would have served to recall their happy trysts together, given the commemorative context of this description in general. Lines 134–35—"Le laüstic li trametrai, / L'aventure li manderai" (I shall send him the nightingale and let him know what has happened)—show her intention to send an account of the adventure, as do lines 139–40—"Sun message li ad chargié, / A sun ami l'ad enveié" (she ... entrusted him with her message and sent him to her beloved)—but it is ambiguous whether this message is indeed what she sewed into the cloth, or whether it is what she simply told her servant to recount to her lover upon presentation of the item. The latter is more probably the case, since we are told, a few lines later in the text, when the messenger presents the bird to the knight, that "Tut sun message [the lady's] li cunta, / Le laüstic li presenta" ([He] related the whole message to him and presented him with the nightingale) (143–44).

Since "sun message" is apparently an oral account of what happened to the nightingale and consequently reveals the reason that she can no longer meet her lover at the window, one wonders why she also felt obligated, like Ovid's Philomela, who herself lacked the ability to speak about her horrible situation, to weave a message into the samite.[55] Pickens has suggested that the oral account of the story sent with the messenger "serves as an interpretation of the tapestry-enshrouded bird."[56] This is very plau-

---

55. For a comparison of Marie de France's textiles to those from the *Philomena*, a medieval adaptation of Ovid's story of Philomela sometimes attributed to Chrétien de Troyes, see Amelia Van Vleck, "Textiles as Testimony in Marie de France and *Philomena*," *Medievalia et Humanistica* 22, no. 1 (1995): 31–60. See also June Hall McCash, "Philomena's Window: Issues of Intertextuality and Influence in Works by Marie de France and Chrétien de Troyes," in Busby, Guidot, and Whalen, *"De sens rassis,"* 415–30.

56. Pickens, "Marie de France and the Body Poetic," 144.

The *Lais*

sible, but I would further suggest that the association of the visible object with the oral discourse improved the potential retention of the episode in the mind of the knight, and this may have been Marie's principal intention.

The concretizing effect that this verbal object has on the message sent by the lady cannot be ignored, and the knight's actions, after he receives the bird, reinforce the commemorative aspect of the tale:

> Un vaisselet ad fet forgier;
> Unques n'i ot fer ne acier,
> Tuz fu d'or fin od bones pieres,
> Mut precïuses e mut chieres;
> Covercle i ot tres bien asis.
> Le laüstic ad dedenz mis,
> Puis fist la chasse enseeler.
> Tuz jurs l'ad fete od lui porter.
> (*La* 149–56)

He had a small vessel prepared, not of iron or steel, but of pure gold with fine stones, very precious and very valuable. On it he carefully placed a lid and put the nightingale in it. Then he had the casket sealed and carried it with him at all times.

Just as the lady rendered visible the discourse of the ordeal she had undergone by wrapping the bird in an embroidered piece of material, so too the knight desires to give form to his memory of the times he had spent with his lover by constructing an elaborate box in which to keep the object of his affection, as it were. The "chasse" and the written message that it contains become for him a constant reminder of his beloved, as he carries it with him at all times.

Not every object that Marie describes in the *Lais* to serve as some sort of visual cue for textual reference contains writing, either explicitly or implicitly. Sometimes the elaborate nature of the description itself, void of any written content that reflects the ac-

The *Lais*

tion of the diegesis, creates an image in our minds that will give us reference and direction as we reconstruct the narrative through memory.

Lanval offers some of the most vivid descriptions of people throughout the whole collection of the *Lais*. The features of the hero, the attendants of the fairy mistress, and the fairy mistress herself are all described in intricate detail. It is not surprising that these characters are so elaborately represented, as the description of physical beauty was common in narratives of Marie's predecessors and contemporaries, especially Chrétien's.[57] Once again, the fascinating aspect of these passages is the number of lines she uses for the task of description in a context where narrative economy is a constant concern. She spends thirteen lines recounting the beauty of the fairy mistress alone, in a *lai* that contains only 646 lines.

Marie also offers a detailed description of the pavilion in which the fairy mistress is housed and, like the description of the fairy's beauty, this description also takes up a significant thirteen lines.[58] The importance of this object lies in the fact that it represents Lanval's first entry into the Other World; until this point he has come into contact only with the attendants of the fairy queen, while remaining in the familiar surroundings of the meadow in

---

57. See Rychner's edition of the *Lais*, 255n. He has identified the source for the description of the fairy mistress as the description of Antigone from the *Roman de Thèbes*.

58. Rychner notes that Ernest Hoepffner has traced the description of this tent back to similar descriptions in the *Thèbes* and in the *Eneas*. See especially p. 63 of Hoepffner's article, "Pour la chronologie des *Lais* de Marie de France," *Romania* 59 (1933): 351–70; *Romania* 60, no. 237 (1934): 36–66. For studies of the descriptions of tents in medieval literature see Emmanuèle Baumgartner, "Peinture et évidence: La description de la tente dans les romans antiques du XIIe siècle," in *Sammlung-Deutung-Wertung: Ergebnisse, Probleme, Tendenzen, und Perspektiven philologischer Arbeit; Mélanges Wolfgang Spiewok*, ed. Danielle Buschinger (Amiens: Université de Picardie, Centre d'Études Médiévales, 1988), 3–11; Marie-Madeleine Castellani, "La description de la tente du roi Bilas dans le roman d'*Athis et Prophilias*," in *Et c'est la fin pour quoy sommes ensemble: Hommage à Jean Dufournet*, ed. J.-C. Aubailly et al., 3 vols. (Paris: Champion, 1993), 1:327–39.

The *Lais*

the Logres countryside. Once he enters the tent of this mysterious lady, however, he has left his own world and is now enclosed entirely within the world of the Other. The elaborate description of the pavilion marks a pivotal moment in the story, for it signals Lanval's meeting with the person who will ultimately be responsible for his defamation of character, redemption, and eventual journey to Avalon. Marie ensures that her readers will not miss the importance of this moment, and that they will be able in the future to call it forth from memory.

A similar narrative strategy is at work in the intricately described ship in the *lai* of *Guigemar*. Marie devotes forty-one consecutive lines to minute details of the vessel, especially of the bed that occupies the center of the ship, including its frame, linens, and pillows. Her *Lais* reveal that she was well acquainted with the *Eneas*, but there are no descriptions of ships in that work to rival the detailed attention she gives the ship.[59] Her treatment of this episode sets her apart from her predecessor, and the amount of space she devotes to it is quite conspicuous in a *lai* of only 886 lines that contains several other long descriptions.

One possible reason for Marie's particular care in describing the ship is that it represents a catalyst for change in the development of the story. The mysterious ship possesses a marvelous quality, as it magically transports Guigemar from the world in which he was wounded to another world in which he will be healed. It therefore functions aesthetically on a narrative level to unite two thematic registers and is consequently vital to the linear development of the plot. As in the case of the tent in *Lanval*, Marie knows that if her audience is able to retain this image in

---

59. For studies on the similarities and differences between the *Eneas* and *Guigemar*, see J.-J. Salverda De Grave, "Marie de France et *Eneas*," *Neophilologus* 10, no. 1 (1925): 56–58; Ernest Hoepffner, "Marie de France et *l'Eneas*," *Studi Medievali*, n.s., 5, no. 1 (1932): 272–308; Earl Jeffrey Richards, "Les rapports entre le *Lai de Guigemar* and le *Roman d'Eneas*: Considérations génériques," in *Le récit bref au moyen âge: actes du colloque des 27, 28, et 29 avril 1979*, ed. Danielle Buschinger (Amiens: Université de Picardie, Centre d'Études Médiévales, and Paris: Champion, 1980), 45–56. See also the notes for the *lai* of *Guigemar* in Rychner's edition of the *Lais*.

The *Lais*

their minds, they will then be capable of connecting the two geographical domains in which the principal adventures of her *lai* take place.

As we have seen, a fascinating element of Marie's literary art is the description of nonverbal objects that enhance the narrative through the aesthetic qualities they impart to the text.[60] These objects are numerous throughout the *Lais* and are frequently described in great detail. These representations are not mere aesthetic adornments, and often the nonverbal object, like the quasi-verbal object, assumes a place in the attention of the audience that is just as significant as the written or spoken word. Unlike the verbal object that has a written text inscribed on its surface, whether the text in question is explicitly or implicitly identified, the "quasi-verbal" refers to an object that contains an allusion to a written text, though no writing actually appears on the object itself.

Memory and *Ekphrasis:* The Case of *Guigemar*

The *lai* of *Guigemar* contains one example of Marie's ability to incorporate a quasi-verbal object into the narration by means of *ekphrasis*.[61] Marie interrupts the action of the narrative to bring

60. Much of the discussion at this point and throughout the rest of this chapter has its source in my article "A Medieval Book-Burning: *Objet d'art* as Narrative Device in the *Lai* of *Guigemar*." *Neophilologus* 80, no. 2 (1996): 205–11.

61. The term is defined in the 1996 edition of the *Oxford Classical Dictionary* as "an extended and detailed literary description of any object, real or imaginary." This definition represents my reference to Marie's detailed description in this episode from *Guigemar*. Contemporary literary theory has inspired quite a fashionable debate over the exact meaning and use of the term. See Murray Krieger, *Ekphrasis: The Illusion of the Natural Sign* (Baltimore: Johns Hopkins University Press, 1992); James Heffernan, *Museum of Words: the Poetics of Ekphrasis from Homer to Ashbery* (Chicago: University of Chicago Press, 1993); Gottfried Boehm and Helmut Pfotenhauer, eds., *Beschreibungskunst—Kuntsbeschreibung: Ekphrasis von der Antike bis zur Gegenwart* (Munich: Wilhelm Fink, 1995); Linda M. Clemente, *Literary Objets d'art: Ekphrasis in Medieval French Romance, 1150–1220* (New York: Peter Lang, 1992); Curtius, *European Literature and the Latin Middle Ages;* François Rigolot, "*Ekphrasis* and the Fantastic: Genesis of an Aberration," *Comparative Literature* 49, no. 2 (1997): 97–112; and, in general, Gotthold E. Lessing, *Laocoon: An Essay on the Limits of Painting and Poetry,* trans. Edward A. McCormick (Baltimore: Johns Hopkins University Press, 1984).

The *Lais*

us a vivid description of a painting that adorns the wall of a castle room in which a jealous husband has imprisoned his wife.[62] François Rigolot notes the power inherent in detailed descriptions of works of art: "Iconic descriptions (i.e., descriptions of which a work of art is the subject), may possess the power—*energeia*—to set before the reader the very object or scene being described."[63] The description of the objects and people associated with this episode—the room, the painting, the maiden who assists the imprisoned wife, and the eunuch priest who stands watch over the room[64]—generates a narrative pause within the text that recalls, by its nature, earlier descriptive passages in the *lai,* especially the mysterious yet marvelously described ship.[65]

These textual elements are distributed among three different segments: the description of the room where the lady is locked up (G 229–45), the description of the maiden (246–54), and the description of the eunuch priest (255–60). Each segment is structured in such a manner that it reflects a recurrent motif in the *lai,* that of imprisonment. For example, the first segment opens with two lines: "Li sire out fait dedenz le mur, / Pur mettre i sa femme a seür" (As a secure place for his wife, the lord had constructed within the enclosure) (229–30). The fourteen lines that follow treat the description of the room and the painting. This first section then ends with one line: "La fu la dame enclose e mise" (In this room the lady was imprisoned) (245). Just as the lady is a pris-

---

[62]. In my article, I refer to this object as nonverbal. After further reflection, and in light of my comments above, I now consider it a quasi-verbal object.

[63]. Rigolot, *"Ekphrasis* and the Fantastic," 110.

[64]. See Robert Hanning, "Courtly Contexts for Urban *Cultus:* Responses to Ovid in Chrétien's *Cligès* and Marie's *Guigemar,*" *Symposium* 35, no. 1 (1981): 34–56. Hanning suggests that this description is analogous to the Ovidian *thalamus:* "The *chambre* recalls Ovid's *thalamus,* bedroom of the *culta puella* and climax of the artful lover's quest.... The heroine's *chambre* in *Guigemar* recalls Ovid's world in that it is guarded by a eunuch, as are the Roman houses in which lovers seek their beloved; and in the presence of a servant who acts as intermediary between the lovers" (49–50).

[65]. For a full discussion of the implications of pauses in the course of narrations, see Gérard Genette, *Figures III* (Paris: Seuil, 1972).

The *Lais*

oner, enclosed within the walls of the castle, so are the descriptive lines enclosed within the nondescriptive ones that open and terminate the first section.[66]

This structure is repeated in the second segment, where one acknowledges two nondescriptive opening lines: "Une pucele a sun servise / Li aveit sis sires bailliee" (The lord had provided her with a noble and intelligent maiden) (246–47), and two closing lines: "Hume ne femme n'i venist, / Ne fors de cel murail n'issist" (No one, man or woman, could have escaped from this walled enclosure) (253–54), while the lines that provide the descriptive details of the maiden are contained between them—she is *franche, enseigniee,* and *fille sa sorur,* and "Entre les deus out grant amur" (The two loved each other dearly) (250).

The third segment does not exemplify this framing structure as explicitly as the previous ones, since the lines that function as textual "walls" in this passage are themselves descriptive or quasi-descriptive by nature: "Uns vielz prestres blancs e floriz / Guardout la clef de cel postiz" (An old priest with hoary-white hair guarded the key to the gate) (255–56), and "Le servise Deu li diseit / E a sun mangier la serveit" (He recited the divine service and served her at table) (259–60). Nonetheless, as in the previous two segments, the most essential information of the description is placed at the midpoint: "Les plus bas membres out perduz, / Autrement ne fust pas creüz" (He had lost his lower members, otherwise he would not have been trusted) (257–58). The whole of these segments and their respective structures inform the reading of the thematic concept of confinement, for the structure it-

---

66. See Keith Busby, "Froissart's Poetic Prison: Enclosure as Image and Structure in the Narrative Poetry," in *Froissart Across the Genres,* ed. Donald Maddox and Sara Sturm-Maddox (Gainesville: University Press of Florida, 1998), 81–100. Busby notices similar images of enclosure in Froissart's narrative poetry, both on a textual and on a codicological level. He shows how lyric insertions such as the *lai, virelai, complainte, ballade,* and *rondeaux* are enclosed with the octosyllabic couplets of the narrative text *Le paradis d'amour* (82). He also demonstrates how some of Froissart's own lyric texts are inserted between longer narratives in BNF, fr. 831 and fr. 830, thereby rendering "imprisonment" on the parchment of the manuscript (97–98).

The *Lais*

self enclosed the descriptive details of the passage within a textual framework.

In addition to its structural function, this theme of confinement serves as the *porte-parole* for yet another, and possibly the most prominent, theme in the text, which is that of repressed or frustrated love, verified by the central allusion of the preceding lines when the narrator describes the painting on the walls of the room. This *objet d'art* functions on different levels within the *lai*. On one level, it participates in a textual *mise-en-abyme;* the reader reads (or the audience hears) a story of love, the *lai* of *Guigemar* in general.[67] Within this *lai,* the narrator tells another story that is depicted by the painting on the walls of the room. Likewise, in the narrative portrayed by the painting of Venus instructing lovers there is yet another story of love, contained within the pages of the unnamed book of Ovid that the goddess of love holds in her hand.

This textual *mise-en-abyme* is echoed by what may be considered a geographical *mise-en-abyme* when judging the location of the room. Much as the modern movie camera first pans over a city, then moves in closer to highlight a particular building, and finally focuses on one single room where the action of that particular scene takes place, the medieval narrator also gradually incorporates this *locus* into the text, methodically progressing from the exterior point of reference in the proximity of the city to an interior position in the exact location of the room. First, Guigemar arrives by boat: "Desuz une antive cité, / Ki esteit chiefs de cel regné" (Below an ancient city, capital of its realm) (207–8). A few lines later, the *locus* becomes more precise: "En un vergier, suz le dongun, / La out un clos tut envirun" (In a garden at the foot of the keep, there was an enclosure) (219–20), and then "De

---

67. For a thorough discussion of the specularity at work in this scene, see Donald Maddox, *Fictions of Identity in Medieval France* (Cambridge: Cambridge University Press, 2000), 34–38. The chapter entitled "The Specular Encounter in Fictions of Reciprocity: The *Lais* of Marie de France" (24–82) treats this subject in all the *lais* in her collection.

The *Lais*

l'altre part fu clos de mer; / Nuls ne pout eissir ne entrer" (The sea enclosed it on the other side, so it was impossible to get in or out) (225–26). Finally, and rather specifically, the room is situated within the walls: "Li sire out fait dedenz le mur, / Pur mettre i sa femme a seür, / Chaumbre" (As a secure place for his wife, the lord had constructed within the enclosure a chamber) (229–31).

In addition to its participation in *mise-en-abyme,* the *objet d'art* in this passage operates on still another, more primary level within the *lai;* the painting, though it contains no explicitly identified written content, becomes a narrative text itself, a sort of *ut pictura poesis* that informs the audience of Marie's authorial intent through her *descriptio:*

> La chaumbre ert peinte tut entur;
> Venus, la deuesse d'amur,
> Fu tres bien mise en la peinture;
> Les traiz mustrout e la nature
> Cument hom deit amur tenir
> E lealment e bien servir.
> Le livre Ovide, ou il enseine
> Comment chascuns s'amur estreine,
> En un fu ardant le gettout,
> E tuz iceus escumengout
> Ki jamais cel livre lirreient
> Ne sun enseignement fereient.
>   (G 231–44)

The walls of the chamber were covered in paintings in which Venus, the goddess of love, was skillfully depicted together with the nature and obligations of love; how it should be observed with loyalty and good service. In the painting Venus was shown as casting into a blazing fire the book in which Ovid teaches the art of controlling love and as excommunicating all those who read this book or adopted its teachings.

It is worth noting that the theme depicted in the painting would most likely recall, in the mind of the medieval reader or auditor, the universal theme of frustrated love, ubiquitous in the *lai.* Furthermore, it is probable that the medieval audience was familiar to some extent with the works of Ovid, whether through direct contact or by assimilation through the writings of medieval authors who themselves, without a doubt, had knowledge of at least part of the Ovidian corpus.

Owing to the ambiguity of the expression *le livre Ovide,* however, which does not designate the exact book that Venus is casting into the fire, different semantic interpretations have been suggested for this passage.[68] Nonetheless, despite the ambiguity of the book in question, at least two things are certain from Marie's text: first, the book teaches how to repress or control love and is consequently contrary to the designs of *fin' amors,* and second, Venus is not at all pleased with its content, even to the extent of excommunicating all who adhere to its teachings. While it is not my intention here to argue for the acceptance of any single work, or of the entire Ovidian corpus for that matter, as that which serves as fuel for Venus's fire, it may in any case be reasonable to consider the *Remedia amoris* as the book in question, especially given the fact that this is, after all, "Le livre Ovide ou il enseine / Comment chascuns s'amur estreine" (The book in which Ovid teaches the art of controlling love) (239–40). The verb *estreindre* in line 240, according to Tobler and Lommatzsch, indicates the action of the German *pressen* or *zusammendrücken,* and Greimas assigns it the

---

68. Some scholars accept the *Remedia amoris* as the book in question; see Paula Clifford, *Marie de France: Lais* (London: Grant & Cutler, 1982), 24; Philippe Ménard, *Les lais de Marie de France* (Paris: Presses Universitaires de France, 1979), 29–30; and Yolande de Pontfarcy, "La souveraineté: Du mythe au lai de *Guigemar,*" *Acta Litteraria Academiae Scientiarum Hungaricae* 32, nos. 1–2 (1990): 153–59, especially 158. However, see Herman Braet, "Note sur Marie de France et Ovide: Lai de *Guigemar,* vv. 233–244," in *Mélanges de philologie et de littératures romanes offerts à Jeanne Wathelet-Willem,* ed. Jacques de Caluwé (Liège: Cahiers de l'A.R.U.Lg., 1978), 21–25. Braet suggests that Marie is ambiguous at this point, whether the *Ars amatoria* or the *Remedia amoris.* See also Hanning, "Courtly Contexts," 34, where he interprets this representation as the entire corpus of Ovid and claims that the text of *Guigemar* is anti-Ovidian. For a thorough study of Ovid and Marie de France, see SunHee Kim Gertz, *Echoes and Reflections: Memory and Memorials in Ovid and Marie de France,* Faux Titre 232 (Amsterdam: Rodopi, 2003). See especially Gertz's discussion of this episode in chapter 2, "Enigmatic Beauty."

The *Lais*

meaning of the French *serrer, presser,* and *tenir rudement*.[69] Furthermore, the *Remedia amoris* seems to accommodate better the construct of the *lai* as a whole, and it reinforces the network of irony, contrast, and comparison that develops when the description of this *objet d'art* briefly becomes the focus of the *lai*.

First, the painting of Venus and the book symbolically unite two textual levels: on the one hand, that of the characters in the *lai* of *Guigemar*, and on the other, the juxtaposition of the poets of the two works—Marie for *Guigemar* and Ovid for his book.[70] In his text, Ovid intends to teach his audience how to repress or control love. However, like Venus, who throws this book into the fire, rejecting the constraints of such an approach to love, so too Marie, through her *lai*, solicits the liberty that love will achieve with those who embrace her text and allow their amorous passions to be fulfilled. Moreover, the poet may have deliberately chosen the image of a love "goddess," rather than a love "god," in order to call attention to the implicit comparison of her own capacity as liberator with that of the deities. In fact, Rychner has noted that a painting metaphor is also found in the *Eneas,* but there it is a "god," not a "goddess," of love who rules.[71]

In addition, this part of the narrative is meaningful in relation to the characters of the *lai* because of the underlying affinity between the story portrayed in the painting and the conditions of Guigemar and the *mal-mariée*. For Guigemar, the room represents the genesis of the healing of his wound, and consequently the remedy for his sexual impotence, since it is here that he is cured by the lady, precisely in accordance with the proleptic discourse of the androgynous hind at the beginning of the *lai*. Also, he is surrounded, during his stay, by the didactic story on the walls of

---

69. Algirdas J. Greimas, ed., *Dictionnaire de l'ancien français* (Paris: Larousse, 2001). See also Frédéric Godefroy, ed., *Dictionnaire de l'ancienne langue française,* 10 vols. (Paris: F. Vieweg, 1881–1902).

70. Hanning, "Courtly Contexts," 45.

71. Rychner's edition of the *Lais,* 244. The lines from the *Eneas* are 7982–84, "Navre Amor et point souvant, / et si est point tot par figure / por demostrer bien sa nature."

The *Lais*

the room that undoubtedly participated in his recovery by convincing him of his need for love.

The textual relationship between painting and characters is even more striking in the figure of the lady, since it is ironic that the room that should serve as a type of prison is so well decorated with a painting narrating a message of liberation. But, even more ironically, it is her jealous husband, a male character who, according to the text, constructed this *locus molestus,* where a female deity reigns.[72] One cannot be sure whether he intended to enlighten his wife, through the story in the painting, on the virtues of unrestrained love, in this case "unrestrained love" for himself. In the end, however, the jealous husband receives his just reward for having imprisoned her when she does in fact allow herself unrestricted love, but for Guigemar rather than for him. In essence, the productive theme of unrestrained love depicted in the painting on the walls stands in sharp contrast to the sterile characters in the castle, with the possible exception of the maiden who already seems to know much about the affairs of love. Each person is in one way or another sexually frustrated: the old, jealous husband, his unhappy wife, Guigemar, and the eunuch priest who "had lost his lower members" (257).[73]

Thus objects and the *objet d'art* are not simply "objects" in Marie's narrative plan; they are in fact catalysts in the generation and transmission of the text, and they represent a decisive part of the art with which she constructs an intricate network of narration. In *Guigemar* they support a structure that accomplishes the narration of the story, not necessarily through explicit discourse in the form of direct or indirect style, but more by means of the art of *descriptio* with which the poet establishes different narrative registers. One has only to consider the central image of the passage under consideration, the painting of Venus, to observe the importance of the object in the poetics of Marie. This particular

---

72. Hanning, "Courtly Contexts," 45.
73. See Rupert T. Pickens, "Thematic Structure in Marie de France's *Guigemar,*" *Romania* 95, nos. 378–79 (1974): 328–41, especially 339.

The *Lais*

description participates in the narration of a story that informs the reading of a fundamental theme in the *lai*—the theme of love.

Furthermore, the use of the painting as narrative device permits the poet to align herself implicitly with the goddess of love in order to communicate her role as authority in the domain of *fin' amors*. In the same manner, the appearance of the book of Ovid justifies Marie's own work through the *topos* of *auctoritas*, placing her *lai* in the same company as that of the ancients. I suggest that the textual significance of this *objet d'art* is surpassed only by its importance as a mnemonic devise, or *aide-mémoire*, which Marie paints into the faculty of memory so that we will one day in the future be able to recall the *lai* of *Guigemar* in general and the poet's lessons of love in particular.

Although not all of Marie de France's *lais* are discussed in this chapter, since the purpose here has been to analyze the most striking descriptions throughout the collection, they all nonetheless demonstrate the author's poetics of memory in some fashion, if, in a few cases, primarily through their opening and closing remarks (as discussed in chapter 2) and through their commemorative function as a *lai*. Sometimes the description of violent events leaves a vivid impression on the audience, as is the case with the werewolf in *Bisclavret* who behaves like a human when he is around the king, and who bites off the nose of his unfaithful wife, or the king and his seneschal's wife, who experience a violent death by drowning in scalding water at the end of *Equitan*. At other times, the description of marvelous creatures captures our attention and helps us to remember the story, as with the hawk that is transformed into a valiant knight in *Yonec*, or the weasel in *Eliduc* that uses an herb to revive its partner, or the androgynous hind in *Guigemar* that speaks and predicts the hero's healing. In one way or another, Marie's poetics, throughout these brief texts based on oral Breton tales, embodies a vivid narrative tableau with lively images that will be easily retained in memory.

4

The *Fables*

The thirteenth and fourteenth centuries saw a pronounced increase in the number of manuscripts containing *Isopets,* or collections of Aesopic fables from the Greek Phaedrean tradition that were accessible to medieval French authors through Latin adaptations, like those of Romulus.[1] The *Isopets* were composed in Old French, especially in octosyllabic rhymed couplets, though sometimes later in prose as well. The abundance of manuscripts bears witness to the success that these brief stories enjoyed during this period, as they used animals, insects, humans, plants, the elements, and inanimate objects to critique contemporary society and culture and to convey moral lessons to an audience that was already accustomed to hearing or reading other short genres such as the *lai* and the fabliau.

The earliest version of the Old French *Isopet,* Marie de France's *Fables* was composed probably between 1167 and 1189.[2] Marie's version of the *Isopet* has survived in twenty-five manuscripts dating from the early thirteenth through the end of the fifteenth century, and the first fifteen lines of one of her fables, *Del fevre e de la*

---

1. The tradition of the Old French *Isopets* is complex. For a concise summary of their sources, see Hans R. Runte, "Fable (Isopet)," in Kibler and Zinn, *Medieval France,* 331–32.

2. For dating, see Françoise Vielliard, "Sur la tradition manuscrite des *Fables* de Marie de France," *Bibliothèque de l'École des Chartes* 147 (1989): 371–97.

The *Fables*

cuinee (The Blacksmith and the Axe),[3] appear in a fragment of Nottingham University Library Mi Lm 6.[4]

The number of manuscripts of Marie's *Fables,* compared with the paucity of manuscripts containing the *Lais,* suggests the popularity of the former during the period in which the tales were composed and copied. The opposite is true of the modern age, the *Lais* having received much more critical attention than the *Fables* during the past three centuries. Renewed interest in Marie's fables in the past fifteen years has produced substantial scholarship, however.[5] It may be worth noting that the revival of her fables is part of a broader renewed interest in short narrative genres as a whole during the last two decades of the twentieth century.

There are either 102 or 103 fables in the most complete collection, depending on whose modern critical edition one follows.[6] Four manuscripts—London, British Library, Harley 978; Paris, Bibliothèque Nationale, fr. 1593, and Arsenal 3142; and Bibliothèque Nationale, fr. 2168—contain the entire collection of fa-

---

3. Though I cite Warnke's edition of the text throughout unless otherwise noted, I use the Old French titles and their English translations from *Marie de France: Fables,* ed. and trans. Harriet Spiegel (Toronto: University of Toronto Press, 1987). London, BL, Harley 978, the base manuscript for Warnke's edition and all subsequent editions, does not contain titles for the fables. Warnke adopts Latin titles found in two different manuscripts, but not in his base manuscript. Modern French titles, based on the Latin titles, are used by Charles Brucker in his translation, *Marie de France: Les fables, édition critique accompagnée d'une introduction, d'une traduction, de notes et d'un glossaire,* 2d ed. (Louvain: Peeters, 1991). Since passages from the fables are cited here in Old French, I opt for the Old French titles in order to facilitate reading. Old French titles are found in seven different manuscripts. See the table in Appendix B.

4. Vielliard, "Tradition manuscrite," 381.

5. See Burgess, *Analytical Bibliography.* He recorded twice as many studies that treated the *Fables* as their principal subject in the years between the publications of the first and second supplements (1985–97) than he did in the years between the publications of the original volume and the first supplement (1977–85). Also, the total number of studies (57) on the *Fables* from 1977–97, a twenty-year period, almost equals all studies (67) on this text published before 1977.

6. Warnke's edition contains 102, as does Brucker's. Martin's translation also contains 102, since it is based on Warnke's edition. Spiegel reads fable 65, *Del lu e de l'escarbot,* and fable 66, *Del gris lu,* as two different texts and thus counts 103 total fables. Warnke and Brucker read the latter as an appendage to the former; I agree with their numbering.

The *Fables*

bles, as well as the prologue and the epilogue, with the exception of the last, which does not have the epilogue.

As for Marie's sources, the first forty fables are based on the Latin *Romulus Nilantii*. The remaining sixty-two fables have sparked much interest in recent years, and the source, or sources, for many of them have not been convincingly identified. Furthermore, Marie's claim to have translated a collection of fables written in English by King Alfred is increasingly viewed with suspicion, and is seen most often as a possible authorial *topos* of self-justification for her own poetic endeavor.[7] Fortunately, research continues in this area, and significant theories have been advanced by scholars like Sahar Amer, who argues that several of Marie's fables bear substantial evidence of Eastern influences.[8]

Narrative Economy and Visual Narrative

Since the time of Aesop, fables have always embodied a critique of the moral, judicial, and political systems of the society in which they are composed. It is no different for Marie de France, writing in twelfth-century England, or even, centuries later, for La Fontaine at the heart of French classicism. The texts of both adamantly reflect and criticize the social climate of their respective periods.[9] While Marie's apparent social and cultural aims in

---

7. See Runte, "Fable (Isopet)." The view that Marie faithfully translated an English collection was held by Eduard Mall, "Zur Geschichte der mittelalterlichen Fabellitteratur und insbesondere des *Esope* der Marie de France," *Zeitschrift für romanische Philologie* 9, no. 1 (1885): 161–203, and by Karl Warnke, "Die Quellen des *Esope* der Marie de France," in *Forschungen zur romanischen Philologie: Festgabe für Hermann Suchier* (Halle: Niemeyer, 1900), 161–284.

8. Sahar Amer, *Ésope au féminin: Marie de France et la politique de l'interculturalité*, Faux Titre 169 (Amsterdam: Rodopi, 1999). Amer argues that although Marie's thematic source is found mainly in the *Romulus Nilantii*, her work nonetheless exhibits a poetic interpretation that reflects more closely an Arab tradition such as that of the *Kalilah wa Dimnah*.

9. For a study that discusses how Marie's treatment of society differs from that of the other fable authors in the two centuries after her, see Charles Brucker, "Société et morale dans la fable ésopique du XIIe et du XIIIe siècle," in *Et c'est la fin pour quoy sommes ensemble: Hommage à Jean Dufournet*, ed. J.-C. Aubailly et al., 3 vols. (Paris:

The *Fables*

the fables are undeniable, my concern here is with the way in which she accomplishes the transmission of her message through strategic description of the narrative elements in question.

If the *lai* discourages the use of detailed descriptions by the constraints on its length, the fable genre presents an even greater challenge in this domain for an author like Marie de France, who relies on the rhetorical use of *descriptio* to enhance her narrative program. In the preceding chapter I demonstrated how Marie embellished her *Lais* with vivid yet economical descriptions that register an image in the mind's eye, and how this type of medieval "objective correlative" will later help the reader or listener recall the story with which it is associated. The *Fables* reveal a similar genius in descriptive design, but in a context that demands even stricter narrative economy than does the *lai;* most fables in her collection are fewer than fifty lines in length, the longest being 124 lines.

That Marie turns her literary attention from the *lai* to the much shorter genre of the fable should come as no surprise when considered in light of her constant concern with memory, as outlined earlier in my discussion of her frequent use of the term "remembrance." The fable, with its focus on the moral lesson, is by its didactic nature constructed to be remembered in association with the objects that it describes. R. Howard Bloch has shown that "the pedagogical paradigm of the *Fables* is every bit as inscribed from the start in a project of memory and of cultural preservation as is that of the *Lais*."[10] Such a narrative blueprint makes few demands on the memory through its combination of mental imagery and spoken or written discourse and follows the same prevailing pattern of mnemonic architecture as found in the *Lais*. Still, Charles Brucker has recognized a fundamental difference in Marie's *Fables* when compared with her Latin counterparts, in that she estab-

---

Champion, 1993), 1:281–92. See also the informative introduction to Martin's English translation of Marie's fables.

10. R. Howard Bloch, *The Anonymous Marie de France* (Chicago: University of Chicago Press, 2003), 113.

The *Fables*

lishes a closer relationship between the story and the moral that follows:"Dans la fable de Marie de France, les éléments descriptifs sont, en fait, des adjuvants de l'action qui doit conduire le lecteur vers le dénouement de l'histoire, mais aussi vers la moralité qu'il importe de tirer de la fable ainsi présentée" (In Marie de France's fable the descriptive elements are in fact facilitators of the action that lead the reader to the outcome of the story, but also to the moral that must be gleaned from the fable presented in this way).[11] Apart from arguing that Marie is more concerned than other authors of fables in the Latin tradition with connecting the moral of the story and the story itself, Brucker highlights the important role that description plays in Marie's fables.

Since Marie's originality in the *Fables* lies partly in the descriptive aspect that she brings to the story, a comparison of certain fables among the first forty from her collection with their treatment in the *Romulus Nilantii* will be helpful in elucidating her contribution in this area. The remaining sixty-two fables are intentionally omitted from discussion here, since for the most part their sources remain unknown and one cannot therefore show the ways in which Marie may have been more descriptive than the originals.[12] It is important to keep in mind that although the *Romulus Nilantii* is the identified source for the first forty fables, Marie's work is in no way a simple translation of them into the vernacular; rather, as Amer suggests, "she is in fact interpreting, rewriting and thus recreating the genre of the fable." In fact, Amer contends that Marie, unlike her sources, questions the didactic nature of the fable, and she sees language as the theme of Marie's

---

11. See Charles Brucker,"La conception du récit dans la fable ésopique en langue vulgaire: De Marie de France à Steinhöwel," in *Le récit bref au moyen âge: Actes du colloque des 27, 28 et 29 avril 1979*, ed. Danielle Buschinger (Amiens: Université de Picardie, Centre d'Études Médiévales; Paris: Champion, 1980), 389–90. My translation.

12. See Sahar Amer's review of Brucker's translation of the *Fables* in *Romance Philology* 48, no. 3 (1995): 309. Amer shows that several fables among the last sixty-two of the collection have possible Eastern (Arabic) sources: 46, 57, 58, 70, 72, 73, 78, 79, 81, 98, 101. She discusses the Eastern influence on Marie's fables throughout *Ésope au féminin*.

The *Fables*

collection.[13] I agree that Marie's principal goal may not have been didactic, but her moral exhortations, while not as authoritative as those of her sources, have a message to convey nonetheless. And while Marie is concerned with language in the *Fables,* it is only one among several themes: memory, political concerns, justice, relationships, and so on.

In the prologue to the *Fables* Marie once again gives credibility to her project, as she did in the General Prologue to the *Lais,* by invoking the authority of the ancients:

> Romulus, ki fu emperere,
> a sun fiz escrit e manda
> e par essample li mustra
> cum se deüst cuntreguaitier
> que hum nel peüst engignier.
> (Prologue 12–16)[14]

Romulus, who was emperor, wrote to his son and declared this, showing him through an exemplum how he should guard himself against being deceived.

---

13. See Sahar Amer, "*L'ésope* de Marie de France: *Translatio* du *Romulus Nilantii*," in *The Medieval Translator,* vol. 5, ed. Roger Ellis and René Tixier (Turnout: Brepols, 1996), 347. While I agree with Amer's premise in this article that Marie's work is not merely a translation of the Latin original and that she brings a new dimension to the fable genre "through her use of the verse and various innovative formal transformations," I remain cautious about her claims that Marie "questions the acceptance of the fable as a didactic instrument," and that "language itself has become the theme of the *Esope* and each fable a reflection on the status of language and its duplicity" (347). For an additional study that champions Marie as author rather than translator, see Hans R. Runte, "Marie de France, traite et retraite," *ALFA: Actes de Langue Française et de Linguistique: Symposium on French Language and Linguistics* 3–4 (1990–91): 229–35.

14. I have chosen to cite Warnke's edition of the *Fables* throughout this study, despite the dangers inherent in the interventionist editorial methods prevalent during the nineteenth century, because I share many of Amer's misgivings, expressed in her review of Brucker's edition of the *Fables.* Like Amer, I believe that no edition since Warnke's, including the most recent by Brucker, has significantly improved upon Warnke's text or choice of base and control manuscripts. In "Tradition manuscrite," Vielliard observes that Chantilly, Musée Condé 474, a manuscript that Warnke did not use to establish his edition but that she has examined in detail, often confirms

The *Fables*

Though it is doubtful that Marie had purely didactic motives when she accepted the task of putting fables into the vernacular, she clearly does not abhor this part of the work, and I agree with Brucker's assessment that this passage supports the moralistic nature of the fables in her collection.[15]

The fable that appears first in all but two of the manuscripts of Marie's *Isopet* is *Del cok e de la gemme (The Cock and the Gem)*. BNF, fr. 4939 does not begin until fable 19, and BNF, fr. 24310 is missing the first twenty-eight texts.[16] For the purposes of this study, the first fable presented by Marie is significant in that it is a perfect example, from the very beginning of her collection, of her tendency, throughout at least the first forty fables for which the source is definitely known, to embellish the original material with elements that make her text more vivid to the imagination.

This text recounts the story of a rooster who discovers a precious gem while scratching for food on top of a dung pile. Marie's source for the fable is the first fable of the first book of the *Romulus Nilantii* collection, *De Gallinacio, qui, in sterquilinio quærens escam, invenit margaritam (The Cock Who Found a Pearl While Looking for Food in a Dung Heap)*.[17] Marie wastes no time in departing from the original text when, in lines 3–4, she interjects a descriptive element that is not found in the Latin version: "sulunc nature purchaçot / sa viande, si cum il sot" (looking for his food in the way he knew best). Just a few lines later she introduces another concept that is absent from her source:

---

his text and corrections against the base manuscript, London, BL, Harley 978 (375). Despite my decision to cite Warnke's edition, my discussion of the differences between Marie's fables and those of her predecessors in this section is greatly indebted to Brucker's insightful commentary in his second, revised edition, in which he notes Marie's divergence from and additions to the Latin texts.

15. Brucker's edition of the *Fables*, 47n.
16. See the useful chart in Spiegel's edition of the *Fables*, 279–82.
17. The Latin titles and text from the *Romulus Nilantii* are from Léopold Hervieux, ed., *Les fabulistes latins, depuis le siècle d'Auguste jusqu'à la fin du Moyen Âge*, 2 vols. (Paris: Firmin-Didot, 1884; 2d ed., 5 vols., 1883–89). The English translations of them are my own.

The *Fables*

> S'uns riches huem ci vus trovast,
> bien sai que d'or vus honurast,
> si acreüst vostre clarté
> par l'or, ki mult a grant bealté.
> (11–14)

> If a rich man had found you, I'm sure he would have graced you with beautiful gold which would have enhanced your brilliance.

Whereas the *Romulus Nilantii* fable is content with the simple discovery of a pearl, Marie has enhanced this image as "une chiere gemme" (a precious gem) and has uniquely associated it with the preciousness of gold in order to call attention to its aesthetic qualities. Not only is her mention of gold new to this fable, but she repeats it within three lines to ensure that it registers in conjunction with the gem.

The addition of just a few descriptive details to the objects of this fable causes the imagery to take on a more visual quality than the dull description of her Latin source and is thus more likely to remain implanted in our memory. Such a style of narration is not limited to this fable alone but is indeed a recurring theme throughout the collection, as Brucker states: "le trait permanent le plus frappant dans ses fables est certainement la concrétisation et l'adaptation à son temps des idées abstraites évoquées dans les fables latines" (the most striking permanent trait in her fables is certainly the concrete expression and adaptation for her time of the abstract ideas evoked in the Latin fables).[18]

At times, the descriptive enrichment has the purpose of intensifying the anthropomorphic qualities of the animals involved by assigning them discourse that stresses the psychological aspect of the situation. This is the case for lines 27–28 of the fable *Del lu e de l'aignel (The Wolf and the Lamb):* "'ja me fez tu ore cuntraire / e chose que tu ne deis faire'" (since you have already annoyed me

---

18. Brucker's edition, 51n.

and done something you shouldn't have). The idea behind these lines does not figure in the source fable, *De agno et lupo ad rivulum potandi causa venientibus (The Lamb and the Wolf Who Came to Drink at a Stream)*, and, as Brucker notes, they "accentuent la tension psychologique entre les deux personnages" (stress the tension between the two characters).[19] Marie also makes the death of the lamb in the next couplet seem more vivid by her addition of the word "estrangle" (strangle), which does not appear in the *Romulus* text: "Dunc prist li lous l'aignel petit, / as denz l'estrangle, si l'ocit" (Thereupon the wolf seized the little lamb, strangled him with his teeth, and killed him) (29–30). Marie emphasizes the psychological dynamics, whereas the source poems neglected them, as is witnessed in several other fables among the ones that draw their inspiration from the *Romulus*: *Del chien e de la brebiz (The Dog and the Ewe), Del corbel e del gupil (The Crow and the Fox),* and *Del l'asne ki volt jüer a sun seignur (The Ass Who Wanted to Play with His Master).*

Marie's penchant for descriptive detail, as compared with her sources, appears on several occasions throughout the fable *De la suriz e de la reine (The Mouse and the Frog)*. Though she has only ninety-two lines in which to narrate the story, she nonetheless spends much of her narrative in lively descriptions that paint a more memorable picture than does her source text. In an effort to make her characters more in tune with the social milieu in which she is writing, she often anthropomorphizes the animals by assigning them attributes that situate them in the economy of daily medieval life, as in lines 24–26: "n'i avrez rien ki vus desplaise; / asez avrez farine e greins / del ble ki remeint as vileins" (You'll find nothing there to displease you, and you'll find quite a bit of

---

19. Ibid., 55n. For a study that compares the orthography and scribal differences of some of the fables in the Anglo-Norman manuscript London, BL, Harley 978, to the same ones from the continental manuscript BNF, fr. 19152, see Bernadette Masters, "*Li lox, lililions* and Their *compaig*: Exemplary Error in the Fables of BNF MS, f. fr. 19152," *Parergon*, n.s., 13, no. 2 (1996): 203–22. Masters argues that orthographical errors are "an integral part of the scribe-artists' creative mandate" (205).

The *Fables*

flour and grains of wheat that are left over by the peasants). This idea is not present in its Latin source, *De mure, qui in transitum fluminis a rana petivit auxilium (The Mouse Who Sought Help While Crossing a River with a Frog)*.

Likewise, the description in lines 48–50, the theme of which is also absent in the Latin source, imparts energy to the narrative: "Li prez fu si plains de rusee / que tute est la suriz muilliee; / dunc quida bien estre neiee" (The meadow was so full of dew and the mouse got so wet that she thought she might well drown). The unprecedented descriptive detail that Marie adds to this scene is similar to another embellishment later in the text:

> La suriz pipe en halt e crie,
> ki quida tute estre perie.
> Uns escufles i vint roant,
> vit la suriz ki vait pipant.
> Les eles clot, a val descent;
> li e la reine ensemble prent
> (amdous furent al fil pendanz).
> La reine fu corsue e granz:
> li escufles par cuveitise
> la suriz lait, la reine a prise
> Mangiee l'a e devoree,
> e la suriz est delivree.
>
> (71–82)

The mouse, who thought all was lost, piped up and started squeaking. A kite came by and saw the squeaking mouse. He folded his wings, dove down, and seized her and the frog together, both hanging from the same thread. The frog was big and fat, so, out of greediness, the kite left the mouse and took the frog. It ate and devoured her, while the mouse was set free.

Marie's deviation here from her source recalls her descriptive style in the *Lais* and serves to enrich the mental tableau that she paints for her audience.

The descriptive technique at work here and throughout the

The *Fables*

Fables brings to mind the mnemonic technique that was used in the Middle Ages to teach moral lessons to students through study of the bestiary. Carruthers offers the example of a copy of the Anglo-Norman version of the bestiary by Philippe de Thaon, London, BL, Cotton Nero A. v., composed during the first half of the twelfth century. For her, this book represents "a particularly provocative study from the standpoint of mnemonic technique," and she notes its importance to the training of memory: "Philippe de Thaon's Bestiary is presented as a memory-book. In each of its 'pictures' of animals, its verses admonish the reader to remember particular pieces of the description as well as the whole: 'Aiez en remembrance • ceo est signefiance' ('It is important to remember them')."[20]

Carruthers observes that the most practical aspect of Philippe's book was not necessarily moral instruction but rather the exercise of mental imagery: "What the Bestiary taught most usefully in the long term of a medieval education was not 'natural history' or moralized instruction (all instruction in the Middle Ages was moralized) but mental imaging, the systematic forming of 'pictures' that would stick in the memory and could be used, like rebuses, homophonies, *imagines rerum,* and other sorts of *notae,* to mark information *within* the grid."[21] The engaging force behind using London, BL, Cotton Nero A. v. to train students in creating mental images is the fact that this bestiary is *not* illustrated. Indeed, no pictures accompany the text; the "pictures," as Carruthers points out, are "entirely verbal," a feature that "forced the students to make the pictures carefully in their minds, to 'paint' mentally."[22] One cannot help but consider the possibility that Marie may have had access to this source, since her narrative technique reflects its manner of instruction. The dating of the manuscript puts it well within Marie's literary time frame, and Carruthers has determined that it was originally in the English Cistercian Library of

---

20. Carruthers, *Book of Memory,* 127.   21. Ibid.
22. Ibid.

The *Fables*

St. Mary's, Holmecultram.[23] If Marie de France was an abbess, the possibility that she may have been influenced by this book becomes even more compelling.

As Marie's texts repeatedly demonstrate, both in the *Lais* and here again in the *Fables,* she is as verbally attentive to painting a mental picture as an artist might be to mixing oils that will be layered upon the canvas. Her ability to accomplish this technique is seen again in the fable *De la suriz de vile e de la suriz de boiz (The City Mouse and the Country Mouse).* This is the tale of a city mouse who crosses the woods to travel to a neighboring town and receives the hospitality of a country-dwelling mouse:

> Quant ele ot piece iluec esté,
> a sa cumpaigne en a parlé;
> dit que sis estres est malvais
> e qu'el n'i vuelt demurer mais;
> od li s'en vienge, si avra
> riches sales, qu'el li durra,
> beles despenses, beals celiers
> e bons beivres e bons mangiers.
> (15–22)

When she had been there a short time, the city mouse spoke to her companion and said that her home was shabby and that she didn't want to stay any longer. If the country mouse would come away with her, she would have lavish rooms, beautiful pantries, lovely cellars, and good food and drink that she would give her.

Brucker remarks that Marie's enumeration in the last three lines is absent from the source fable in the *Romulus Nilantii, De mure rurali a mure urbano in hospitium recepto (The Country Mouse Who Received the City Mouse in Her Home),* and that the Latin version offers a dry presentation of this exchange between the two mice.[24]

Though operating within a conservative textual economy that

---

23. Ibid.
24. Brucker's edition, 81n.

The *Fables*

discourages narrative digressions, Marie nonetheless takes care, as is often the case in her fables, to go beyond her sources in describing the objects or the scene at hand so that they become more real and vivid to us, more concrete to our imagination. The first six lines of *Del corbel e del gupil (The Crow and the Fox)*, as well as the first eight lines of *De l'arunde e del lin (The Swallow and the Linseed)*, further demonstrate Marie's descriptive style through her attention to detail, an aspect that is lacking in the Latin version of these fables. Likewise, in *De la femme ki fist pendre sun mari (The Widow Who Hanged Her Husband)*[25] she simply adds three lines not found in the *Romulus,* and thereby gives greater drama to the episode:[26] "Cuintement a a li parlé; / dit li qu'ele se cunfortast, / mult sereit liez, s'ele l'amast" (He spoke to her slyly, saying that she should be comforted and that he would be delighted if she were to love him) (20–23).

The fable *Del lëun e del vilein (The Lion and the Peasant)* has a description of a painting that recalls the painting of Venus on the castle walls in the *lai* of *Guigemar* discussed above.[27] Marie's narrative handling of this scene privileges the object over the action that takes place in the opening lines of the text, unlike the opening of the same fable in her source of the *Romulus Nilantii, De contentione habita inter hominem et leonem quis esset illorum audacior et superior (The Dispute between a Man and a Lion about Who Was More Courageous and Noble)*. The Latin title suggests the emphasis of the fable, as it begins by highlighting the tension between the

---

25. This fable, though taken from the *Romulus Nilantii (De Muliere, quæ, corpus mariti sui defuncti de tumulo elevans, in cruce suspendit)* like the rest of the first forty fables in her collection, has its ultimate source in the *Matron of Ephesus* tale by Petronius. For a detailed study on the anecdotal character of this fable in Marie, see Hans R. Runte, "'Alfred's Book,' Marie de France, and the Matron of Ephesus," *Romance Philology* 36, no. 4 (1983): 556–71. Runte does not agree with the appellation of "Schwank" that was assigned to Marie's version by earlier scholars. Marie's version of the tale is sometimes compared with the fabliau *Cele qui se fist foutre sur la fosse de son mari.* See Norris J. Lacy, *Reading Fabliaux* (New York: Garland, 1993), 1–17.

26. Brucker's edition, 135n.

27. The iconographical representation of the painting from this fable in the manuscript tradition of Marie's *Isopet* is discussed below.

The *Fables*

lion and the man: "Jam dudum Homo et Leo quamdam inter se contencionem habuerunt quis esset illorum audacior aut superior" (Now for a long time there was a dispute between a man and a lion over who was more courageous and noble) (3.8).[28] Amer notes the difference between the focus of the Latin fable and its French *translatio* by pointing out that the former centers on a quarrel between the lion and man over the issue of their valor, "quis esset illorum audacior aut superior," whereas Marie's version stresses an entirely philosophical discussion about the nature of truth and misrepresentation, that which is real and that which imitates reality.[29]

Instead of a quarrel between the lion and the man, Marie actually insists on their friendship from the very beginning of her text, through the term "cumpaignun":

> Ci nus recunte d'un liün,
> qu'uns vilains prist a cumpaignun.
> Entre eles cunterent lur parage,
> si parlerent de lur lignage.
> Li liüns dist: "Fiz sui a rei."
>
> (1–5)

There once was a man who took up with a lion as a companion. They were discussing their parentage and talking about their lineage. The lion said, "I am the son of a king."

Brucker reminds us that the idea of a conversation concerning their lineage does not appear in the Latin source and that line 5, in which the lion asserts his royal heritage, is unique to Marie.[30] The topic of lineage that she introduces in the fable is significant in regard to the present inquiry, for any discussion of lineage is implicitly a discussion that calls forth from memory images of the past.

Upon the lion's announcement of his royal descent, the man

---

28. My translation.
29. Amer, "*L'ésope* de Marie de France," 353.
30. Brucker's edition, 173n.

The *Fables*

leads him to a wall upon which there is a painting depicting a man and a lion, the former killing the latter with an axe:

> A un mur sunt amdui venu.
> Iluec a li leüns veü
> desur la piere une peinture
> cum uns vileins par aventure
> od sa hache oscist un leün.
>
> (7–11)

Together they came to a wall, and there on the stone the lion saw a painting of how a man happened to kill a lion with his axe.

Marie's originality does not lie in the specularity of this narration, that is to say, in the fact that it tells the story of a man and a lion within a story of a man and a lion; the source for her fable in the *Romulus Nilantii* depicts the same *mise-en-abyme*. Instead, her contribution comes once again in the form of descriptive detail that adds energy to the image.

The *Romulus* fable simply states that a lion is killed by a man: "ymaginem Leonis occisi ab homine" (the image of a lion killed by a man) (3.8). By contrast, Marie tells us how the killing is done. Just the two additional details, that the man commits this act intentionally and that he does so with an axe, certainly makes the scene portrayed in the painting more vivid to the imagination than the simple statement of fact in the Latin version of the fable. Consequently, Marie's image is much easier to enter into our storehouse of memory, and much more likely to remain there.

Both in Marie's text and in the Latin source, a discussion between the man and lion ensues after they have viewed the painting. The difference in these two dialogues has already been noticed by Amer, who shows that in the Latin version the lion dwells on the fact that the painting would have been executed differently if it had been done by a lion: "At si Leo pingeret, Hominem a Leone superatum pingeret" (If a lion had painted it, he would have made the lion superior to the man), whereas in the French retelling the lion has no such opinion to express.[31] Rather, Marie's text records the lion's commentary in the form of an observation that puts the emphasis on the creative capabilities of humans in comparison with those of animals, specifically lions:

> 'Ceo fist uns huem', dist li vileins,
> 'od ses engins e od ses meins.'
> Dunc a li liüns respundu:
> 'C'est a tut pueple coneü
> qu'um set entaillier e purtraire,
> mes li leüns nel set pas faire.'
> (15–20)

"A man painted it," said the peasant, "with his brushes and his hands." Then the lion answered, "Everyone knows that man can sculpt and paint, but the lion can't."

The accent in Marie's text is placed squarely on the process of creating art, and, more important for the theme of this fable, visual art. The Latin source only mentions the art of painting; Marie not only invokes this art and reinforces the objective quality of it in the words of the man—"with his brushes and his hands"—she also includes the art of sculpting, "entaillier," in line 19. This is yet another example of how Marie attaches narrative importance to that which can be seen with the mind's eye so that it can be recorded in memory.

At the end of this dialogue the lion leads the man to a castle where an emperor has an unfaithful baron, who had been accused of treason, put to death. This scene differs as well from the *Romulus* text, which depicts the lion leading the man to an amphitheater where many accused persons are imprisoned. Marie's representation of this episode is enhanced with several details for which no Latin analogue exists:[32]

---

31. Amer, "*L'ésope* de Marie de France," 353. She reminds the reader of the mention of this fable in Chaucer's *Wife of Bath*.
32. Brucker's edition, 175.

The *Fables*

> ... sil fist geter a sun liün,
> ki lung tens ot esté guardez
> dedenz sa curt enchaenez,
> e il l'ocist ignelepas;
> ainz n'i guarda armes ne dras.
>
> (28–32)

> ... and so the emperor had him thrown to his lion which had been kept chained up for a long time in the court. Soon the baron was stripped of weapons and clothes, and the emperor's lion killed him straitway [*sic*].

Her enhancement of this scene by describing the lion, which has been chained in the court for a long time and must be famished, reinforces the brutality of its killing of the baron with no attention to his weapons or clothing. It is complementary to the brutality of the axe in the French version of the fable. These depictions, which receive much livelier treatment in Marie's hands than they do in her Latin predecessor's, produce a more ardent image to be burned into the psyche. As Amer remarks, "Chez Marie, l'action tire sa force de persuasion, et donc sa supériorité sur le langage, du fait qu'elle pose le lion et le paysan en témoins oculaires de la scène de condamnation du baron. Nous notons un glissement par rapport au *RN* puisque dans la version française, ce n'est pas l'action en tant que telle qui est opposée au langage, mais plutôt ce qui est vu" (With Marie, the action draws its strength from persuasion, and thus its superiority over language, owing to the fact that she presents the lion and the peasant as eye witnesses of the condemnation of the baron. We note a shift in relation to the *RN* [*Romulus Nilantii*] since in the French version, it is not the action itself that is opposed to language, rather that which is seen).[33] Amer recognizes in this episode the same type of visual dimension that is at work throughout Marie's narratives.

While the Latin fable ends after the brief trip to the amphitheater, Marie de France adds an entirely new episode after the

---

33. Amer, "*L'ésope* de Marie de France," 355.

The *Fables*

execution of the baron. This description involves a meeting with another lion that, upon seeing his own species associating with a human, promptly offers to kill the man. As this beast reminds the other lion, a man is capable of making traps that lions can fall into: "ki set la fosse apareillier / u il purreient trebuchier" (who knew how to prepare pits into which they might fall) (41–42). The man's companion protests and warns that he will never allow the other lion to kill his friend: "ne sufferreit qu'il l'ocesist / pur nule rien; ne l'en peist ja!" (he would not allow him to kill the man for a trifle—so now he should mind his own business!) (46–47).

The lion's preventing his human companion from being devoured sets the stage for the final dialogue and moral of the fable:

> Li liüns li a demandé
> se li semblot cum einz ot fet.
> Dist li vileins: 'Altrement vet!'
> 'Jol vus dis einz', fet li liüns.
> Ainz que nus fussuns cumpaignuns,
> me mustras tu une peinture
> sur une piere d'aventure;[34]
> mes jeo t'ai puis uevre mustree,
> a descuvert l'as esguardee.'
> (50–58)

The lion asked him if he felt the same as before. The man said, "Quite different!" "I'll tell you how it is now," said the lion. "Before we were friends, you showed me a painting of an incident on a stone. But I have shown you deeds that you have seen before your very eyes."

---

34. Warnke corrects the reading "par aventure" found in his base manuscript, London, BL, Harley 978, since that reading makes the line hypermetric. However, his substitution of "d'aventure," while solving the problem of meter, is nonetheless puzzling because it makes the word "aventure" appear to be representative of the stone's composition or quality. One would have preferred the variant reading offered by BNF, fr. 2168, "a aventure," both to preserve scansion and possibly to give the word a meaning that better accommodates the context. Tobler and Lommatzsch offer no reference to a "piere d'aventure." Therefore, taking into consideration the problem of

The *Fables*

The lion's words here recall the painting at the beginning of the fable, as it makes a contrast between the image that the man presented and the living example that the lion has just shown the man by preventing his death. These last few lines prepare the audience for Marie's moral, which follows:

> Par essample nus vuelt aprendre
> que nuls ne deit niënt entendre
> a fable, ki est de mençunge,
> n'a peinture, ki semble sunge;
> c'est a creire dunt hum veit l'uevre,
> ki la verité en descuevre.
> (59–64)

From this fable we should learn not to believe anything from a lying story or a dreamlike painting. Believe only what is evident and has been revealed as true.

At first glance, these lines seem not only to contradict Marie's choice of the fable genre—"ki est de mençunge" (a lying story)—but also her own narrative descriptions, particularly in the form of a medium such as painting—"ki semble sunge" (dreamlike)—that she employs so successfully here and elsewhere in her *lai Guigemar*. I propose, however, that just the opposite is true, and that what Marie is really stressing in this moral is indeed the visual dimension. What we as audience are to believe and remember is not the painting as it might appear on the wall, but rather the image that we create in our minds from her descriptions, much like the medieval student who used the pictureless bestiary to create his or her own mental pictures.

In this regard, Marie's poetry prefigures by centuries the goal of the modern French poets of the twentieth century who were concerned with iconic form, poets such as René Char, who began with an abstract idea and solidified it into a concrete image

---

meter, I read lines 54–56 as, "Before we were companions, you showed me a painting, by chance, on a stone." Both Spiegel and Brucker read "par aventure," leaving the line hypermetric.

The *Fables*

through his selection of the *mot juste*, or Paul Eluard, who posited the inseparable relationship between art and poetry, both through his poems and through his essays on the topic such as those in *Donner à voir*.[35] Marie's poems and the descriptions within them are given to us to be "seen" as much as they are to be heard or read. They are bound neither to the manuscript folio nor to the page of the printed edition, but rather come alive as images in our minds through her nuanced *descriptio*.

Memory, Moral, and Manuscript Tradition

A closer reading of Marie de France's *Fables*, and the fact that they exist in far more manuscripts than do the *Lais*, arouse curiosity about the written tradition of these brief narrative texts, and about any clues it might offer into the memory-oriented aspect of Marie de France's works as a whole.[36] Specifically, the visual aspect of the tales as they were recorded on manuscript folios during the centuries following their composition helps to situate them within the broader context of a mnemonic architecture of description that reveals itself to be the hallmark of Marie's literary talent.

Consultation of more than fifty manuscripts in the bestiary and *Isopet* tradition that date from the early thirteenth century through the late fifteenth century allows us to draw certain con-

---

35. René Char, *Œuvres complètes* (Paris: Gallimard, 1983), and Paul Eluard, *Donner à voir* (Paris: Gallimard, 1939).

36. My analysis of the manuscript tradition of the *Fables* owes much to Busby, *Codex and Context: Reading Old French Verse Narrative in Manuscript*, 2 vols. (Amsterdam: Rodopi, 2002). His book contains reproductions of some of the images discussed in this chapter; see especially 471–77: Paris, BNF, fr. 1446, fol. 88rb, Paris, BNF, fr. 2173, fols. 58ra and 93rb, and Paris, Arsenal 3142, fols. 256ra and 273ra. I also examine some of the author portraits from this chapter in my article "*Ex libris Mariae:* Courtly Book Iconography in the Illuminated Manuscripts of Marie de France," in *Courtly Arts and the Art of Courtliness,* ed. Keith Busby and Christopher Kleinhenz (Woodbridge, UK: Boydell & Brewer, 2006), 745–53. My discussion in this article centers on the iconography of the book in some of the illuminations from these same manuscripts.

The *Fables*

clusions about the scribal and iconographical tendencies evident throughout the manuscripts of Marie's fables.[37] In this section I depart from a purely textual investigation of Marie's narrative craft as author and adopt an approach that examines the visual dimension of the manuscript page as it appeared before the eyes of the medieval scribe, illuminator, and reader several decades, and even centuries, after the original composition of her work. Although the discussion that follows will primarily examine iconography, it is nonetheless essential to keep in mind the textual analysis of her fables, since the evidence offered here demonstrates the *mise-en-page* of Marie's program of memory and moral instruction as it is eventually received and interpreted. This discussion of visual and codicological details of the manuscripts aims precisely to show how the scribes and illuminators incorporated their own understanding of Marie's message into the execution of their craft, and to explore what possible implications their interpretations brought to bear on the reception and performance of the text by subsequent readers.

Memory is one of Marie's principal concerns in the *Fables,* as we have seen in her use of the verb "remembrer" in the prologue to this collection and in her famous use of "remembrance" in the epilogue, where she identifies herself, as discussed in chapter 2. The verb "trover" in the prologue evokes the process of medieval literary *inventio,* taken in its context with the verbs "escrire" and "remembrer" of line 6. In other words, medieval poets "found" preexisting material in the storehouse of their memory and then, through their treatment of that material, composed a work that

---

[37]. I have consulted *in situ* all the extant medieval manuscripts of Marie's corpus, with the exception of Cologny, Bodmer 113, an exact copy of both text and images in BNF, fr. 2173, and with the exception of the fifteen lines of the fable from the Nottingham fragment mentioned earlier. London, BL, Harley 978, though not illuminated, contains all the fables and all the *lais*. For the purposes of this book, I do not take into account the manuscripts of Marie's *Fables* from the eighteenth century: Paris, Arsenal 3124, La Haye, Bibliothèque Royale 71 G 68, La Haye, BR 71 E 48, and BNF, Moreau 1603. These manuscripts are copies of medieval manuscripts of Marie's fables that are discussed here.

The *Fables*

revealed their own *ingenium*. This use of "remembrerent" in the prologue to her *Fables* brings to mind Chaucer's use of "remembrance" in *The Legend of Good Women*:

> And if that olde bokes weren aweye,
> Yloren were of remembrance the keye.
> Wel oughte us thanne on olde bokes leve,
> There as there is non other assay by preve.
> (25–28; text G)

For Chaucer, as for Marie before him, the act of writing was an act of remembering, that is, the transfer of knowledge from the past to the present and on to the future; it ensures cultural memory. Robert Payne observes, in reference to Chaucer's use of "remembrance," that the past is kept alive as it is made meaningful to experience in the present: "History had its most real and fruitful existence in the minds of men, so that the first thing we must note in considering Chaucer's uses of the past is that the past was for him primarily an intellectual phenomenon which continued in remembrance just so long as it could be made meaningful to experience."[38]

Just as the *Fables* open with an invocation of memory, so they end by recalling its importance: "me numerai pur remembrance: MARIE ai num, si sui de FRANCE" (I shall name myself for posterity: Marie is my name, and I am from France) (Epilogue 1–4). In the prologue, "remembrer" stresses the recall of textual material that gives way to moral lessons, whereas the use of this same word in the epilogue refers to a record of Marie de France's name and place of origin. Both examples are representative of collective memory.

Marie not only wanted her audience to remember her work in general, but she seems to have been especially concerned that they would commit to memory the morals, or lessons, of the fables: the "moralité." In a prologue of forty lines, she uses the terms

---

38. Robert Payne, *The Key to Remembrance: A Study of Chaucer's Poetics* (New Haven: Yale University Press, 1963), 65.

The *Fables*

"essamples" (three times), and "diz," "moralité," and "proverbes," invoking the moral aspect of the fable genre, a total of six times. This frequency of reference reinforces the didactic nature of her text, and we are told from the very beginning that the ancients recorded these brief stories for moral edification:

> Par moralité escriveient
> les bons proverbes qu'il oeient,
> que cil amender s'en poïssent
> ki lur entente en bien meïssent.
> Ceo firent li ancïen pere.
> (Prologue 7–11)

> For the ancients who wrote down these good proverbs that they heard did so for the purpose of moral edification, in order that those who set their mind upon the good might improve themselves.

It is interesting that the scribes and illuminators were quick to note the importance of this concern on Marie's part, and the manuscripts clearly demonstrate that they were preoccupied with conveying the importance of the lessons to future readers of the text. They consistently ensured that the moral of the story, in addition to the beginning of each new fable, would be set off from the rest of the text for purposes of emphasis. It was their way of pointing out the significance of the story, much as we do today when we wish to call attention to the didactic part of a story, or to the punch line of a joke, by saying, "and the moral of *this* story is . . ."

Chantal Maréchal reminds us, quoting J. J. G. Alexander, that "the initial at all times . . . had a function as a signpost to the reader."[39] Almost all of the extant manuscripts of Marie's fables visually emphasize the moral of the story in some fashion. In fact,

---

39. See Chantal Maréchal, "Marie de France as *Sapientia:* Author Portraits in the Manuscripts of the *Fables*," *Le Cygne: Bulletin of the International Marie de France Society* 3 (spring 1997): 46. She quotes J. J. G. Alexander, *The Decorated Letter* (New York: G. Braziller, 1978), 21.

The *Fables*

only BNF, fr. 12603 and fr. 1822, both dating from the thirteenth century, do not mark the morals in any way, although both do set off the beginning of each fable with a long flourished initial that is two lines high in red and blue.[40] Maréchal has suggested that the reason for the lack of marked morals in these two manuscripts is that they were "clearly intended for an aristocratic audience, concerned more with pleasure and entertainment than with moral edification," and she notes that BNF, fr. 12603 contains, in addition to the fables, romances of antiquity, courtly romances, fabliaux, and epics.[41] As tempting and plausible as this point of view may seem, it must nonetheless be approached with caution, for while this is indeed the case for fr. 12603, it is certainly not so for fr. 1822, which also contains several other moral texts, including *Sermones de voragine en prose, Sermon de la croix en vers,* and *Le petit livre de moralité en prose.*

All in all, the stress on the moral in the manuscript tradition of Marie's fables is fairly consistent, and the fashion in which they are set off from the rest of the text includes the use of bold, flourished initials in red, blue, or green, and more elaborately decorated or even historiated initials. These almost always alternate in color. One example of a conservative marking is found in Oxford, Bodleian Library, Douce 132, a thirteenth-century manuscript that also contains a bestiary. Apart from the "C" of "Cil, ki sevent de letreüre," which opens the prologue and is always significantly larger than the other initials on the first folio of each manuscript, the reader is immediately struck by the initials on folio 35rb and their aesthetic arrangement on the page. It is worth noting that the *mise-en-page* has assigned equal visual value to the fable and its ensuing moral. The red "D" of *Del cok et de la gemme (The Cock and the Gem)* is two lines in height with fine pen flourishes.[42] Like-

---

40. See the table in Appendix B for details in the discussion to follow.

41. Maréchal, "Marie de France as *Sapientia,*" 47.

42. When quoting lines of text from specific manuscripts under discussion, the reading follows that particular manuscript, and not any one edition of Marie's *Fables.*

The *Fables*

wise, the blue "A" that opens the moral with "Altresi est de mainte gent" is two lines high with long pen flourishes. There is also a *pied de mouche* just above and to the left of the flourished "A" of the moral. Although the *pieds de mouche* are not entirely consistent throughout this manuscript, and although they are used at times to mark the beginning of the fables as well, they do appear frequently enough next to the morals to be considered yet another way of drawing attention to the lessons. Folio 56a of Douce 132 also reveals the significance devoted to the "moralité" when one considers that the initial blue "P," opening the first line of the moral "Par ceste essample nus asume," is four lines high, with long flourishes.[43] The opening letter of this moral is twice the height of the initial red "D" in the line that opens the fable to which it belongs, *Del sengler e de l'asne (The Boar and the Ass)* and almost the same size as the initial red "I" that opens the fable immediately following it, *Del teissun e des pors (The Badger and the Pigs)*.

BNF, fr. 2168 is one of only five manuscripts among twenty-five in which the colors of the initials do not alternate between blue and red to highlight the beginning of the fables and the introduction to their accompanying morals. However, in this manuscript, as well as in BNF, fr. 24428, in Vatican City, Bibliotheca Apostolica Vaticana (hereafter BAV), Ottob. Lat. 3064, and in BNF, fr. 4939, the moral of the fable is explicitly marked by words that alert the reader to the lesson of the text. In the case of BNF, fr. 2168, the capital letters that mark the beginning of each fable and each moral are simply bold, unflourished initials throughout. The moral of the story is further accentuated by the word "l'essample," as on folio 159rb, or in all other cases throughout this manuscript with the words "ves chi l'essample" (here is the moral), as on folio 160rab of the same manuscript. This admonition to "see" the example reinforces the visual importance that the scribe or ru-

---

43. For a study of the instances in which Marie addresses the audience with such formulae, see Hans R. Runte, "Marie de France dans ses *Fables*," in *In Search of Marie de France: A Twelfth-Century Poet*, ed. Chantal Maréchal (Lewiston, Maine: Edwin Mellen, 1992), 28–44.

The *Fables*

bricator attached to the text.[44] Furthermore, in this manuscript one notices French titles, in red, preceding each fable. In fact, nine of the twenty-five manuscripts contain titles before each fable, mostly in French, but in two different manuscripts the titles are in Latin.

The other three manuscripts that indicate the moral of the text with a rubric use the term "moralité" instead of "essample." BNF, fr. 24428 offers a striking example of this word choice on folio 89v. Marking the morals in such a manner is particularly significant in this case because it occurs in one of only three manuscripts of Marie's fables that are fully illuminated. One notices, in addition to the alternation in color of the opening initials to the fables and the morals, that the colors of the "moralité" line alternate here as well. In column "a," the expression "moralité de la fable" appears entirely in blue in a line just above the lesson of the text. By contrast, the marker in column "b" is arranged in such a way that the word "moralité" is in red, while the rest of the expression, "de la fable," is in blue. This is the only instance in this manuscript of colors that alternate within the same line of a moral marker. Otherwise, the expressions "la moralité de la fable," "moralité de ceste fable," and "moralité" are entirely in blue or red.

Moreover, the position of the moral indicator on the page varies throughout this manuscript so that most of the occurrences are in the line just above the lesson of the text, as is the case on folio 89v, but six times it is placed in the margin, as on folio 97r, just to the right of column b. One cannot help but wonder whether this was the original intention of the rubricator or whether this person simply forgot, or failed to notice, the division of the moral and the fable, and was later obligated to add the word "moralité" in the margin. The visual synergy of this manuscript is particularly remarkable, as it combines four different aesthetic qualities that help the reader remember the text and image: large bold and flourished initials mark the beginning of each fable and moral,

---

44. "Ves" is the imperative of the verb "veoir" (to see) in Old French. The expression "ves chi" is the equivalent of modern French "voici" (here is).

The *Fables*

and they alternate in color; the moral markers are in red or blue; the title of each fable is in red just above the illumination; and the colorful illuminations themselves add to the appearance.

Visual symmetry appears to be a concern for the scribes and illuminators of BNF, fr. 24428. The script of the text, the moral markers, and the titles are all very neatly aligned on the page and executed in a clean hand. The miniatures are fairly consistent in size, most measuring 60 × 70 mm. The borders alternate in blue and red and are always flush with the edge of the columns (60 mm wide), never extending over the ruled area. They are immediately preceded by the title of the fable, always in red, and immediately followed by the text. All these elements combine to make the images on the page easier to view and easier to recall.

A similar visual synergy is present on certain folios of BAV, Ottob. Lat. 3064. Like BNF, fr. 24428, this manuscript combines several visual elements of alternating colors, red titles, and red moral indicators on the same page to create an aesthetic reading of the text and to draw attention to important details. This aesthetic arrangement is particularly striking on folio 237r, where there are eight bold colored initials with long, sharp pen flourishes, alternating in red and blue.

Within an iconographic program that is strong on visually marking the text of the fables and their accompanying morals in these ways, there is yet another important dimension to these memory-oriented manuscripts, namely, the illuminations themselves. BNF, fr. 2173, a thirteenth-century manuscript of continental provenance, contains unbordered sketches in pastel colors from an Italian school of illumination.[45] These illuminations are different from the otherwise bordered and rather stylized miniatures in the two other fully illuminated manuscripts of Marie's *Fables* in that they seem to attempt a certain realism in their depictions. The representation of the fable *Del leün e del vilein (The*

---

45. Vielliard, "Tradition manuscrite," 382–83. See also François Avril and Marie-Thérèse Gousset, *Manuscrits enluminés d'origine italienne* (Paris: Bibliothèque Nationale, 1984), 9–10, and Busby, *Codex and Context,* 1:474n165.

The *Fables*

Lion and the Peasant) at the top of folio 74rb visually sums up both the fable and its moral, and provides the reader with a visual cue that will serve as a future *aide-mémoire*. In other words, after reading the fable and the moral, and after "reading" the miniature, the reader will be able in the future to call up the image of the illumination, and by extension the moral lesson it conveys.

This drawing also functions as an iconographical *mise-en-abyme* within a context that demands narrative economy. It clearly depicts a man pointing to a painting; his head is turned toward the lion at the left side of the column, and his gesture calls attention to the action taking place. When this painting is enlarged with the help of a magnifying glass, it reveals a man hitting a lion with an object, presumably the axe that Marie uses in the story. The depiction of this same fable in Paris, Ars. 3142 is even more telling, because the borders of its more stylized miniature on folio 262va further reinforce the technique of iconographical specularity; the viewer is truly struck in this instance by the reality of a painting within a painting. Marie's moral, as discussed above, is an admonition to visual verification. Her moral and the illumination that accompanies it serve to stress the importance of seeing the "moralité," either as it appears on the manuscript folio in written and painted form or as it is shown to our mind's eye through the oral description of the narrative text as it is read aloud.

Another visual aspect of Marie de France's fable manuscripts that holds interest for the study of memory is the way in which illuminators represented the poet herself within the iconographical program.[46] In the twenty-five manuscripts, there are five different miniatures that depict a female subject, presumably Marie. These author portraits appear either at the beginning of the text,

---

46. In addition to Maréchal's "Marie de France as *Sapientia*," the subject is treated by two essays in Lesley Smith and Jane H. M. Taylor, eds., *Women and the Book: Assessing the Visual Evidence* (Toronto: University of Toronto Press, 1997): Sandra Hindman, "Æsop's Cock and Marie's Hen: Gendered Authorship in Text and Image in Manuscripts of Marie de France's *Fables*," 45–56, and Susan L. Ward, "Fables for the Court: Illustrations of Marie de France's *Fables* in Paris, BNF, MS Arsenal 3142," 190–203. See also my article, *"Ex Libris Mariae."*

The *Fables*

situated next to the prologue, or at the end, next to the epilogue; in one instance they appear both at the beginning and at the end of the fables. Folio 88v of BNF, fr. 1446 depicts Marie seated, with her left hand resting on an object that Maréchal identifies as an inkwell and her right hand extended as if teaching or reading aloud a text.[47] The rubric just above the miniature that opens the collection of fables supports the performative aspect of the text: "Ici apriez porres oïr les provierbs ysopet" (Now you will hear the proverbs [fables] of Aesop). What is particularly fascinating about this illustration, apart from the fact that Marie is portrayed as a teacher or performer, is the absence of a written source before her on the table. If she is indeed reciting the fables that are to follow, does this indicate that Marie will perform the task from memory? The verb "oïr" reinforces the oral dimension of the text and stands in contrast to the indicator of visual recognition, "ves chi l'essample," of BNF, fr. 2168.

By comparison, the collection of fables in fr. 2173 opens on folio 58ra with a historiated initial that depicts a scholarly male figure seated at a desk and in the act of writing. Maréchal has suggested that this illumination represents the original author of the text and continues the iconographic tradition of the eleventh-century Latin Aesop of the Codex Avianus, "though the author has assumed the attitude and adopted the attire of a thirteenth-century scholar (with cap and gown)."[48]

The last illumination of the manuscript appears on folio 93rb, just above the beginning of the epilogue. The image in question is one of Marie, seated at a desk with a book in her left hand and a pen in her right. The initial representation of the author portrait at the beginning of the fables has been replaced by a "translator" portrait at the epilogue in the form of Marie. This interpretation is perfectly in keeping with the opening lines of the epilogue that it introduces, where she names herself at the end of the text that she has "written and narrated in French." Thus the manuscript

---

47. Maréchal, "Marie de France as *Sapientia*," 51.
48. Ibid., 49.

The *Fables*

doubly promotes recognition of Marie—by the discourse of the written word and by the visual embodiment of her as translator and poet on the manuscript page for all future readers of the text to see and later recall.

Paris, Ars. 3142 also bears an authorial representation at the beginning and again at the end of the fables, but unlike BNF, fr. 2173, it portrays Marie in both locations. The miniature at the top of folio 256ra shows Marie seated at a desk with a parchment scraper in her left hand and a writing instrument in her right. She appears to be writing. In contrast to fr. 2173, she is presented at the beginning of the text as the author of the fables to follow. It is significant that she appears to be writing and not necessarily copying another book. Does this suggest that Marie is writing from her storehouse of memory, which contains the works she has gathered in the past? This question, though purely speculative, suggests an answer that would reveal the illuminator's own perception of Marie's literary practices.

The emphasis in the historiated initial that introduces the epilogue at the top of folio 273ra has shifted from that of the opening miniature on folio 256ra. Here Marie is no longer a writer, having moved from the desk to a chair, but is possibly a performer of the text she has just recorded. This illumination raises several questions. Is she, in fact, reading the book, or is she presenting it to someone else, even perhaps to the reader? If she is reading, is it to an audience, or is she reading to herself to commit this work to memory? Or better yet, is she inviting us as future readers to commit the book to our own memory? And why did the illuminator choose to place a table full of other books in front of Marie at this point? If these were to represent her written sources, it would have made more sense to include them in the opening illumination, which depicts the act of writing. Indeed, it was not uncommon to represent the written sources for a scribe or author in the same miniature that demonstrated the act of copying or writing. An example of such iconography is seen in the illumination on folio 1v of the fourteenth-century *Isopet-Avionnet* in BNF,

The *Fables*

fr. 1594, not Marie's collection of fables, where the scribe is depicted at the beginning of the text with a table of books, presumably his sources, before him.

This same motif of including other books in an illustration that focuses on a specific work appears in one of Marie's own fable manuscripts. Folio 235 of BAV, Ottob. Lat. 3064 contains one of the most vivid representations of Marie among all the manuscripts. She is seated in a covered space in the left third of the illumination, where she is either writing or reading, though it is difficult to discern which from the miniature. The right third of the miniature is occupied by four figures who seem to be looking toward Marie and listening intently to instruction, therefore making a case for her reading rather than writing. The first of these figures is kneeling, while his right hand is extended toward the center of the illustration in a sort of receiving gesture. But as important as the human figures appear to be to the overall meaning of this representation, the center space is nonetheless reserved for a three-tiered table that supports two important elements: four books and a pentagonal building with a small opening on the side facing Marie.

The books are so arranged as to occupy the center-front space of the illumination. The position of the desk and the direction that Marie is facing, as well as the gestures and positions of the other four figures, are all directed toward the center and serve to accentuate the foregrounding of these objects. This image raises several questions that may be difficult if not impossible to answer. For example, who are these four courtly figures, and what is their role? What is Marie's function? Is she teacher or is she author? Or is she both here? But to my mind springs an entirely different kind of question. What are these books with clasps that lie so prominently in a privileged space within the miniature? And what of this building that sits atop the books on this stand?

While it may never be possible to establish definitively the role of the male figures in this miniature, it is difficult not to speculate. Are they patrons of the court, possibly offering the books on the table to Marie to translate? Could they be her pupils, or simply her audience? Or could they be the authors of the books on the table, her sources from the past, represented in a prosopopoeial manner? I would like to suggest the possibility that the books that appear before the reader here may represent those works Marie mentions in the prologue to her fables: the "bons livres," the "escriz," the "essamples," and the "diz" that the "philosophe" called forth from the faculty of memory through "remembrer," and upon which she now constructs her own work. Furthermore, it is plausible that the building in the center space of this illumination is intended to evoke the storehouse of memory, especially given that the *artes memorativae* referred to memory as an edifice or storehouse in which information was kept in various rooms, or *loci*.

It seems almost ironic that many centuries removed from the production of these manuscripts, and at the height of an age like our own, which is so visually oriented, we nonetheless do not employ the same techniques that our ancestors used to encourage the retention of the literary text in the faculty of memory when dealing with medieval texts. I know of no modern edition of Marie's fables that includes images and text on the same page, except Spiegel's English verse translation, and even in that case the illuminations are neither systematically nor consistently reproduced. It is as if, for all of our technological progress, we still do not understand, as did Marie de France, her scribes, and her illuminators, the importance of the visual dimension of the narrative text and its ultimate value to our memory.

As the first poet to record an Old French version of Aesopic fables in the Phadrean tradition, Marie de France recognized before her contemporaries did the usefulness of these tales for edifying her audience and for subtly critiquing the moral, judicial, and political systems of the society in which she wrote. She imbued them with her own narrative art of description, which brought the morals and certain other key elements of the story to life, thereby creating an energy that encouraged the retention of the

The *Fables*

lessons in the storehouse of memory for future recall. Moreover, the reception of her fables, and their subsequent textual and iconographical interpretation by scribes and illuminators responsible for the *mise-en-page* decades, even centuries, later, reveal the way in which the written text and the image on the manuscript page ultimately work together to ensure the performance of her work.

5

The *Espurgatoire seint Patriz* and *La vie seinte Audree*

Marie de France's *Lais* and *Fables* reveal a poetics of memory through vocabulary that implicitly or explicitly evokes this aspect of literary topical invention, and through a plan of detailed descriptions that render objects and events visible to the imagination, helping the audience later to recall the narrative sequence. Both of these texts demonstrate her creative art of finding preexisting material, committing it to memory, embellishing it with descriptive detail, and arranging it in an order that generates a new conception of the work.

Like the two narrative texts before them, the *Espurgatoire seint Patriz* and *La vie seinte Audree* display literary characteristics that are meaningful to Marie. In the *Espurgatoire* the reader or listener navigates a story in which successful linear development of the narrative depends on the ability of a character to remember past information during his journey through an underworld rich in the *merveille* of vividly described objects, people, and places. The *Audree,* while not as rich in vivid, energetic descriptions as the *Espurgatoire,* nonetheless bears the mark of the author's ability to adorn her source through her own poetic craft. Her version of the story depends on a discursive construction and vocabulary that stress the necessity of memory to preserve the celebration of one of medieval literature's most venerated female saints, St. Etheldreda.

The *Espurgatoire* and the *Audree*

To our understanding, the *Lais* and the *Fables* represent Marie's reworking of material largely through her own imagination. The works she adapts in the former apparently came to her from oral sources. In the latter, the first forty fables are rewritten from the *Romulus Nilantii*, but the majority of them are derived from sources that have not been sufficiently identified for comparison with her renditions of them. By contrast, the *Espurgatoire seint Patriz* and *La vie seinte Audree* are translations of known Latin texts that have come down to us in manuscript form: H. of Saltrey's *De Purgatorio Sancti Patricii* for the *Espurgatoire,* and, for the *Audree,* a text close to a tripartite *Vita sancte Ætheldrede, De secunda translatione,* and *Miracula* (hereafter collectively referred to as *The Life of St. Etheldreda*).[1]

Marie's shift of approach at this point in her life seems significant in light of what we know about her stated purpose in earlier prologues, but one wonders to what extent it would be so notable if we did not possess the two sources she translates to compare with her own versions of the texts. The *Espurgatoire* and the *Audree* suggest that Marie's focus as author changes from literary to hagiographic, but a close reading shows that her vernacular

---

1. For an updated and thorough study of the *De Purgatorio Sancti Patricii* and its relationship to Marie's text, see Pontfarcy's edition of the *Espurgatoire,* 1–70. She notes that the word "tractatus" does not appear in any of the extant manuscripts of this work, so I have omitted it in my references to the full title of the work. Pickens has studied closely the source for the *Audree* in its manuscript context. In a paper read at the 2003 International Medieval Congress, University of Leeds, UK, July 16, 2003, he offered a thorough analysis on this subject, on which he provided a detailed handout. Marie's exemplar is very close to the text in BL, Cotton, Domitian A xv, fols. 9v–75r (a transcription of this manuscript served as the basis for St. Etheldreda's Life in the *Acta sanctorum*). As this book was going to press, he had significantly expanded his commentary on these sources as part of a forthcoming larger project on *La vie seinte Audree.* See the introductions to Östen Södergård's edition, *La vie seinte Audree: Poème anglo-normand du XIIIe siècle,* Uppsala Universitets Årsskrift 11 (Uppsala: Lundequistska Bokhandeln, 1955), and to McCash and Barban's edition of *The Life of Saint Audrey,* in which they cite the work of Pickens mentioned above. See also chapter 4, "'La gloriuse seint Audree / Une noble eglise a fundee': Chastity, Widowhood, and Aristocratic Patronage (ca. 1189–1416)," in Virginia Blanton, *Signs of Devotion: The Cult of St. Ethelthryth in Medieval England, 695–1615* (University Park: Pennsylvania State University Press, 2007).

The *Espurgatoire* and the *Audree*

training in the arts of poetry and prose still informs the narratives, and even clearly manifests its presence at times as she brings these two stories to a lay audience. For reasons of thematic unity, I have chosen to discuss these works together in this final chapter, beginning with the *Espurgatoire seint Patriz*.

The *Espurgatoire* and the Art of *Translatio*

Marie's translation of the monk of Saltrey's text consists of 2,302 lines arranged in octosyllabic rhymed couplets and is preserved in a single manuscript dating from the end of the thirteenth century, Paris, BNF, fr. 25407.[2] It is likely that she wrote the *Espurgatoire* sometime between 1190 and the turn of the century.[3] The legend of St. Patrick's discovery of Purgatory is the source of H. of Saltrey's text and eventually of Marie's translation.[4] According to the legend as developed by H. of Saltrey, St. Patrick has a church and monastery built in an attempt to evangelize the area around Lough Derg in Ireland. After the local inhabitants fail to heed his admonitions to lead a purer life, he prays for God's assistance, which arrives in the form of revelation of the entrance to Purgatory. He makes the journey there and sees both the torment of sinners and the eventual bliss of those who enter the celestial paradise. He returns, has a wall constructed around the entrance,

---

2. For descriptions of this manuscript, see Pontfarcy's *Espurgatoire*, 19–22, and Warnke's *Espurgatoire*, 65.

3. See Bruckner, "Marie de France," in Kibler and Zinn, *Medieval France;* Emanuel J. Mickel Jr., *Marie de France* (New York: Twayne, 1974), 41; and Pontfarcy's edition of the *Espurgatoire*, 4–10. For dating that differs considerably from the commonly accepted view, see Eduard Mall, *De aetate rebusque Mariae Franciceae nova quaestio instituitur* (Halle, 1867). Though he held the same sequence of composition that was later accepted by most scholars—*Lais, Fables,* and *Espurgatoire*—he offered much later possible dates of composition: for the *Lais,* 1245; for the *Fables,* 1248; and for the *Espurgatoire,* 1250. For a different sequence, and an earlier date of 1185 for the *Espurgatoire,* see Ezio Levi, "Sulla cronologia della opera di Maria di Francia," *Nuovi Studi Medievali* 1, no. 1 (1923): 41–72. Levi proposes that the *Espurgatoire* was written after the *Lais* but before the *Fables.*

4. The brief résumé of the legend and of H. of Saltrey's and Marie's versions that I make here owes much to Mickel, *Marie de France,* 41–49.

The *Espurgatoire* and the *Audree*

and leaves the area in the charge of the monastery. The monks later record various accounts of Purgatory provided by others who made the journey and returned safely. Emanuel J. Mickel Jr. has shown that the story of St. Patrick's Purgatory enjoyed great success in medieval literature for more than three hundred years, and that references to it appeared in literature that followed.[5]

The theme of journeys to the underworld dates back at least to the Greek and Roman epics of Homer and Virgil. The innovation of medieval literature of the twelfth century is that the visits to the Other World begin to become the core narrative of the entire story rather than a mere interpolation in it, as Peter Dewilde notes: "A cette époque la visite de l'au-delà, cessant de s'intégrer dans le récit hagiographique ou historique, accède au statut de genre autonome" (During this period, the visit to the Other World became an autonomous genre, ceasing to be integrated in hagiographic and historical texts).[6] In the legend of St. Patrick's Purgatory, an example of the newly developed autonomous otherworldly literature of this period, H. of Saltrey's original contribution is his account of the adventures of an Irish knight named Owein who enters the underworld passage. According to Mickel, H.'s version of this tale enjoyed great success during the Middle Ages and is the first of its kind to appear in the Purgatory tradition, since its theme of knightly adventure is absent from contemporary narratives about Purgatory.[7] Attesting to the literary success of this tale, Yolande de Pontfarcy has recorded more than 150 extant manuscripts of H. of Saltrey's version of the *Purgatorio*.[8]

There are two versions of H.'s *Purgatorio,* a long version and a short one, which represent two groups of manuscripts. Marie

---

5. Ibid., 42.

6. See Peter Dewilde, "Le système descriptif des visions de l'autre monde dans le *Purgatoire de saint Patrice*," in *La description au Moyen Âge: Actes du Colloque du Centre d'Études Médiévales et Dialectales de Lille III, Université Charles-de-Gaulle-Lille III, 25–26 septembre 1992,* ed. Aimé Petit Villeneuve d'Ascq (Université de Lille III, 1993), 144.

7. Mickel, *Marie de France,* 42.

8. See Michael Haren and Yolande de Pontfarcy, *The Medieval Pilgrimage to St. Patrick's Purgatory: Lough Derg and the European Tradition* (Enniskillen, Ireland: Clogher

The *Espurgatoire* and the *Audree*

translated the shorter version of the legend, but since her text contains elements from both the long and short versions, Warnke and editors following him—Thomas A. Jenkins and Pontfarcy—have held that she worked from an exemplar containing a combination of the two versions.[9] Surprisingly, scholars have neglected the possibility that she could have used manuscripts from both the long and the short versions as she was translating. This method of treating her exemplars would mirror the process of *inventio* through which material was gathered from disparate sources and given form in a single new conception. In any case, hers was apparently the first translation of the *Purgatorio* into French among at least six other French verse translations, and Michael Curley notes that there were many French prose translations, as well as translations of the tale into many other languages during the Middle Ages.[10]

Apart from Marie's own prologue, epilogue, and a few other original lines, her version of the tale follows the events in H.'s

---

Historical Society, 1988), 212–14. They list fifty-four manuscripts and incunabula of the *Purgatorio*. In Pontfarcy's edition of the *Espurgatoire*, 11n, she has increased the list of extant manuscripts of the *Purgatorio* legend to more than 150, the same number that appears in the works of Robert Easting, *St. Patrick's Purgatory: Two Versions of Owayne Miles and The Vision of William of Stranton Together with the Long Text of the Tractatus de Purgatorio Sancti Patricii* (Oxford: Oxford University Press, 1991), lxxxiv–lxxxvii, and in Curley's translation, *Saint Patrick's Purgatory*, 14. See Mickel, *Marie de France*, 42, where he puts the number of extant manuscripts at more than thirty, but the more recent works of Curley and Pontfarcy were not available to him at the time.

9. See Pontfarcy's *Espurgatoire*, 2–4. She notes, "Marie traduit le texte de la version courte et donne la plupart des additions de la version longue" (2). For the correspondence of segments of Marie's text with segments in different manuscripts of H.'s text, see the chart in Mickel, *Marie de France*, 43, which he reproduces from Thomas A. Jenkins, ed., *The Espurgatoire Seint Patriz of Marie de France with a Text of the Latin Original* (Chicago: Decennial Publications of the University of Chicago, 1903).

10. Curley's translation, *Saint Patrick's Purgatory*, 2. For a study of the French verse translations, see Kurt Ringger, "Die altfranzösischen Verspurgatorien," *Zeitschrift für romanische Philologie* 88, nos. 4–6 (1972): 389–402. See also Haren and Pontfarcy, *Medieval Pilgrimage to St. Patrick's Purgatory,* 83–98, and D. D. R. Owen, *The Vision of Hell: Infernal Journeys in Medieval French Literature* (Edinburgh: Scottish Academic Press, 1970), 51–141.

The *Espurgatoire* and the *Audree*

diligently, but she distinguishes herself by the narrative energy she brings to the tale. In this way, her creative method places her squarely in the tradition of *translatio studii,* the retelling of a preexisting story in her own words to transfer knowledge from one culture to another, as in the case of the *Lais* and the *Fables.* The exemplar from which she copied is now lost, but H.'s Latin elements for the majority of her lines can be identified in manuscripts of his *Purgatorio.*[11] Mickel notes that a close comparison of certain passages of Marie's text with corresponding ones found in a manuscript of the monk of Saltrey's text, London, BL, Harley 3846, reveals that "when she departs from the text, it is to clarify an ambiguous Latin passage or to develop clearly what is implied in the original."[12] This is true for lines 185–88, discussed below, in which she evokes the process of *inventio* through her arrangement of rhetorical vocabulary belonging to the arts of poetry and prose at a point in the text where her source states the matter rather simply.

Why Marie chooses at this point to turn her attention to projects that embrace translation more closely than her previous two collections did is impossible to determine conclusively from the surviving textual evidence. Indeed, her decision appears to refute her stated desire, found in the General Prologue to the *Lais:*

> Pur ceo començai a penser
> D'aukune bone estoire faire
> E de latin en romaunz traire;
> Mais ne me fust guaires de pris:
> Itant s'en sunt altre entremis!
>
> (28–32)

---

11. For a study of the manuscript tradition of H.'s *Purgatorio,* see Lucien Foulet, "Marie de France et la légende du Purgatoire de Saint Patrice," *Romanische Forschungen* 22, no. 4 (1908): 599–627; Jenkins's *Espurgatoire,* 236–327; Pontfarcy's *Espurgatoire,* 11–14; and Warnke's *Espurgatoire,* 7–9.

12. Mickel, *Marie de France,* 47.

The *Espurgatoire* and the *Audree*

> For this reason I began to think of working on some good story and translating a Latin text into French, but this would scarcely have been worthwhile, for others have undertaken a similar task.

It should be remembered that Marie did not wait until the *Espurgatoire* to depart from this position. As mentioned above, the first forty fables from her *Isopet*, which was composed after the *Lais*, are taken from the Latin text of the *Romulus Nilantii*.

Was Marie simply tired of continuing in the same generic direction, and was she searching for a new type of literary challenge, or did she expressly begin to think of material that was more religious in theme than her previous selections had been? Whatever her reasons may have been—edification, entertainment, both, or something entirely different—her eventual purpose is to make this Latin story available to her audience in the vernacular:

> Jo, *Marie,* ai mis, en memoire,
> le livre de l'Espurgatoire
> en Romanz, qu'il seit entendables
> a laie gent e convenables.
> (2296–300)

> I, Marie, have put
> The Book of Purgatory into French,
> As a record, so that it might be intelligible
> And suited to lay folk.

A telling part of her stated purpose is that she put the story "en memoire." In fact, the significant emphasis on memory in hagiographic texts could have been one of the reasons, among others, that inspired Marie to compose vernacular versions of H. of Saltrey's text and of the *Life of St. Etheldreda,* instead of other Latin texts that contained religious themes, such as bestiaries or certain chronicles.

That Marie's religious concerns have become more transparent in this work should not be surprising given her possible ecclesiastical ties. Moreover, her interest in Purgatory was timely. As

The *Espurgatoire* and the *Audree*

Curley remarks, the doctrine of the Church concerning Purgatory was very much in transition at this time, being reevaluated and conveyed by philosophers and theologians such as Bernard of Clairvaux, Hugh of St. Victor, Peter Lombard, and Gratian: "The period from 1170–1200 in particular saw the doctrine of purgatory assume what would remain for centuries its canonical form. The *Tractatus de Purgatorio Sancti Patricii* by the English Cistercian H. of Saltrey, the source of Marie's *Espurgatoire,* figured prominently in the dissemination of the concept of purgatory during the Middle Ages."[13] While one cannot neglect the role that the religious milieu played in attracting Marie to this legend,[14] it is likely that H.'s original contribution to the tale, namely, the descent of a knight into Purgatory, played at least an equal role in the appeal of his version to a poet writing for the court of England.

Indeed, it may have been the combination of elements that prompted Marie to bring this text to her lay audience, both the religious and didactic aspects, as well as the dimensions of *aventure*.[15] Curley notes that "Marie's *Espurgatoire* served not only to transmit this image of Purgatory to a French-speaking public, but also to refashion the story of Owein's experiences into the idiom of the *conte d'aventure,* which she and her contemporaries, Chrétien de Troyes and Wolfram von Eschenbach, did so much to popularize."[16]

---

13. Curley's translation, *Saint Patrick's Purgatory,* 1.
14. See Jeanette M. A. Beer, *Narrative Conventions of Truth in the Middle Ages* (Geneva: Droz, 1981), 69. Beer states that "Marie's translation *L'Espurgatoire Seint Patriz* was dedicated exclusively to Christian truth." Since Marie's narrative interventions in H.'s text privilege a lay perspective over an ecclesiastical one, this position exaggerates the poet's religious intentions.
15. See Owen, *Vision of Hell,* 66: "It seems fair to conclude that if one quality that drew Marie's attention to the *Tractatus* was its salutary moral tone, another was its value as an adventure story. This would be in keeping with her personality as it emerges from her other works."
16. Curley's translation, *Saint Patrick's Purgatory,* 2. H.'s addition of a knight in the legend and its rapport with medieval courtly society has been noticed by most critics. See especially Mickel, *Marie de France,* 48–49, where he compares Owein's vari-

The *Espurgatoire* and the *Audree*

The *Espurgatoire* and a New Audience

When Curley refers to Marie's putting the story into the "idiom of the *conte d'aventure*," what must be understood is the way in which she omits certain monastic elements at times in the narrative to emphasize the adventurous elements and to make the story more appealing to her lay audience.[17] Her reference to the knight by name seven times stands in striking contrast to H.'s single mention of Owein's name at the beginning of his text.[18] They way she describes the scene in which Owein consults the king in making a decision to remain a knight and not to enter holy orders also highlights the courtly over the monastic. However, H. of Saltrey's version of the story is already partly "courtly" ipso facto: as Mickel observes, some fifteen hundred of the twenty-three hundred lines deal with the adventures of the knight.[19]

By engaging her audience through courtly discourse, Marie makes it clear in the *Espurgatoire* that she is an author of vernacular training, and that she has not abandoned her original regard for *descriptio* and memory prevalent throughout the first two texts she composed, works that the same audience undoubtedly knew well. She keeps the consideration of memory before her public through repeated references to this cognitive act, usually through the specific mention of the term "remembrance" or "memoire." The prologue to the *Espurgatoire* puts such an emphasis on the act

---

ous encounters in Purgatory with the themes found in the *roman* and the *chansons de geste*. He specifically recalls the *Joie de la Cort* and sword-bridge episodes from Chrétien for romance, and Owein's struggle with the enemies of God for the *chansons de geste*. See also Curley's translation, *Saint Patrick's Purgatory*, 33–34, where he compares Owein's adventures in Purgatory to the adventures of Lanval, Muldumarec, and Eliduc in Marie's *Lais*.

17. For a discussion of Marie's creative art as translator, especially her use of rhetorical techniques that render her version of the tale more concise than that of the source, see Rupert T. Pickens, "Marie de France: Translatrix," *Le Cygne: Journal of the International Marie de France Society*, n.s., 1 (fall 2002): 7–24.

18. Curley's translation, *Saint Patrick's Purgatory*, 24. H. uses Owein's name only once. Otherwise, he refers to him as *vir* or *miles*.

19. Mickel, *Marie de France*, 48.

The *Espurgatoire* and the *Audree*

of memory that it uses both of these terms within a single line of the text, "en remembrance e en memoire" (5).[20] The focus in her prologue to the *Espurgatoire* is not on the eventual bliss of paradise that will be encountered in the story, but rather on the "peines" to be portrayed along the purgatorial voyage. She wants to ensure that her audience does not forget the sufferings that are about to be depicted.[21]

Literary representations of Hell through graphic descriptions of suffering were found in texts from antiquity, such as those in Book 6 of Virgil's *Aeneid* and in Book 10 of Ovid's *Metamorphoses*. These texts were popular throughout the Middle Ages and were accessible to authors as early as the twelfth century.[22] In addition to these texts, Marie would also have had access to other works that vividly recounted sufferings in an underworld context, as in the *Dialogues* of Pope Gregory the Great, the *Vision of Saint Paul,* and Benedeit's *Voyage of Saint Brendan,* among others.[23] The important role that description and memory played in purgatorial literature raises the possibility that their design is one reason, combined with the other courtly and religious ones, that she chose to adapt H. of Saltrey's *Purgatorio* for a lay audience.

Memory in the Journey through Hell

As the lines from the prologue and epilogue indicate, the *Espurgatoire,* like the *Lais* and the *Fables* before it, begins and ends by calling attention to memory. The cognitive process of remembering is associated with writing, and more specifically, in both

---

20. See chapter 1, in which I discuss the terms "memoire" and "remembrance" in Old French as treated by Stefenelli.

21. See Bonnie H. Leonard, "The Inscription of a New Audience: Marie de France's *Espurgatoire Saint Patriz,*" *Romance Languages Annual* 5 (1993): 57–62. Leonard stresses Marie's role in bringing a religious message to a French-speaking audience.

22. Owen, *Vision of Hell,* xi.

23. For a discussion of the impact of these texts on French literature of the Middle Ages, see ibid., chapters 1–4.

The *Espurgatoire* and the *Audree*

instances, with a book. Not only does the juxtaposition of memory and books call to mind Chaucer's similar association in the prologue to the *Legend of Good Women,* discussed in the previous chapter, it also recalls Dante's famous opening phrase in the *Vita nuova,* quoted in the Introduction.

Memory, as we have seen, is not only necessary to preserve material from the past and to create new literature to transfer from one generation to the next, it is also useful for future moral reference and self-edification through the recall of precepts drawn from the material in question. Marie achieves the same results as she did in her previous works by handing down to a vernacular public a literature that can be "seen" with the mind's eye as easily as it can be read or heard.

It is significant that Marie focuses on the faculty of memory in most of the lines that can be considered entirely original with her. Apart from four couplets—1019–20, 1053–54, 1119–20, and 1667–68—Marie's additions consist of the prologue (1–8) and the epilogue (2297–302).[24] Both of these passages center on remembering the work at hand. In this way, Marie envelops H.'s text in the act of memory by reminding the audience of its importance, both at the beginning of the narration and again at its conclusion.

For his part, at a strategic moment in his prefatory comments just before the opening of the narration proper, H. indicates that he tells this story from memory: "Quam quidem narrationem, si

---

24. Ibid., 65. He refers to these couplets as "quite commonplace pious interjections," adding that, "as for the omissions and discrepancies between Marie's text and the *Tractatus* as we know it, these are very small matters and contribute in no way to our knowledge of the authoress or her text." The four couplets are "Chaitis est cil ki en tel peine / pur ses pechiez se trait e meine!" (1019–20), "A las, se nuls deit deservir / que tel peine deie sufrir!" (1053–54), "mult est cist nuns bons a nomer, / par quei um se puet delivrer" (1119–20), and "Or nus doint Deus ço deservir / qu'a cez joies puissuns venir!" (1667–68). In relation to my study, the first three couplets hold more significance than Owen ascribes to them, and they all occur within the context of the ten torments, a passage of the *Espurgatoire* that Marie would have particularly wanted her audience to remember.

147

The *Espurgatoire* and the *Audree*

bene memini, ita exorsus est" (If I remember correctly, the story certainly begins in this manner) (II, 14).[25] Marie's text renders the Latin original as follows:

> Se j'ai bien eü en memoire
> ço que j'ai oï en *l'estoire,*
> je vus dirrai veraiement,
> en *ordre,* le comencement.
> (185–88, emphasis added)

> If I have well retained in memory
> What I have heard in the story,
> I shall truly recount to you
> The beginning, in an orderly fashion.

Marie's terms "remembrance" and "memoire" in line 5 of the prologue cited above are echoes of H.'s expression of the same idea in his phrase "si bene memini," which she translates at this point in the text as "Se j'ai bien eü en memoire."

Another point about Marie's translation in lines 185–88 centers on her use of the terms "estoire" and "ordre," for both belong to the paradigm of medieval topical invention as *historia* and *ordo.* Marie explicitly emphasizes the technique of *inventio* through her choice of rhetorical vocabulary. While the monk of Saltrey simply announces that he will relate the tale in an orderly fashion, Marie, as a vernacular poet well trained in literary composition, reveals an understanding of how this process works when she names specific stages in *inventio: memoria, historia,* and *ordo,* as posited in the art of rhetoric.

Historia, taken in its rhetorical context, refers to the first part of medieval literary invention in which source material is located, namely, the *materia* that will inform the new conception of the work.[26] *Historia,* in a broader medieval understanding, was passed

---

25. All references to H. of Saltrey's *Purgatorio* are taken from Warnke's edition of the *Espurgatoire,* which also reproduces the Latin source on the page facing the Old French text. The translation here is my own.
26. Kelly, *Art of Medieval French Romance,* 44.

The *Espurgatoire* and the *Audree*

down through annals, chronicles, biographies, and hagiography, and regardless of whether this material was accepted as truth, its value to the art of poetry was appreciated by medieval authors, as Kelly notes: "The historical paradigm, although by and large an illusion, was apparently taken quite seriously by medieval authors and audiences. It contributed to the romancer's conception of *conte,* and thus to the art of inventing *matiere* and *sen.*"[27]

Ordo in the rhetoric of medieval literary composition is associated with *figura,* "the stamp of auctorial conception on the work's *materia.*"[28] There were two types of order in the Middle Ages, natural and artificial, the former referring to a chronologically correct sequence of narration, the latter meaning that the order of the narration was not bound by chronology, such as in the account in Chrétien's *Yvain* that Kelly cites as an example: "Calogrenant's presence at Arthur's court precedes the chronologically earlier adventures he relates there about his defeat at the fountain."[29] When Marie uses the terms "estoire" and "ordre," she assures her audience that H.'s text is coming to them, through her own version of it, by a technique analogous to the process of *inventio.* Her reference here takes on even greater significance if she indeed copied his story from two or more manuscripts at the same time, instead of using a single exemplar, a method that would mirror the art of *inventio.*

The role of memory in the *Espurgatoire* is not limited to authorial exhortation or invocation at the outset or end of the narration, both for H. in his text and for Marie in her version, but is also instrumental in the linear development of the story. Owein's journey into the underworld includes passage through ten different torments, in which he is taunted and tortured by devils and during which he witnesses souls undergo various forms of punishments for their earthly sins. Upon his entrance into the pit of Pur-

---

27. Ibid., 86.
28. Ibid., 61.
29. Ibid., 264–69. For a full discussion of *ordo* as a division in the medieval literary paradigm, see 263–305.

The *Espurgatoire* and the *Audree*

gatory, he is greeted by fifteen holy figures, one of which appears to be a Prior, who instructs him in the importance of memory throughout his journey: "'Ferme creance aies en tei! / Retien ço que tu oz de mei'" (Keep your faith strong within you: / Remember what you have heard from me) (729–30). He tells Owein that his only hope in Purgatory will be to remember God: "'E aiez tuz jurs en memoire / Deu ki est sire e reis de gloire'" (Always remember God, / Who is Lord and King of Glory!) (771–72).

The Prior tells Owein that he will be approached by devils who will not only torture him but will also attempt to deceive him:

> "Grant multitudine i verras
> des diables, n'en dute pas,
> ki granz turmenz te musterrunt,
> de greignurs te manacerunt.
> Se en lur cunseil vus metez
> e se creire les en volez,
> il vus prometrunt veirement
> que hors vus merrunt salvement
> a l'entree, dunt vus venistes
> quant dedenz cest clos vus mesistes;
> si vus quiderunt engignier."
>
> (733–43)

> "You will see, have no doubt,
> A huge crowd of devils
> Who will show great suffering to you,
> And threaten you with greater suffering;
> If you show trust in their advice
> And believe what they say,
> They will promise solemnly
> To lead you back safely
> To the gate by which you entered
> When you first placed yourself inside this enclosure.
> Thus they will think they have fooled you."

The *Espurgatoire* and the *Audree*

The admonition to avoid believing plausible-sounding lies recalls Marie's moral to the fable *Del lëun e del vilein (The Lion and the Peasant)*, in which she addresses her audience in a similar way:

> Par essample nus vuelt aprendre
> que nuls ne deit nïent entendre
> a fable, ki est de mençunge,
> n'a peinture, ki semble sunge.
> (59–62)

From this fable we should learn not to believe anything from a lying story or a dreamlike painting.

At this point in the narrative, Marie must have remembered her own words, which were an original addition to the Latin source of her fable.

Owein's need for a reliable memory is further stressed by the Prior because it is the only way in which he will be able to overcome the torment of the devils and resist putting faith in their deceptive words:

> "En quel liu que seiez menez
> e quel turment que vus sentez,
> le nun Ihesucrist apelez:
> guardez que vus ne l'obliëz!
> Delivres serrez par cel nun,
> par la Deu grace le savum."
> (777–82)

> "In whatever place where you are led,
> And whatever torment you will experience,
> Call on the name of Jesus Christ.
> Take care that you do not forget,
> For you will be delivered by his name.
> We know this through the grace of God."

At the end of each of the ten torments that Owein must endure throughout his journey in Purgatory, he remembers to call on God's name and is saved from the torture and deception of the devils.

The *Espurgatoire* and the *Audree*

It is significant that Marie makes one of her completely original additions to H.'s text precisely at one of the moments when memory serves Owein and saves him from perdition. At the end of his fifth torment, the halfway mark of the trials in Purgatory, and just after Owein has saved himself by remembering to invoke his Lord's name, Marie addresses her audience and reminds them that "mult est cist nuns bons a nomer, / par quei um se puet delivrer" (This name is a very good one to name, / For by this act one can deliver oneself) (1119–20). Through her textual interjection and descriptive embellishment in this couplet, Marie depicts the power of God's name in the struggle of good and evil, while at the same time implicitly highlighting the role that memory plays in this battle.

The art of memory operates on at least two levels in this text. On a narrative level, the story can progress because the knight faithfully remembers to invoke God's name at the end of each torment and is thereby delivered from suffering at the hands of the devils. Likewise, the lay audience of Marie's *Espurgatoire*, who could not read the Latin of the monk of Saltrey's text, are encouraged to remember the images of suffering that they will encounter on their own journey through Purgatory, horrible images that Marie describes in detail, including burning bodies, people nailed to the ground by their hands and feet, people being devoured by dragons, serpents and toads tearing out the hearts of those being tormented, people hanging by various parts of their bodies from burning chains and hooks (even by their eyes and genitals), people attached to burning wheels, and people being boiled alive in liquid metal. These are precisely the types of highly charged descriptions that easily register in the audience's memory.

Description and *Merveille* in the *Espurgatoire*

If the primary role of memory throughout the *Purgatorio* that Marie translates reflects its importance in her first two narra-

The *Espurgatoire* and the *Audree*

tive works, the elaborate descriptions found at the beginning and end of the purgatorial journey recall similar descriptions from the *Lais*. Whereas the vivid depictions of torture are designed to remind us of the importance of avoiding sin, the beautiful accounts of the entrance to Purgatory and to the celestial city of paradise are intended to recall the rewards for living a righteous life.

Marie's choice of vernacular vocabulary at this point makes the objects under consideration visible to our imagination through her descriptive art. When Owein first enters the pit of Purgatory he is struck by the marvel of a house and wall that he discovers there:

> Tant a erré par desuz terre
> qu'il vint al champ qu'il alout querre.
> Une maisun vit bele e grant,
> dunt il oï parler devant.
> Tel lumiere a iluec trovee
> cum est d'yver en l'avespree.
> Icist palais aveit en sei
> en tur une entiere parei;
> faiz fu a piliers e a arches
> a volsurs e a wandiches.[30]
> Cloistre resemblout envirun
> cum a gent de religiün.
> Li chevaliers s'esmerveilla
> de l'ovraigne qu'il esguarda.
> Quant le palais out esguardé
> dehors e tut en tur alé,
> hastivement dedenz entra.
> Asez plus sei esmerveilla
> de ço qu'il a dedenz veü.
> A tant s'assist, loant Ihesu.
> Ses ueilz turna e sus e jus;
> merveilla sei, ne poeit plus:

---

30. "Wandiches" is a *hapax legomenon*. See the note in Curley's translation, *Saint Patrick's Purgatory*, 81.

The *Espurgatoire* and the *Audree*

ne quida pas, c'en est la sume,
que cele uevre fust de main d'ume.
(681–704)

He wandered far underground
Until he came upon the field that he sought.
He saw a large and lovely house
Which he had heard spoken of before.
The light he saw there
Was like winter light at dusk.
The palace had all around it
One continuous wall,
Constructed of columns, arches,
Vaults and *wandiches*.
It resembled a cloister,
Suited for men of religion.
The knight marvelled
At the work he observed.
When he had looked the place over
From without, and had gone all around it,
He went inside quickly.
There he marvelled even more
At what he saw,
And sat down praising Jesus.
Casting his eyes up and down,
He could not have marvelled more,
Nor could he believe, to sum it up,
That this was the work of human hand.

If her audience was familiar with Marie's *Lais,* this descriptive passage would remind them of her depiction of the castle, its wall, and the painting of Venus from *Guigemar,* as well as the marvelous description of the ship, both discussed in chapter 4. In lines 675–704, some form of the Latin *mirabilis* appears four times, rendered in the vernacular by Marie as *merveille, s'esmerveilla, esmerveilla,* and *merveilla.* Descriptions of the marvelous, as we know, represent a fundamental thematic element in courtly literature, as in the genres of romance and *lai,* for example.

The *Espurgatoire* and the *Audree*

Marie does not limit her choice of *merveille* to scenes of beauty but employs the term in unpleasant contexts as well. In the eighth torment, Owein marvels at the pain he sees before him, "Li chevaliers s'esmerveilla / de cele gent qu'il esguarda" (The knight marvelled at those / He now gazed upon) (1235–36), and in the ninth torment he stands in awe of the dangerous situation in which he finds himself, "Une piece suls i estout; / mult s'esmerveilla u il fu" (Where he paused for a moment, / And marvelled at where he was) (1306–7).

Marie also uses the term strategically to add energy to her description of the suffering that sinners endure during several of the ten torments that occupy nearly five hundred lines of the *Espurgatoire*. At the beginning of the first torment, the devils set fire to the house in which Owein awaits their arrival: "Un feu firent demeintenant / en la maisun, merveilles grant" (And immediately [they] set / A huge fire in the house) (887–88). Her use of "merveilles grant" in this couplet is absent from H.'s account, and it serves to underscore the seriousness of the scene she describes as the devils launch their program of torture. She uses the same expression fewer than one hundred lines later in the story, when she recounts a horrible torment that Owein witnesses:

> Crapolz i vit, merveilles granz,
> ço li ert vis, trestuz ardanz.
> Sur les piz des alquanz seeient;
> od lur bes, qu'orribles aveient,
> a grant force erent ententis
> de traire les quers des chaitis.
>
> (1007–12)

> He also saw huge toads,
> Burning fiercely, and perched
> On the breasts of some of these people.
> With enormous force they attempted
> To tear out the hearts of their captives.

Although her passage conveys the same idea as the Latin exemplar, Marie's choice of "merveilles granz" differs from H.'s vocab-

The *Espurgatoire* and the *Audree*

ulary and makes the scene more vivid than it is in the source. She repeats this same construction later, in the sixth torment:

> Un torment vit, merveilles grant:
> une roe ardant e fuïne;
> desuz ert la flame sulphrine.
> A la roe, u li rai sunt mis,
> ot cros de fer ardant asis;
> fichié furent espessement.
> Sur cez cros pendeient la gent.
>   (1122–28)

> A terrible punishment: he saw a fiery wheel,
> Burning with sulfurous flame.
> On the rim of that wheel where the spokes touch
> Were flaming irons hooks,
> Affixed thickly all around.
> On these hooks people were impaled.

Here again, her vernacular expression renders the torment more lively than it appears in her source, while its use also accommodates a lay audience accustomed to hearing the term in regard to the description of spectacular events.

Likewise, during the fifth torment, Marie uses the word "merveille" to interrupt the narrative and to interject a line that is entirely absent from her model in the scene that depicts people hanging from flaming hooks:

> Li un pendeient cruëlement
> a cros ardanz diversement:
> par ueilz, par nes et par oreilles,
> —de cels i aveit il merveilles—
> par col, par buche et par mentun
> e par mameles, ço trovun,
> par genitailles, par aillurs,
> e par les joues les plusurs.
>   (1083–90)

> Others were hung cruelly
> From flaming hooks:

The *Espurgatoire* and the *Audree*

> Some by their eyes, others by their noses or ears
> (This was a great wonder),
> Or neck, or mouth, or jaw,
> Or by their breasts we find.
> Some were hung by their genitals,
> And many others by their cheeks.

One has the impression that the events in this scene were so striking to Marie herself that she felt the need to express her own wonder.

After Owein successfully passes through the torments of Purgatory, he arrives at the gates of the celestial paradise. Like the account of the house he discovered at the beginning of his journey, the narration of this scene calls to mind the earlier descriptive passages from Marie's *Guigemar*:

> Devant lui vit un mur si grant,
> halt de la terre, en l'air a munt.
> Les merveilles ki del mur sunt
> ne purreit nuls cunter ne dire,
> ne l'ovraigne ne la matire.
> Une porte a el mur veüe,
> bien l'a de loinz aparceüe.
> De preciüs metals fu faite
> e gloriusement portraite:
> porsise esteit de bones pieres,
> mult preciüses e mult chieres.
> Li chevaliers s'esmerveilla
> de la porte, qu'il esguarda,
> pur la clarté qu'ele rendeit,
> ki des chieres pieres eisseit.
>
> (1488–1502)

> And he came to a huge
> Wall rising high up from the earth.
> No one could recount
> The marvelous nature of this wall,
> Or its design or material.
> He saw from afar

The *Espurgatoire* and the *Audree*

> That the wall had a gate
> Made of precious metals
> Splendidly inlaid,
> Containing lovely, rare,
> And very costly stones.
> The knight marvelled
> At the door he was observing,
> On account of the brightness
> Given off by its costly stones.

Again, the treatment of the *merveilleux* is emphasized in these lines as in the lines discussed above, not only by the repetition of the word itself but also by the magical quality that the door seems to possess in giving off radiant light from its precious stones. As in the *Lais,* the use of the term "merveille" here has special significance to the act of remembering. Tobler and Lommatzsch attest that the etymology for the Old French "merveille" is Latin *mirabilia,* or German *Wunder,* that which is marvelous, unusual, or wonderful to behold. By giving an object unusual qualities, an author assists the audience in the process of creating a lasting image in the faculty of memory.

In addition to the ability of these descriptive lines to help us create a picture of the scene in our imagination and then enter it into our storehouse of memory, much like the medieval student would have done from the pictureless descriptions in the *Bestiaire* of Philippe de Thaon, these passages also serve a structural function within the text. Just as the lines that speak of the act of memory in Marie's prologue and epilogue enclose the memory-oriented narrative of the *Espurgatoire* in a general sense, so too do the descriptive scenes of the marvelous objects at the beginning and end of the journey in Purgatory frame the episode of the ten torments and Owein's repeated victory through the act of memory.

The courtly and religious dimensions of H. of Saltrey's account of St. Patrick's Purgatory were no doubt important considerations for Marie, but she was equally interested in presenting her lay public with a text that reflected her own poetics, one that incorporated detailed descriptions of events and objects and

The *Espurgatoire* and the *Audree*

privileged the act of memory. When Marie translates H.'s *Purgatorio*, she not only takes literature from one language to another and passes it along to a new audience, she also transfers memory, what I would call a *translatio memoriae*, as she brings to her public a text that accentuates the significance of this faculty.

La vie seinte Audree and the Question of Authorship

I originally intended to include a chapter on each of the three narrative texts that scholarship, through general consensus over the years, has confidently attributed to Marie de France. In the July 2002 issue of *Speculum*, however, June Hall McCash revived a debate over authorship that had lain dormant for several years when she revisited the long-accepted attribution of a late twelfth- or early thirteenth-century French narrative text, *La vie seinte Audree*, to an author known simply as "Marie."[31] Through a cogent linguistic and stylistic argument that compares this text to the *Espurgatoire seint Patriz* discussed above, and through reconsidering the dating of the *Audree*, McCash presents a convincing case that both narratives are the work of the same author, France's first known feminine voice of the Middle Ages, whom we traditionally know as Marie de France.

Based on McCash's evidence, on Pickens's recent research, and on my own subsequent reading and analysis of the text and its manuscript in light of her poetics of memory, it is now my conviction that *La vie seinte Audree* merits inclusion in her corpus, as the discussion to follow seeks to demonstrate. Indeed, Pickens declares that, "thanks to June Hall McCash, no one can pretend any more to write comprehensively on Marie de France while ignoring the *seinte Audree*."[32] It is not my intention here to argue for Marie's specific identity as a nun or otherwise, and this issue

---

31. The discussion at this point, and throughout the rest of the chapter, owes much to June Hall McCash, "*La vie seinte Audree:* A Fourth Text by Marie de France?" *Speculum* 77, no. 3 (2002): 744–77.

32. See note 1 above.

The *Espurgatoire* and the *Audree*

has been exhaustively debated for many years.[33] Rather, I suggest that the evidence continues to come forth in support of including the *Audree* among the three other texts in which she identifies herself simply as Marie, and once as Marie de France. Much has in fact been made of her anonymity, most recently by Bloch's book, *The Anonymous Marie de France,* in which the author argues that she was intentionally anonymous. As an author in early medieval culture, however, Marie is much less anonymous than others writing during her period, owing to the very fact that she names herself in all four works—many, if not most, authors at this time do not, and as such they remain truly anonymous. She is, in fact, no more anonymous than her contemporary, Chrétien de Troyes, who also names himself in his texts. As with Chrétien, it is true that we have very few details of her life, and even those about which we are relatively confident have been debated—she was a woman from France and she wrote for the court of Henry II in England. Nonetheless, in the true sense of the word she is not anonymous, and the fact that the author of these four texts showed remarkable concern that we record her name in memory remains significant.

To begin, a brief summary of the theories associated with the authorship of *La vie seinte Audree* clarifies the position of McCash and others, including myself, who share her view and who currently work on Marie de France. The controversy over Marie de France's possible authorship of the *Audree* dates back at least to Richard Baum's 1968 study,[34] in which Baum actually challenges her authorship of the three texts from the end of the twelfth century that are now confidently ascribed to her: the *Lais,* the *Isopet*

---

33. The articles devoted to the subject of Marie de France's identity are too numerous to cite. See Burgess, *Analytical Bibliography.* However, a recent study worth highlighting broadens our understanding of traditional arguments surrounding her identity: see Rupert T. Pickens, "*En bien parler* and *mesparler:* Fecundity and Sterility in the Works of Marie de France," *Le Cygne: Journal of the International Marie de France Society,* n.s., 3 (fall 2005): 20n23.

34. Baum, *Recherches sur les œuvres attribuées à Marie de France.*

The *Espurgatoire* and the *Audree*

(*Fables*), and the *Espurgatoire*. Baum's assertions—and a dubious view posited by Jean-Charles Huchet in 1981 contending that the *Lais* were composed by a man rather than a woman—have now been largely discredited.[35] Baum's most lasting contribution to the recently reborn question may in fact be his contention that the *Audree* deserves to be reckoned with, alongside the three other texts, in any consideration of their authorship.[36]

A few years after Baum's study, Mickel, in his book on Marie de France published in the Twayne Series in 1974, proposed the need for a close linguistic investigation of the *Audree* and stated that it may have "as much right to be placed among Marie [de France]'s work as any of the other three."[37] Likewise, Curley refers the reader to lines 4624–25 in the epilogue of the *seinte Audree*—"Ici escris mon non Marie / Pur ce ke soie remembree" (Here I write my name "Marie" / so that I may be remembered)—and he notes that "both the sentiments and the language expressed here closely parallel passages in Marie's *Fables* and in [the] *Espurgatoire*, which raises the possibility that Marie de France was the author of four works rather than three."[38] The corresponding passages in both texts are lines 3 and 4 from the epilogue of the *Fables* and lines 2297 and 2298 from the epilogue to the *Espurgatoire*, quoted above. The years following Curley's comments saw little discussion about Marie de France's possible authorship of *La vie seinte Audree* until McCash's sound argument on the subject in *Speculum*.[39]

La vie seinte Audree is recorded in a single thirteenth- or early fourteenth-century manuscript, London, BL, Add. 70513, and has only recently been edited again since the edition in 1955 by Östen Södergård.[40] The story recounts various events associated with the

---

35. McCash, "A Fourth Text," 745n.
36. Ibid., 744–45.
37. See ibid., 745, where McCash quotes Mickel.
38. Curley's translation, *Saint Patrick's Purgatory*, 7.
39. See McCash, "A Fourth Text," 745. She notes that Jocelyn-Wogan Browne and Virginia Blanton-Whetsell have worked on the provenance and patronage of the *Audree* manuscript.
40. Södergård's edition of *Vie seinte Audree*. The manuscript that measures

The *Espurgatoire* and the *Audree*

life and death of the saint, including her two marriages, the founding of Ely Cathedral, the second translation of her body, and a series of miracles.[41] The manuscript contains exclusively thirteen lives of saints in its 265 folios, the life of St. Etheldreda of Ely (St. Audree) occupying folios 100v–134v.[42] Of the thirteen texts presented in the collection, six of them open with a small miniature of a portrait of the saint whose story follows.[43] In the case of St. Audree, one of these six decorated opening initials, the 30 × 30 mm illumination on folio 100v, depicts the saint standing in frontal pose and reading from a book on a podium in front of her. She holds a small cathedral (Ely) in her right hand and gestures toward it with her left hand. Virginia Blanton-Whetsell has noted that iconography up to that time had portrayed St. Audree with a crozier, highlighting her role as abbess. She points out that the substitution here of the miniature church for the crozier underscores her role as founder of the Ely Cathedral, and that it represents her "telling her own story as patron of religious institutions."[44] Interestingly, the iconography here, specifically the way in which St. Audree is

---

250 × 170 mm, with a ruled text area of 190 × 135 mm, was formerly Welbeck Abbey MS. I.C.1. The most recent edition is McCash and Barban, *Life of Saint Audrey.*

41. See the beginning of this chapter and note 1.

42. I thank Mr. Joe Maldonado and Mr. Michael J. Boggan of the Manuscripts Reading Room at the British Library in London for their assistance during my consultation of this manuscript and for providing valuable information about it. The lives of the saints appear in the following order: fols. 1r–4r, St. Elizabeth of Hungary; fols. 4r–5v, St. Paphnutius; fols. 6r–8r, St. Paul the Hermit; fols. 9r–50v, St. Thomas Becket; fols. 50v–55v, St. Mary Magdelen; fols. 55v–85v, St. Edward the Confessor; fols. 85v–100r, St. Edmund, Archbishop of Canterbury; fols. 100v–134v, St. Etheldreda of Ely (St. Audree); fols. 134v–147v, St. Osyth; fols. 147v–156v, St. Faith; fols. 156v–222r, St. Modwenna; fols. 222r–244v, St. Richard of Wych, Bishop of Chichester; fols. 246r–265v, St. Catherine of Alexandria.

43. Edward the Confessor, fol. 55v; St. Etheldreda (St. Audree), fol. 100v; St. Osyth, fol. 134v; St. Modwenna, fol. 156v; St. Richard de Wych, fol. 222r; St. Catherine of Alexandria, fol. 246r.

44. See Virginia Blanton-Whetsell, "*Imagines Ætheldredae:* Mapping Hagiographic Representations of Abbatial Power and Religious Patronage," *Studies in Iconography* 23 (2002): 74–80. She describes the image in detail and provides two reproductions, one as it appears in relation to the entire manuscript folio, fig. 11 (76), and one enlargement of the illumination alone, fig. 12 (76).

The *Espurgatoire* and the *Audree*

positioned, recalls the author portraits of Marie de France from some of the *Fable* manuscripts discussed in chapter 4.[45] Although purely speculative in nature, this similarity invites us to consider whether or not the illuminator of BL, Add. 70513, or the scribe who left instructions for the illumination, was familiar with Marie de France's *Fables* manuscripts, from roughly the same period, that contain her portrait. Even though Marie de France, or at least the female figure depicted in the *Fables* manuscripts in question, is presented as the author of the text, whereas the woman shown in Add. 70513 is obviously the saint whose subject is recounted in the narrative, it is nevertheless possible to imagine that the scribe or illuminator associated the Marie who names herself at the end of the *Audree* with the Marie of the *Fables,* at least from an iconographical perspective.

With this brief summary in mind, the following analysis treats the use of rhetorical memory in the *Audree* to demonstrate the discursive relationship between it and Marie's other works, especially the *Espurgatoire*. While McCash's article has already dealt with several stylistic and thematic similarities that I highlight in this discussion, I focus on the author's use of rhetorical memory and the medieval art of *inventio*, an aspect of her narrative art that she emphasizes in the texts discussed in the previous chapters.

The *Audree* and Marie's Poetics of Memory

Marie exhibits an accomplished understanding of the medieval arts of poetry and prose in the *Espurgatoire,* as is evidenced by her references to rhetorical terms from the paradigm of literary invention. In the *Audree* she employs a similar rhetorical vo-

---

45. See chapter 4, and my article, *"Ex Libris Mariae,"* for a discussion of the images in question: Paris, BNF, fr. 2173, fol. 93r.; BNF, fr. 1446, fol. 88v; Paris, Arsenal 3142, fols. 256r and 273r. The author portrait in Vatican, BAV, Ottob. Lat. 3042, fol. 235r, is most probably later than BL, Add. 70513. Furthermore, her position in the Vatican manuscript illumination is slightly different than it is in the *Isopet* manuscripts that precede it, in that she is sitting at a covered desk and leaning forward before four male figures. See Busby, *Codex and Context,* 478.

The *Espurgatoire* and the *Audree*

cabulary when she brings her version into the vernacular, and the terms she chooses are sometimes absent from the source material, as we have already seen in the *Espurgatoire*. One passage in particular from the *Audree* confirms this occurrence toward the beginning of the text, where she enlists the expressions *venir a la matere, trovom en escrit,* and *mostre l'estoire,* terms that are designed to give credibility to the work at hand through the rhetorical implications of *captatio benevolentiae* and *auctoritas*:

> Pour la grant bonté de ceo roy
> Et pur s'onesté et sa foy,
> Com il fu bon rei et bon pere
> Et pur venir a la matere,
> Avom de li parlé et dist
> Ceo que nos trovom en escrit.
> De Kenewal, un roy puissant,
> Mostre l'estoire ici avant.
>   (525–32)[46]

> In order to get to the main story
> we have told at length
> what we find in the written record about this king
> because of his goodness,
> his honor, and his faith,
> and because he was a good king and a good father.
> Now I will tell the story
> of Cenwald, a powerful king.

This narrative strategy is particularly apparent in regard to the use of words associated with memory where Marie uses terms that her source does not.[47] In fact, throughout the *Audree*, she

---

46. Other passages where Marie includes these and similar terms not found in her source are lines 315–16, 484, 562, 603, 636–38, 811, 919, 1799, 1992–94, 2899, 2905–6, 3637–38.

47. Marie records the term, while her source does not, in the following lines from the *Audree: memoire* (rhymed with *estoire*) in 399–400, 855–56; *remembrance* in 1103–6; *recorder* in 1444; *remembra* in 3427–31. At times, Marie uses a form of *remembrer* where her source uses *memoria*: 1129, 1443.

164

The *Espurgatoire* and the *Audree*

seems quite intent on conveying to her audience the importance of memory by invoking this faculty at least sixteen times in the 4,625 lines in the text with expressions like "mettre en memoire," "remembrer/membrer," and "faire la memoire."[48]

Reading the prologues and epilogues of Marie de France's *Lais, Isopet,* and *Espurgatoire* against the exordial and closing lines in the *Audree* reveals a shared rhetorical discourse among the four narratives. The author pays particular attention throughout the prologues and epilogues of her works, discussed earlier, to the techniques of *descriptio* and *memoria*, both fundamental parts of *inventio* that imbued the medieval arts of poetry and prose.[49] She also opens the *Audree* by invoking the faculty of memory:

> An bon hovre e en bon porpens
> Devroit chascun user son tens.
> Pur sage devroit hon tenir
> Celui ke porroit *sovenir*
> Dont il est fait, qui le cria,
> Et quel part il *revertira*.
>
> (1–6, emphasis added)
>
> For a good work and for a good purpose
> should each person use his time.

---

48. "Membra lui par religion," 113; "Ceste matere lais issi, / Kar revertir voil a l'estoire / Dont en romanz fas la memoire," 318–20; "Ky en chercha la veire estoire / Pur mestre la vie en memoire," 399–400; "De cui vie et de cui victoire / En cel livre mis en memoire," 657–58; "En cel tens, si com ge recort," 778; "Ou quart livre de ceste estoire / Dont seint Bede feit la memoire," 855–56; "A la mateire revendrons," 919; "En l'onor Deu par remembrance / L'eglise fait une monstrance," 1103–4 (these lines are marked in the margin on fol. 108v, line 19, of the manuscript with a large plus symbol [+]); "Li uns avoit l'autre en memoire," 1109; "Ky poet remembrer en corage," 1129; "Digne chose est a remembrer / La seinteté et recorder / De la roïne sainte Audree," 1443–45 (cf. *Espurgatoire*, 771–82); "Si com nos reconte l'estoire / Ke saint Bede mist en memoire," 2381–82; "En son quer prist a remembrer / De seinte Audree et de sa vie," 3302–3; "En ses tormenz li remembra / De Brustan ke Deu delivra," 3427–28; "Li sovint et ad remembré / De seinte Audree la roïne," 3572–73; "Ne voil nul mettrë en obli," 4616; "Mut par est fol ki se oblie. / Ici escris mon non Marie / Pur ce ke soie remembree," 4623–25.

49. See chapters 1 and 2.

The *Espurgatoire* and the *Audree*

> It would be wise
> for everyone to remember
> what he is made of, who made him,
> and whither he shall return.

Both of the verbs *sovenir* and *revertir* are etymologically related to memory, the latter of which in Old French can mean to return, to come back, or to return to one's senses, in other words, to *re-member* who you are. Indeed, the noun based on the verb—*reverteure*—indicates a "souvenir" or "memory" of something. As I have shown in chapter 2, Marie de France's *exordia* consistently express a concern with memory. It should also be noted that the first two lines of the *Audree*—"An bon hovre e en bon porpens / Devroit chascun user son tens" (For a good work and for a good purpose / should each person use his time)—are very close to those that open the General Prologue to the *Lais:* "Ki Deus ad duné escïence / E de parler bone eloquence / Ne s'en deit taisir ne celer" (Anyone who has received from God the gift of knowledge and true eloquence has a duty not to remain silent), evoking the rhetorical device of *causa scribendi*.

Furthermore, Marie ends the *Audree* with an epilogue that also points to the importance of memory by syntactically juxtaposing her name with the past participle *remembree* and with the verb *oblïer* (or its negation, as the encouragement is not to forget), a strategy similar to that found in the epilogues to her earlier works:

> Issi ay ceo livre finé
> En romanz dit et translaté
> De la vie seintë Audree
> Si com en latin l'ay trové,
> Et les miracles ay oÿ,
> Ne voil nul mettrë en obli.
> Pur ce depri la glorïuse
> Seinte Audree la precïeuse
> Par sa pité k'a moy entende
> Et ce servise a m'ame rende,
> Et ceus pur ki ge la depri

The *Espurgatoire* and the *Audree*

> K'el lur aït par sa merci.
> Mut par est fol ki se oblie.
> Ici escris mon non Marie
> Pur ce ke soie remembree.
>   (4611–25)

> Now I have finished this book,
> told and translated into French
> the life of Saint Audrey
> just as I found it in Latin,
> along with the miracles I have heard.
> I do not wish to let anything be forgotten.
> Therefore I beseech glorious,
> precious Saint Audrey
> to hear me out of compassion
> and give aid to my soul,
> as well as to those for whom I pray:
> may she help them through her mercy.
> One is indeed foolish who forgets herself:
> here I write my name "Marie"
> so that I may be remembered.

Although the *Lais* do not contain a formal epilogue, *Eliduc*, the last text in the collection, ends with its own epilogue, which serves to frame the entire work: the opening references to the faculty of memory in the General Prologue and the prologue of *Guigemar* function as one "bookend," and the direct appeal to this faculty in the epilogue of *Eliduc* functions as the other.

In addition to the affinity of opening and closing material in the four texts under consideration here, a stylistic comparison of the narrations themselves in the two texts that are most thematically alike, the *Espurgatoire* and the *Audree,* reveals a shared concern with the application of *memoria* as it is expressed in the art of literary composition. McCash has already exposed the significance of this similarity by pointing to the paucity of references to memory in other hagiographic texts of the same period: only three times in Clemence of Barking's *La vie de Seinte Catherine d'Alexandrie* and only four times in the anonymous Nun of Bark-

The *Espurgatoire* and the *Audree*

ing's *Vie d'Edouard le Confesseur,* for example.[50] By contrast, the *Audree* offers numerous mentions of memory. McCash is quick to acknowledge that vernacular hagiographic writers use memory to a slightly different end than do authors of secular romance narratives, the former focusing more on "the celebration of shared memory" of a saint who already exists "en memoire," the latter desiring to preserve the memory of the past through rhetorical devices that included, but were not limited to, such techniques as *translatio studii* and *imperii, ordo, descriptio,* and *amplificatio;* in sum, they were more interested in the process of "mettre en memoire," or putting the material into memory, both for their own audiences and, as Marie de France makes explicit, for posterity.[51]

In the *Espurgatoire* and the *Audree* Marie's comprehension and implementation of this process shows that she was an author accustomed to secular vernacular narrative, even though she is now working in the domain of hagiography in translating the lives of the saints from their Latin models into Old French.[52] Lines 185–88 of the *Espurgatoire,* as discussed above, reveal her understanding of *inventio* as it emerges from her interpretation of the source material, H. of Saltrey's *Purgatorio.* Likewise, the *Audree* demonstrates her training and knowledge in the arts of poetry and prose. She states clearly in line 318 that she will leave aside the *matere* of her narrative digression and pick up again the *historia* of her source material so that she will not transgress the order *(ordo)* of the work at hand that she is putting "en memoire":

> Ceste matere lais issi,
> Kar revertir voil a l'estoire
> Dont en romanz fas la memoire.
> Sainte Audree dont nos parlon
> Fu mut de grant religion.
>
> (318–22)

---

50. See McCash, "A Fourth Text," 752. McCash refers to Clemence of Barking's *La vie de Seinte Catherine d'Alexandrie,* 384, 483, and 2608, and the anonymous Nun of Barking's *Vie d'Edouard le Confesseur,* 2079, 2797, 2844, and 6385.

51. Ibid., 752.   52. Ibid., 753.

The *Espurgatoire* and the *Audree*

> But I will not pursue this subject,
> for I wish to return to the main story
> which I am recording in French.
> Saint Audrey, of whom we are speaking,
> was devoutly religious.

In fact, numerous passages throughout the *Audree* reveal a certain obsession on the part of the author with *estoire* and *matere*.[53]

It is worth mentioning that the *Espurgatoire* and the *Audree* share yet another resemblance, apart from the design of memory, in their common use of courtly language. By putting the story "en memoire" for her lay audience, as she states in the epilogue of the *Espurgatoire*, Marie de France has helped her readers and listeners understand its message by means of the *aventure* to which they are accustomed.[54] Curley's observations on her method of putting the religious story of the *Espurgatoire* into the "idiom of the conte d'aventure" can be extended to the *Audree,* in which Marie generously and consistently employs the word *aventure* throughout the entirety of her text. In comparable fashion, both texts narrate the importance of the role that holy names play in acts of deliverance from peril. For the *Audree,* the very memory of the name of the saint represents assurance: "Digne chose est a remembrer / La seinteté et recorder / De la roïne sainte Audree / Ke a Deu out s'amur donee" (It is well worth remembering / her righteousness and recalling / how queen Saint Audrey / had given her love to God) (1443–46).[55] In the *Espurgatoire,* memory assures Owein of a means of escaping difficult circumstances, as he is encouraged to remember the name of Jesus Christ.[56] The vocabulary in these passages is similar to vocabulary in several other passages throughout both texts in which the author adopts a strikingly parallel discourse in bringing her Latin sources into the vernacular.

---

53. See notes 47–49, above.

54. See Leonard, "Inscription of a New Audience," 57–62, as discussed earlier in this chapter.

55. This theme recurs often throughout the text: 1129–30, 3337–38, 3427–29, 3572–73, and 3838–40. See also notes 46–48, above.

56. See, for example, 771–72 and 1119–20 of the *Espurgatoire*.

The *Espurgatoire* and the *Audree*

Description and *Merveille* in the *Audree*

In both works a similar strategy is used for describing objects that will help the audience remember key episodes and themes in the story. The knight in Marie de France's *Laüstic* creates a small and decorative container to house the dead nightingale that is wrapped in a precious samite cloth embroidered in gold, which will serve as a memorial of the love of his lady. In like fashion, and with much the same vocabulary, the two decorative *objets* that St. Audree makes, the elaborate stole and maniple for priestly service, are associated with the act of remembering, as the author informs us that these items are kept in Durham in God's honor *par remembrance:*

> D'or et de saie sainte Audree
> Fist une estole bien ovree
> Et un fanon k'el li tramist;
> Pieres precïeuses i mist.
> Ces aornemenz sont gardé
> A Durthaim par [mut] grant chierté;
> En l'onor Deu par remembrance
> L'eglise fait une monstrance.
> L'amur des deus ert covenable,
> Kar ele ert a Deu acceptable:
> Virges furent et chastement
> Tindrent lur vie et seintement;
> Li uns avoit l'autre en memoire
> Ke Deus le menast en sa gloire.
> (1097–110)

Saint Audrey made a finely worked stole
and maniple out of gold and silk,
adorned it with precious stones
and gave it to him.
These adornments are still kept
with great affection in Durham.
To honor God in memory of Saint Cuthbert
the church made a monstrance for them.

The *Espurgatoire* and the *Audree*

> The love between these two [Cuthbert and Audrey] was proper
> and acceptable to God
> for they were both virgins who led
> chaste and holy lives.
> One was always mindful of the other,
> [praying] that God would bring each of them into His glory.

Whether *eros* for the knight-lover in the *lai* of *Laüstic,* or *caritas* for the *Audree,* these passages demonstrate the author's desire to adorn objects descriptively and render them more accessible in our memory.

Moreover, Marie employs the term *merveille,* as she did in the *Espurgatoire,* when describing scenes that are particularly important to her. Here again, her audience would be used to hearing this expression in vernacular descriptions of people, places, objects, and events. She uses it in the beginning of her narrative to enhance her description of St. Audree's virginity:

> Sainte Audree dont nos parlon
> Fu mut de grant religion
> Pur Deu garda virginité
> Et toz jurs menoit en chasté:
> Ceuz ke la virge conoiseient
> A grant merveillie le teneient
> K'ele gardoit en mariage
> Virginité et pucelage.
> (321–28)

> Saint Audrey, of whom we are speaking,
> was devoutly religious.
> She kept her virginity for God
> and lived a chaste life daily.
> Those who knew the virgin
> marveled at her,
> for though she was a married woman, she kept
> her virginity and maidenhood.

The *grant merveillie* of line 326 recalls the use of the same expression throughout the *Espurgatoire* and calls attention to her de-

The *Espurgatoire* and the *Audree*

scription at this point. She chooses this construction again, later in the text, when she speaks about the virginity of the saint: "Grant merveillie fu de la foy / K'ele garda a Jhesu Crist / A cui virginité promist" (It was a great miracle of faith / that she remained faithful to Jesus Christ, / to whom she had promised her virginity) (1258–60). In fact, as in the *Espurgatoire,* she uses *merveille* regularly throughout the story to add descriptive energy to the scene.[57] Virginia Blanton has shown that Marie's focus on St. Audree's virginity and sexual desires from her daily life is original and cannot be found in sources prior to her vernacular version of the life.[58]

Marie consistently embellishes her version of the events from the Latin model with descriptions rich in vocabulary belonging to secular literature. At another point in the narrative in which St. Audree's chastity is emphasized, the author uses the same construction she has employed twice earlier to address the subject of virginity, but this time with yet another discursive dimension her audience would have no doubt known:

> Une haute roche i avoit
> Ke un de[s] costés aceignoit,
> Entaillié ert la pere dure:
> C'estoit merveillieuse aventure;
> Et la mer ke desouz estoit
> Ou ele au tertre se tenoit
> En pes se tint sanz departir
> Si ke hom ne poet avenir.
>
> (1355–62)
>
> There was a high rock
> that formed part of the coastline.
> The hard stone had been hollowed out.
> This was a miraculous occurrence,
> the water at the base

---

57. Similar uses of *merveille* are found in lines 1358, 1430, 1532, 2058, 2105, 2187, 2241, 2273, 2283, 2317, 2332, 2498, 2564, 2715, 2744, 3052, 3455, and 4279.
58. Blanton, *Signs of Devotion,* chapter 4.

The *Espurgatoire* and the *Audree*

> of the hill where she stood
> stayed there without moving,
> so that no one could come near her.

To the term *merveillieuse* Marie has added the element of *aventure* in this account of a miracle that saves the saint from the advances of King Egfrid. The juxtaposition of these two terms, which belong to the discourse of courtly literature, cannot be coincidental, and they betray the talents of an author well trained in the art of literary composition.[59]

The preponderance of references to memory and the act of remembering in the *Espurgatoire* and the *Audree,* the way in which Marie frames her works in these references, her demonstration of competence in the process of medieval literary *inventio* and its vocabulary, the regular occurrence of the courtly register in the descriptions, and the fact that the author syntactically associates her name in the epilogues with memory, represent more than mere artistic coincidence. These characteristics reveal an author with training in the vernacular, someone well versed in the arts of poetry and prose as they were understood during the last quarter of the twelfth century, an artist accomplished in *translatio studii,* in bringing preexisting material to a new, lay audience through her own conception of the work. Whether we call her simply Marie or Marie de France, the poetics of memory that emerge from the *Lais,* the *Isopet,* the *Espurgatoire,* and the *Audree* point rather convincingly to the same author, not an anonymous ghost hiding in her narratives, but a poet who wants to be remembered.

---

59. In fact, Marie uses *aventure* and the verb *avenir* numerous times throughout the *Audree,* especially when she recounts the miracles, to which she often refers as *aventure.*

Conclusion

Marie de France's use of *descriptio* and her concern with memory reveal a proficient training in the medieval arts of poetry and prose. *Descriptio* and *memoria,* two essential elements of topical invention, entered medieval instruction in literary composition through the study of authorities on rhetoric and grammar from antiquity, such as Cicero, the author of the *Rhetorica ad Herennium,* and Priscian. The art of *inventio* that developed in the Middle Ages honed the ability to find preexisting *materia,* commit that material to memory, and later arrange the disparate parts into a new whole that displayed the author's *ingenium.*

Marie de France's implementation of *inventio,* while not neglecting the use of rhetorical devices like *captatio benevolentiae* and *ordo,* privileges *descriptio* and *memoria* over other aspects of the process. We have seen how she combines these elements to construct an architecture of memory built upon vivid descriptions that impart a visual dimension to the narrative. Her literary plan consistently reminds the audience of the importance of remembering the story she treats, whether a moral fable, an adventurous *lai,* or a hagiographic tale that celebrates the life of a venerated saint. To facilitate the future recall of this material she embellishes her sources with descriptive detail, imparting energy to the episode in question and making it visible to the mind's eye and easy to register in the faculty of memory.

While Marie's narratives draw from the past, they also ensure its preservation through *translatio studii,* the transfer of knowledge from one culture to another or from one generation to the next. Her method of literary composition reflects the rhetorical practices of authorities from antiquity and helps to keep that tradition alive for her own period and for posterity. Likewise, her discov-

Conclusion

ery of material in preexisting sources and its subsequent reshaping into a work that accommodates the interests of her audience guarantees the preservation of literature that might otherwise have disappeared. In Marie's case, *translatio* applies not only to textual material but also to the survival of a medium: Marie puts the mostly oral tradition of the lyrical Breton *lai* into written narrative form, a genre that the authors of the *lais anonymes* continue in the thirteenth century.

But as much as Marie's corpus ensures the memory of past literature for her twelfth-century courtly audience, it also looks forward to works, both literary and scholastic, in the two centuries that follow. I have shown that she was writing just before the development of treatises devoted solely to the art of memory. Yet her narratives clearly reveal that she operated with the same concern for memory that characterizes these later treatises. I hope that further research will establish exactly how Marie was able to make a connection between the descriptive narration of literary texts and the medieval principles of memory years before they were actually codified in the writings of such authors as Albertus Magnus and Thomas Bradwardine. In light of the evidence presented here, I am convinced that Marie's synthesis of this mnemonic narrative architecture and her mentally visual descriptions surpassed the basic instruction she would have received from rhetorical and grammatical training in the arts of poetry and prose of the mid- to late twelfth century. Indeed, she may have been at least partly guided by the same sources that ultimately led to the development of the *artes memorativae* not long after she wrote. She was in all probability influenced to some degree by the various artistic media prevalent in her own culture, to which she would have been exposed through her association with the court in England. These included stained glass windows, frescoes, statues carved on churches and cathedrals, and manuscript illuminations, and they represented images, often in narrative sequence, that had the power to preserve in the minds of their public important secular and religious events.

The same type of relationship that Marie noticed and developed between vivid narrative descriptions and their benefits to

Conclusion

the faculty of memory was quickly passed on from memory treatises to literary texts of the thirteenth and fourteenth centuries, not only in France but in other European countries as well. Approximately fifty years after she translated the *Espurgatoire seint Patriz* and *La vie seinte Audree,* Richard de Fournival made a significant connection, similar to Marie's, between the written word and the image it could produce in the imagination. I have attempted to demonstrate how his intimate link between *painture* and *parole* is an echo of Marie's descriptive narration, which creates mentally visual images. Carruthers observes that Richard believed that one could "see" the events of a story, whether through actual pictures on a page or through the words that described them, creating a picture in the mind.[1]

In the fourteenth century, Chaucer also recognized the ability of *parole* to take visible form, and Carruthers cites an example of this understanding in the English poet's *House of Fame:* voices rise to Fame's house, where they take the shape of those who spoke them and eventually become clothed in red or black.[2] In like fashion, the wall paintings in the *Knight's Tale* exemplify the relationship between textual description, mentally visual form, and memory. Having described several depictions from the wall, the narrator tells the reader that his memory is full of many more, similar representations: "Ther saugh I many another wonder storie, / The which me list nat drawen to memorie" (1.2073–74). These pictures recount a story through the description of their contents, and they allow the audience to create a visual image that will register the story in the faculty of memory. This passage from Chaucer recalls Marie's use of the same narrative technique through the painting of Venus in the *lai* of *Guigemar,* as discussed in chapter 3.

Guillaume de Lorris, writing approximately twenty-five to fifty years after Marie,[3] noticed the same value of narrative description and "remembrance" that she did. Soon after the dream

---

1. Carruthers, *Book of Memory,* 224.   2. Ibid., 225.

3. For dating Guillaume de Lorris, see Félix Lecoy, ed., *Le roman de la rose,* 3 vols., Classiques Français du Moyen Age 92, 95, 98 (Paris: Champion, 1970–73), 1:viii. The citation is from this edition. The translation is mine.

Conclusion

sequence begins in the *Roman de la Rose*, the narrator stumbles upon an orchard enclosed by high walls. These walls are decorated with vivid depictions of allegorical figures:[4]

> Les ymages et les pointures
> dou mur volentiers remirai;
> si vos conterai et dirai
> de ces ymages la semblance,
> si com moi vient a remembrance.
> (134–39)

I will gladly recall the images and paintings on the wall; I will recount the appearance of the images as I remember them.

Guillaume makes a clear connection between the appearance of these images and the faculty of memory through his rhyme of "semblance" and "remembrance." During the 320 lines of text that follow, the narrator draws upon the memory of his dream to offer detailed descriptions of each allegorical figure in the paintings.

The relation between narrative description and the faculty of memory that Marie understood at an early period in the Middle Ages may have eventually realized its fullest expression in the works of Dante in the early fourteenth century. In the *Vita nuova*, he uses the metaphor of memory as a book that will serve him as he recalls his encounter with Beatrice. This memory will continue to play a key role for him in the *Commedia* as it ensures the omnipresence of historical consciousness on his journey through the underworld. For the poet, memory is the mother of the muses, invoked in the second canto of his *Inferno* by the term "mente": "O Muse, o alto ingegno, or m'aiutate; / o mente che scrivesti ciò ch'io vidi, / qui si parrà la tua nobilitate" (O Muses, o high genius, help me now; / o memory that set down what I saw, / here shall your excellence reveal itself!) (7–9).[5]

---

4. See lines 139–460: Haine, Felonie, Vilanie, Covoitise, Avarice, Envie, Vielleice, Papelardie, and Povreté.

5. The English translation is from *The Divine Comedy of Dante Alighieri: Inferno*, trans. Allen Mandelbaum (New York: Bantam Books, 1982).

Conclusion

As in the examples we have seen in H. of Saltrey's and Marie de France's purgatorial texts, the vivid descriptions in Dante's *Inferno* are the catalysts for registering the various scenes in the *loci* of our mental storehouses. One can never forget the representation of Paolo and Francesca (5.73–142), swept up in an eternal whirlwind, or the Provençal poet, Bertran de Born, condemned to walking in a circle for all eternity while holding his severed head in his hand (28.118–142). The intricate descriptions of rooms, gates, and walls found in Marie's narratives have their counterparts in the Italian poet's work years later.[6]

Thus Marie de France enjoys an auspicious position in the history of medieval literature. Long before Guillaume de Lorris, Richard de Fournival, Chaucer, and Dante, she highlighted the faculty of memory through her creative craft of description and through her generous and strategic arrangement of language associated with the act of remembering. Furthermore, no other author of vernacular literature during her time shares her design of opening and closing her stories with terms that evoke memory, including her famous contemporary Chrétien de Troyes; all four of her narrative texts clearly demonstrate this framing technique. Her method of literary composition embodied an ability to gather secular or religious material from the past and shape it into a new form that accommodated her own audience's understanding. Marie's poetics of memory throughout the *Lais,* the *Fables,* the *Espurgatoire seint Patriz,* and *La vie seinte Audree* not only guaranteed her endurance, they also assured the transmission of her texts to future generations, who she hoped would add their own *surplus de sen.*

---

6. See *Purgatorio,* 10.28–96, where he offers a lively description of images on a bank of the first terrace. These examples of the Virgin Mary, David, and the emperor Trajan truly take on a narrative life of their own, leading Dante to remark that they seem to be able to speak. The textual energy of these artistic descriptions is reminiscent not only of Marie's wall painting in *Guigemar,* but also of the entrance to Purgatory (671–704) and the wall of paradise (1488–530) in the *Espurgatoire.*

APPENDIX A

Priscian's *Institutiones grammaticae* and *Praeexercitamina*

The following passages are taken from Heinrich Keil, ed. *Grammatici Latini,* 8 vols. (Leipzig, 1855–80; reprint, Hildesheim: Georg Olms, 1961). Martin Hertz has edited the *Institutiones grammaticae* in this collection, vols. 2 and 3, and Keil has edited the *Opera minora* (including the *Praeexercitamina*), vol. 3.

Institutiones grammaticae

Cum omnis eloquentiae doctrinam et omne studiorum genus sapientiae luce praefulgens a Graecorum fontibus derivatum Latinos proprio sermone invenio celebrasse et in omnibus illorum vestigia liberalibus consecutos artibus video, nec solum ea, quae emendate ab illis sunt prolata, sed etiam quosdam errores eorum amore doctorum deceptos imitari, in quibus maxime vetustissima grammatica ars arguitur peccasse, *cuius auctores, quanto sunt iuniores, tanto perspicaciores, et ingeniis floruisse et diligentia valuisse omnium iudicio confirmantur eruditissimorum*—quid enim Herodiani artibus certius, quid Apollonii scrupulosis quaestionibus enucleatius possit inveniri?—cum igitur eos omnia fere vitia, quaecumque antiquorum Graecorum commentariis sunt relicta artis grammaticae, expurgasse comperio certisque rationis legibus emendasse, nostrorum autem neminem post illos imitatorem eorum extitisse, quippe in neglegentiam cadentibus studiis literarum propter inopiam scriptorum, quamvis audacter, sed non impudenter, ut puto, conatus sum pro viribus rem arduam quidem, sed officio professionis non indebitam, supra nominatorum praecepta virorum, quae congrua sunt visa, in Latinum transferre sermonem, collectis etiam omnibus fere, quaecumque necessaria nostrorum quoque inveniuntur artium commentariis grammaticorum, quod gratum fore credidi temperamentum, si ex utriusque linguae

Appendix A

moderatoribus elegantiora in unum coeant corpus meo labore faciente, quia nec vituperandum me esse credo, si eos imitor, qui principatum inter scriptores Graios artis grammaticae possident, cum veteres nostri in erroribus etiam, ut dictum est, Graecos aequiperantes maximam tamen laudem sunt consecuti. (§§ 1–3, pp. 1–2, emphasis added)

Praeexercitamina (De laude)

Consimiliter tamen muta quoque animalia quomodo convenit. et a loco in quo nascuntur laudentur et a deis, in quorum sunt tutela, ut columba Veneri, equus Neptuno dicitur esse consecratus. praeterea dices, quomodo pascitur, qualem habeat animum, quale corpus, quid opus aut quid utilitatis, quale spatium temporis vitae. nec non etiam comparatione et omnibus accidentibus locis uteris. res autem laudes ad inventoribus, ut venationem Diana invenit et Apollo, et ab his qui ea usi sunt, heroes venationibus utebantur. maxima autem facultas in huiuscemodi rerum laudationibus datur ex contemplatione eorum qui eas res affectant, quales sunt tam animis quam corporibus, ut venantes fortes audaces acuti integri corporibus. hinc non ignores, quomodo etiam deos debeas laudare. similiter arbores a loco in quo gignuntur et a deo in cuius sunt tutela, *ut* oliva Minervae, laurus Apollini; et a pastu, quomodo pascuntur, et si multa cura egent, id mireris, sin parva, id quoque laudabis. dices autem, quomodo de corpore, staturam pulchritudinem pullulationem, quomodo de mali arbore, et quid utile habeat, in quo maxime morandum. comparationes autem ubique assumendae. quin etiam urbium laudes ex huiuscemodi locis non difficulter adquires. dices enim de genere, quod indigenae, et de victu, quod a deis nutriti, et de eruditione, quod a deis eruditi sunt. tractes vero, quomodo de homine, quali sit structura, quibus professionibus est usa, quid gesserit? (§§ 23–24, pp. 436–37)

Praeexercitamina (De descriptione)

Descriptio est oratio colligens et praesentans oculis quod demonstrat. fiunt autem descriptiones tam personarum quam rerum et temporum et status et locorum et multorum aliorum: personarum quidem, ut apud Virgilium

> virginis os habitumque gerens et virginis arma Spartanae;

rerum vero, ut pedestris proelii vel navalis pugnae descriptio; temporum autem, ut veris aestatis; status, *ut* pacis vel belli; locorum, ut litoris campi montium urbium. potest autem et commixta esse demonstratio, ut, siquis

describat nocturnam pugnam, simul et tempus et rem demonstrat. conemur igitur res quidem describere ab ante factis, et quae in ipsis eveniunt vel aguntur, ut, si belli dicamus descriptionem, primum quidem ante bellum dicere debemus dilectus habitos, sumptus paratos, timores qui fuerunt; hinc congressus, caedes, mortes, victorias, laudes victorum, illorum vero qui victi sunt lacrimas, servitutem. sin vero loca vel tempora vel personas describamus, habebimus aliquam et a narratione, de qua supra docuimus, et a bono vel utili vel laudabili rationem. virtus autem descriptionis maxime planities et praesentia vel significantia est. oportet enim elocutionem paene per aures oculis praesentiam facere ipsius rei et exaequare dignitati rerum stilum elocutionis. si clara res est, sit et oratio similis; sin summissa, huic quoque aptetur qualitas verborum. sciendum autem, quod quidam non posuerunt descriptionem in praeexercitamentis, quasi praeoccupatam et in fabula et in narratione: in illis enim quoque describimus et loca et fluvios et personas et res. sed quoniam eam quoque quidam eloquentissimorum tradidere inter praeexercitationes, non incongruum est eos imitari.
(§§ 29–30, pp. 438–39)

APPENDIX B

Table of Extant Medieval Manuscripts of Marie de France's *Isopet*

	Manuscript	Illum.	Number of fables	Image of Marie	Prologue	Epilogue	Moral marked
αA	BL, Harley 978		102		•	•	•
αD	BL, Douce 132		100		•	•	•
αM	BNF, fr. 1822		97		•		
αY	York Minster XVI K12		69		•		•
βB	BL, Vesp. XIV		61		[1]		•
βE	Camb., Univ. Lib. Ee.6.11		68		•		•
βN	BNF, fr. 1593		102		•	•	•
βQ	BNF, fr. 2173	•	101	•	•	•	•
βT	BNF, fr. 24428	•	64		•		•
γC	BL, Harley 4333		87		•	•	•
γF	BNF, fr. 12603		101		•	•	
γH	Paris, Arsenal 3142	•	102	•	•	•	•
γL	BNF, fr. 25406	[2]	55		•	[3]	•
γO	BNF, fr. 1446	[4]	100	•	•	•	•
γP	BNF, fr. 2168		103		•		•
γS	BNF, fr. 19152		67		•	•	•
X[5]	Chantilly, Musée Condé 474		76		•	•	•
βZ	BAV, Ottob. Lat. 3064	[6]	23	•	•		•
γK	BNF, fr. 25545		64		•		•
γR	BNF, fr. 14971		98		•	•	•
γV	BNF, fr. 25405		92		•	•	•

Medieval Manuscripts of *Isopet*

Manuscript		Illum.	Number of fables	Image of Marie	Prologue	Epilogue	Moral marked
βG	BNF, fr. 4939		37				•
βI	BNF, fr. 24130	7	50				•
γW	Brussels, Bib. Royale 10296		91		•	•	•
Q⁸	Cologny, Bodmer 113⁹	•	101	•	•	•	•

Notes: The information in this table is from my consultation of the manuscripts. However, I am also indebted here to observations on the manuscripts by Julia Bastin, ed., *Recueil général des Isopets,* 2 vols. (Paris: Société des Anciens Textes Français, 1929, 1930); Burgess, *Analytical Bibiography;* Busby, *Codex and Context;* Hervieux, *Fabulistes latins;* Jambeck's edition of the *Fables;* Kenneth McKenzie and William A. Oldfather, eds., *Ysopet-Avionnet: The Latin and French Texts* (Urbana: University of Illinois Press, 1919); Kurt Ringger, "Prolégomènes à l'iconographie des œuvres de Marie de France," in *Orbis Mediævalis* (Bern: Francke, 1978), 329–42; and Warnke's edition of the *Fables.* I also consulted the catalogues of the collections to which the manuscript belongs. I have not included in the table Nottingham, University Lib. Mi Lm 6, a fragment that contains the first fifteen verses of *Del fevre e de la cuinee,* or the manuscripts of Marie's *Fables* from the eighteenth century, i.e., Paris, Arsenal 3124, La Haye, Bibliothèque Royale 71 G 68, La Haye, Bib. Royale 71 E 48, and BNF, Moreau 1603. The sigla and the number of fables are taken from Warnke's edition. The bullets indicate that the element of that column appears in the manuscript.

1. The *Fables* begin on folio 19r. The two folios before folio 19 appear to have been cut out. What remains of Marie's prologue, which obviously began on the now missing previous folio, continues on folio 19r with the lines, "Et qüt tel home nen ad requise / Ne voil laisser en nul guise."
2. Spaces left, but miniatures never executed.
3. The *Fables* end with the words "Explicunt fabule Ysopi Deo gratis amen." Marie's epilogue was then inserted by a later hand.
4. One illumination of Marie or another female figure at the beginning of the collection.
5. Vielliard's siglum in "Tradition manuscrite."
6. One illumination of Marie or another female figure at the beginning of the collection.
7. Spaces left, but miniatures never executed.
8. Vielliard's siglum in "Tradition manuscrite."
9. Almost an exact copy of the text and images from BNF, fr. 2173.

Bibliography

Alexander, J. J. G. *The Decorated Letter*. New York: G. Braziller, 1978.
Amer, Sahar. Review of *Marie de France: Les fables, édition critique accompagnée d'une introduction, d'une traduction, de notes et d'un glossaire*, ed. Charles Brucker. *Romance Philology* 48, no. 3 (1995): 306–11.
———. "*L'ésope* de Marie de France: *Translatio* du *Romulus Nilantii*." In *The Medieval Translator*, vol. 5, ed. Roger Ellis and René Tixier, 347–61. Turnout: Brepols, 1996.
———. *Ésope au féminin: Marie de France et la politique de l'interculturalité*. Faux Titre 169. Amsterdam: Rodopi, 1999.
Armstrong, Grace Morgan. "Engendering the Text: Marie de France and Dhouda." In *Translatio Studii: Essays by His Students in Honor of Karl D. Uitti for His Sixty-Fifth Birthday*, ed. Renate Blumenfeld-Kosinski et al., 27–49. Faux Titre 179. Amsterdam: Rodopi, 2000.
Avril, François, and Marie-Thérèse Gousset. *Manuscrits enluminés d'origine italienne*. Paris: Bibliothèque Nationale, 1984.
Bastin, Julia, ed. *Recueil général des Isopets*. 2 vols. Paris: Société des Anciens Textes Français, 1929, 1930.
Baum, Richard. *Recherches sur les œuvres attribuées à Marie de France*. Heidelberg: Carl Winter, 1968.
Baumgartner, Emmanuèle. "Peinture et évidence: La description de la tente dans les romans antiques du XIIe siècle." In *Sammlung-Deutung-Wertung: Ergebnisse, Probleme, Tendenzen, und Perspektiven philologischer Arbeit; Mélanges Wolfgang Spiewok*, ed. Danielle Buschinger, 3–11. Amiens: Université de Picardie, Centre d'Études Médiévales, 1988.
Baylé, Maylis. "La Tapisserie de Bayeux et l'ornementation dans l'Europe du nord-œust." In *La Tapisserie de Bayeux: L'art de broder l'histoire*, ed. Pierre Bouet, Brian Levy, and François Neveux, 303–25. Caen: Presses Universitaires de Caen, 2004.
Bédier, Joseph. *Les légendes épiques*. 3d ed. 4 vols. Paris: Champion, 1926–29.
Beer, Jeanette M. A. *Narrative Conventions of Truth in the Middle Ages*. Geneva: Droz, 1981.

Bibliography

Blanton, Virginia. *Signs of Devotion: The Cult of St. Ethelthryth in Medieval England, 695–1615*. University Park: Pennsylvania State University Press, 2007.

Blanton-Whetsell, Virginia. "*Imagines Ætheldredae:* Mapping Hagiographic Representations of Abbatial Power and Religious Patronage." *Studies in Iconography* 23 (2002): 55–107.

Bloch, R. Howard. *The Anonymous Marie de France*. Chicago: University of Chicago Press, 2003.

Boehm, Gottfried, and Helmut Pfotenhauer, eds. *Beschreibungskunst—Kuntsbeschreibung: Ekphrasis von der Antike bis zur Gegenwart*. Munich: Wilhelm Fink, 1995.

Boldrick, Stacy L. "Romanesque Art." In *Medieval France: An Encyclopedia,* ed. William W. Kibler and Grover A. Zinn, 816–19. New York: Garland, 1995.

Braet, Herman. "Marie de France et l'obscurité des anciens." *Neuphilologische Mitteilungen* 79, no. 2 (1978): 180–84.

———. "Note sur Marie de France et Ovide: Lai de *Guigemar*, vv. 233–244." In *Mélanges de philologie et de littératures romanes offerts à Jeanne Wathelet-Willem,* ed. Jacques de Caluwé, 21–25. Liège: Cahiers de l'A.R.U.Lg., 1978.

Brown, Shirley Ann. *The Bayeux Tapestry: History and Bibliography*. Woodbridge, UK: Boydell & Brewer, 1988.

Brucker, Charles. "La conception du récit dans la fable ésopique en langue vulgaire: De Marie de France à Steinhöwel." In *Le récit bref au moyen âge: Actes du colloque des 27, 28 et 29 avril 1979,* ed. Danielle Buschinger, 387–427. Paris: Champion, 1980.

———. "Société et morale dans la fable ésopique du XIIe et du XIIIe siècle." In *Et c'est la fin pour quoy sommes ensemble: Hommage à Jean Dufournet,* ed. J.-C. Aubailly et al., 3 vols., 1:281–92. Paris: Champion, 1993.

Bruckner, Matilda Tomaryn. "Marie de France." In *Medieval France: An Encyclopedia,* ed. William W. Kibler and Grover A. Zinn, 589–91. New York: Garland, 1995.

Burch, Sally L. "The Prologue to Marie's *Lais:* Back to the *Littera.*" *AUMLA: Journal of the Australian Universities Language and Literature Association* 89 (May 1998): 15–42.

Burgess, Glyn S. *Marie de France: An Analytical Bibliography*. London: Grant and Cutler, 1977. Supplement no. 1, 1986. Supplement no. 2, 1997. Supplement no. 3, 2007.

———. "The Problem of Internal Chronology in the *Lais* of Marie de France." *Zeitschrift für französische Sprache und Literatur* 91, no. 2 (1981): 133–55.

Bibliography

———. *The Lais of Marie de France: Text and Context.* Athens: University of Georgia Press, 1987.

———. *The Old French Narrative Lay: An Analytical Bibliography.* Woodbridge, UK: D. S. Brewer, 1995.

———. "The *Fables* of Marie de France: Some Recent Scholarship." *French Studies Bulletin* 61, no. 1 (1996): 8–13.

Busby, Keith, ed. *Towards a Synthesis? Essays on the New Philology.* Amsterdam: Rodopi, 1993.

———. "'Ceo fu la summe de l'escrit' (*Chevrefoil,* line 61) Again." *Philological Quarterly* 74, no. 1 (1995): 1–15.

———. "Froissart's Poetic Prison: Enclosure as Image and Structure in the Narrative Poetry." In *Froissart Across the Genres,* ed. Donald Maddox and Sara Sturm-Maddox, 81–100. Gainesville: University Press of Florida, 1998.

———. *Codex and Context: Reading Old French Verse Narrative in Manuscript.* 2 vols. Amsterdam: Rodopi, 2002.

Cagnon, Maurice. "*Chievrefeuil* and the Ogamic Tradition." *Romania* 91, no. 362 (1970): 238–55.

Calkins, Robert. *Illuminated Books of the Middle Ages.* Ithaca: Cornell University Press, 1983.

Carnes, Pack. *Fable Scholarship: An Annotated Bibliography.* New York: Garland, 1985.

Carruthers, Mary. "The Wife of Bath and the Painting of Lions." *PMLA* 94, no. 2 (1979): 209–22.

———. *The Book of Memory: A Study of Memory in Medieval Culture.* Cambridge: Cambridge University Press, 1990.

———. "The Poet as Master Builder: Composition and Locational Memory in the Middle Ages." *New Literary History* 24, no. 4 (1993): 881–904.

———. "Boncompagno at the Cutting-edge of Rhetoric: Rhetorical *Memoria* and the Craft of Memory." *Journal of Medieval Latin* 6 (1996): 44–64.

Castellani, Marie-Madeleine. "La description de la tente du roi Bilas dans le roman d'*Athis et Prophilias.*" In *Et c'est la fin pour quoy sommes ensemble: Hommage à Jean Dufournet,* ed. J.-C. Aubailly et al., 3 vols., 1:327–39. Paris: Champion, 1993.

Cather, Sharon, David Park, and Paul Williamson, eds. *Early Medieval Wall Painting and Painted Sculpture in England.* Oxford: BAR, 1990.

Caviness, Madeleine H. *The Early Stained Glass of Canterbury Cathedral: Circa 1175–1220.* Princeton: Princeton University Press, 1977.

———. *The Windows of Christ Church Cathedral Canterbury.* Oxford: Oxford University Press, 1981.

Bibliography

———. *Stained Glass Windows*. Turnhout: Brepols, 1996.
———. *Paintings on Glass: Studies in Romanesque and Gothic Monumental Art*. Aldershot: Ashgate, 1997.
———. *Art in the Medieval West and Its Audience*. Aldershot: Ashgate, 2001.
Char, René. *Œuvres complètes*. Paris: Gallimard, 1983.
Chaucer, Geoffrey. *The Riverside Chaucer*. Ed. Larry D. Benson et al. 3d ed. Boston: Houghton Mifflin, 1987.
Chefneux, Hélène. "Les fables dans la tapisserie de Bayeux." *Romania* 60, no. 237 (1934): 1–35; no. 238 (1934): 153–94.
Chrétien de Troyes. *Erec und Enide*. Ed. Wendelin Foerster. Halle: Niemeyer, 1934.
———. *Yvain: Le chevalier au lion*. Ed. Wendelin Foerster. Manchester: Manchester University Press, 1942.
———. *Cligés*. Ed. Claude Luttrell and Stewart Gregory. Cambridge: D. S. Brewer, 1993.
———. *Le roman de Perceval ou le conte du Graal*. Ed. Keith Busby. Tübingen: Niemeyer, 1993.
Cicero. *De inventione: De optimo genere oratorum; topica*. Trans. H. M. Hubbell. Cambridge, Mass.: Harvard University Press, 1949.
———. *Ad C. Herennium de ratione dicendi*. Trans. Harry Caplan. Cambridge, Mass.: Harvard University Press, 1954.
Cirlot, J. E. *A Dictionary of Symbols*. Trans. Jack Sage. 2d ed. New York: Philosophical Library, 1971.
Clemente, Linda M. *Literary objets d'art: Ekphrasis in Medieval French Romance, 1150–1220*. New York: Peter Lang, 1992.
Clifford, Paula. *Marie de France: Lais*. London: Grant & Cutler, 1982.
Cohen, Gustave. "Marie de France, le lai des *Deux Amants*." *Mercure de France* 265 (1936): 61–68.
Corbellari, Alain. "Les jeux de l'anneau: Fonctions et trajets d'un objet dans la littérature narrative médiévale." In *"De sens rassis": Essays in Honor of Rupert T. Pickens*, ed. Keith Busby, Bernard Guidot, and Logan E. Whalen, 157–67. Amsterdam: Rodopi, 2005.
Cowell, Andrew. "Deadly Letters: '*Deus Amans*,' Marie's 'Prologue' to the *Lais*, and the Dangerous Nature of the Gloss." *Romanic Review* 88, no. 3 (1997): 337–56.
Curtius, Ernst Robert. *European Literature and the Latin Middle Ages*. Trans. Willard R. Trask. Princeton: Princeton University Press, 1953.
Dante Alighieri. *Le opere di Dante*. Ed. Michele Barbi. Florence: R. Bemporad et Figlio, 1921.
———. *The Divine Comedy of Dante Alighieri: Inferno*. Trans. Allen Mandelbaum. New York: Bantam Books, 1982.

Bibliography

———. *Dante Alighieri: Vita Nuova*. Trans. Mark Musa. Oxford: Oxford University Press, 1992.

De Grave, J.-J. Salverda. "Marie de France et *Eneas*." *Neophilologus* 10, no. 1 (1925): 56–58.

Delclos, Jean-Claude. "Encore le prologue des *Lais* de Marie de France." *Le Moyen Âge* 90, no. 2 (1984): 223–32.

Dembowski, Peter F. "Vocabulary of Old French Courtly Lyrics—Difficulties and Hidden Meanings." *Critical Inquiry* 2, no. 4 (1976): 763–79.

Dewilde, Peter. "Le système descriptif des visions de l'autre monde dans le *Purgatoire de saint Patrice*." In *La description au Moyen Âge: Actes du Colloque du Centre d'Études Médiévales et Dialectales de Lille III, Université Charles-de-Gaulle-Lille III, 25–26 Septembre 1992*, ed. Aimé Petit Villeneuve d'Ascq, 143–46. Université de Lille III: 1993.

Donovan, Mortimer. "Priscian and the Obscurity of the Ancients." *Speculum* 36, no. 1 (1961): 75–80.

Easting, Robert. *St. Patrick's Purgatory: Two Versions of Owayne Miles and the Vision of William of Stranton Together with the Long Text of the Tractatus de Purgatorio Sancti Patricii*. Oxford: Oxford University Press, 1991.

Eluard, Paul. *Donner à voir*. Paris: Gallimard, 1939.

Faral, Edmond. *Les arts poétiques du XIIe et du XIIIe siècle: Recherches et documents sur la technique littéraire du moyen âge*. Paris: Champion, 1924.

Fasciano, Domenico. "La mythologie du lai *Les Deux Amants*." *Rivista di Cultura Classica e Medioevale* 16, no. 1 (1974): 79–85.

Fitz, Brewster. "The Prologue to the *Lais* of Marie de France and the *Parable of the Talents*: Gloss and Monetary Metaphor." *Modern Language Notes* 90, no. 4 (1995): 558–64.

Foulet, Alfred, and Karl D. Uitti. "The Prologue to the *Lais* of Marie de France: A Reconsideration." *Romance Philology* 35, no. 1 (1981–82): 242–49.

Foulet, Lucien. "Marie de France et les lais bretons." *Zeitschrift für romanische Philologie* 29, no. 1 (1905): 19–56, 293–322.

———. "Marie de France et la légende du Purgatoire de Saint Patrice." *Romanische Forschungen* 22, no. 4 (1908): 599–627.

Fournival, Richard de. *Li bestiaires d'amour*. Ed. Cesare Segré. Milan: Riccardi, 1957.

France, Peter, ed. *The New Oxford Companion to Literature in French*. Oxford: Clarendon Press, 1995.

Frappier, Jean, ed. *La littérature narrative de l'imagination, des genres littéraires aux techniques de l'expression*. Paris: Presses Universitaires de France, 1961.

Bibliography

French, Jean M. "Romanesque Sculpture." In *Medieval France: An Encyclopedia,* ed. William W. Kibler and Grover A. Zinn, 819–21. New York: Garland, 1995.

Genette, Gérard. *Figures III.* Paris: Seuil, 1972.

Gertz, SunHee Kim. *Echoes and Reflections: Memory and Memorials in Ovid and Marie de France.* Faux Titre 232. Amsterdam: Rodopi, 2003.

Godefroy, Frédéric, ed. *Dictionnaire de l'ancienne langue française.* 10 vols. Paris: F. Vieweg, 1881–1902.

Greimas, Algirdas J., ed. *Dictionnaire de l'ancien français.* Paris: Larousse, 2001.

Grodecki, Louis. *Le vitrail roman.* Fribourg: Office du Livre, 1977.

Hanning, Robert. "Courtly Contexts for Urban *Cultus:* Responses to Ovid in Chrétien's *Cligès* and Marie's *Guigemar.*" *Symposium* 35, no. 1 (1981): 34–56.

Haren, Michael, and Yolande de Pontfarcy. *The Medieval Pilgrimage to St. Patrick's Purgatory: Lough Derg and the European Tradition.* Enniskillen, Ireland: Clogher Historical Society, 1988.

Heffernan, James. *Museum of Words: The Poetics of Ekphrasis from Homer to Ashbery.* Chicago: University of Chicago Press, 1993.

Hervieux, Léopold, ed. *Les fabulistes latins, depuis le siècle d'Auguste jusqu'à la fin du Moyen Âge.* 2 vols. Paris: Firmin-Didot, 1884. Second ed., 5 vols., Paris: Firmin-Didot, 1883–89. Reprint, New York: Burt Franklin, 1972.

Hindman, Sandra. "Æsop's Cock and Marie's Hen: Gendered Authorship in Text and Image in Manuscripts of Marie de France's *Fables.*" In *Women and the Book: Assessing the Visual Evidence,* ed. Lesley Smith and Jane H. M. Taylor, 45–56. Toronto: University of Toronto Press, 1997.

Hoepffner, Ernest. "Marie de France et *l'Eneas.*" *Studi Medievali,* n.s., 5, no. 1 (1932): 272–308.

———. "Pour la chronologie des *Lais* de Marie de France." *Romania* 59 (1933): 351–70; 60, no. 237 (1934): 36–66.

Holzbacher, Ana-María. "El Prólogo de los *Lais:* No se ha dicho aún la última palabra." *Boletín de la Real Academia de Buenas Letras de Barcelona* 41 (1987–88): 227–57.

Hornblower, Simon, and Anthony Spawforth, eds. *The Oxford Classical Dictionary.* 3d ed. Oxford: Oxford University Press, 1996.

Hunt, Tony. "Glossing Marie de France." *Romanische Forschungen* 86, nos. 3–4 (1974): 396–418.

Irvine, Martin. *The Making of Textual Culture: "Grammatica" and Literary Theory, 350–1100.* Cambridge: Cambridge University Press, 1994.

Bibliography

Kahn, Deborah. *Canterbury Cathedral and Its Romanesque Sculpture.* Austin: University of Texas Press, 1991.

Keil, Heinrich, ed. *Grammatici Latini.* 8 vols. Leipzig, 1855–80. Reprint, Hildesheim: Georg Olms, 1961.

Kelly, Douglas. *Sens and Conjointure in the Chevalier de la Charrette.* The Hague: Mouton, 1966.

———. *The Medieval Imagination: Rhetoric and the Poetry of Courtly Love.* Madison: University of Wisconsin Press, 1978.

———. "Obscurity and Memory: Sources for Invention in Medieval French Literature." In *Vernacular Poetics in the Middle Ages,* ed. Lois Ebin, 33–56. Kalamazoo: Western Michigan University, Medieval Institute, 1984.

———. "The Art of Description." In *The Legacy of Chrétien de Troyes,* ed. Norris J. Lacy, Douglas Kelly, and Keith Busby, 2 vols., 1:191–221. Amsterdam: Rodopi, 1987.

———. *The Art of Medieval French Romance.* Madison: University of Wisconsin Press, 1992.

Kibler, William W., and Grover A. Zinn, eds. *Medieval France: An Encyclopedia.* New York: Garland, 1995.

Knapton, Antoinette. "La poésie enluminée de Marie de France." *Romance Philology* 30, no. 1 (1976–77): 177–87.

Krieger, Murray. *Ekphrasis: The Illusion of the Natural Sign.* Baltimore: Johns Hopkins University Press, 1992.

Lacy, Norris J. *Reading Fabliaux.* New York: Garland, 1993.

Leonard, Bonnie H. "The Inscription of a New Audience: Marie de France's *Espurgatoire Saint Patriz.*" *Romance Languages Annual* 5 (1993): 57–62.

Lessing, Gotthold E. *Laocoon: An Essay on the Limits of Painting and Poetry.* Trans. Edward A. McCormick. Baltimore: Johns Hopkins University Press, 1984.

Leupin, Alexandre. "The Impossible Task of Manifesting 'Literature': On Marie de France's Obscurity." *Exemplaria* 3, no. 1 (1991): 241–42.

Levi, Ezio. "Sulla cronologia della opera di Maria di Francia." *Nuovi Studi Medievali* 1, no. 1 (1923): 41–72.

Lewis, Charlton T., and Charles Short, eds. *A Latin Dictionary.* 1879. Reprint, Cambridge: Clarendon Press, 1962.

Lorris, Guillaume de, and Jean de Meun. *Le roman de la rose.* Ed. Félix Lecoy. 3 vols. Classiques Français du Moyen Age 92, 95, 98. Paris: Champion, 1970–73.

Maddox, Donald. *Fictions of Identity in Medieval France.* Cambridge: Cambridge University Press, 2000.

Bibliography

Mall, Eduard. *De aetate rebusque Mariae Francicae nova quaestio instituitur.* Halle, 1867.

———. "Zur Geschichte der mittelalterlichen Fabellitteratur und insbesondere des *Esope* der Marie de France." *Zeitschrift für romanische Philologie* 9, no. 1 (1885): 161–203.

Maréchal, Chantal. "Marie de France as *Sapientia:* Author Portraits in the Manuscripts of the *Fables.*" *Le Cygne: Bulletin of the International Marie de France Society* 3 (spring 1997): 45–58.

Marie de France. *Die Fabeln der Marie de France.* Ed. Karl Warnke. Halle: Niemeyer, 1898.

———. *The Espurgatoire Seint Patriz of Marie de France with a Text of the Latin Original.* Ed. T. A. Jenkins. Chicago: Decennial Publications of the University of Chicago, 1903.

———. *Die Lais der Marie de France.* Ed. Karl Warnke. 3d ed. Halle: Niemeyer, 1925.

———. *Das Buch vom Espurgatoire S. Patrice der Marie de France und seine Quelle.* Ed. Karl Warnke. Halle: Niemeyer, 1938.

———. *Marie de France: Fables.* Ed. Alfred Ewert and Ronald C. Johnston. Oxford: Blackwell, 1942.

———. *Marie de France: Lais.* Ed. Alfred Ewert. Oxford: Blackwell, 1944.

———. *La vie seinte Audree: Poème anglo-normand du XIIIe siècle.* Ed. Östen Södergård. Uppsala Universitets Årsskrift 11. Uppsala: Lundequistska Bokhandeln, 1955.

———. *The Lais of Marie de France.* Trans. Robert Hanning and Joan Ferrante. New York: Dutton, 1978.

———. *Les fables de Marie de France: Édition critique de fables choisies.* Ed. Karen Jambeck. Ph.D. diss., University of Connecticut-Storrs, 1980. *Dissertation Abstracts International* 41, no. 8 (1981): 3570A.

———. *The Fables of Marie de France: An English Translation.* Trans. Mary-Lou Martin. Birmingham, Ala.: Summa Publications, 1982.

———. *Les lais de Marie de France.* Ed. Jean Rychner. Classiques Français du Moyen Age 93. Paris: Champion, 1983.

———. *Marie de France: Fables.* Ed. and trans. Harriet Spiegel. Toronto: University of Toronto Press, 1987.

———. *Marie de France: Œuvres complètes.* Ed. Yorio Otaka. Tokyo: Maison d'Edition Kazama, 1987.

———. *Marie de France: Les fables, édition critique accompagnée d'une introduction, d'une traduction, de notes et d'un glossaire.* Ed. and trans. Charles Brucker. 2d ed. Louvain: Peeters, 1991.

———. *Saint Patrick's Purgatory: A Poem by Marie de France.* Trans. Mi-

Bibliography

chael J. Curley. New York: Center for Medieval and Early Renaissance Texts and Studies, 1993.

———. *Marie de France, L'Espurgatoire Seint Patriz: Nouvelle édition critique accompagnée du De Purgatorio Sancti Patricii (éd. de Warnke), d'une introduction, d'une traduction, de notes et d'un glossaire.* Ed. and trans. Yolande de Pontfarcy. Louvain: Peeters, 1995.

———. *The Lais of Marie de France.* Trans. Glyn S. Burgess and Keith Busby. 2d ed. London: Penguin, 1999.

———. *The Life of Saint Audrey: A Text by Marie de France.* Ed. and trans. June Hall McCash and Judith Clark Barban. Jefferson, N.C.: McFarland & Co., 2006.

Masters, Bernadette. "*Li lox, lililions* and Their *compaig:* Exemplary Error in the Fables of BN MS, f. fr. 19152." *Parergon,* n.s., 13, no. 2 (1996): 203–22.

McCash, June Hall. "'Ensemble poënt bien durer': Time and Timelessness in the *Chevrefoil* of Marie de France." *Arthuriana* 9, no. 4 (1999): 32–44.

———. "*La vie seinte Audree:* A Fourth Text by Marie de France?" *Speculum* 77, no. 3 (2002): 744–77.

———. "Philomena's Window: Issues of Intertextuality and Influence in Works by Marie de France and Chrétien de Troyes." In *"De sens rassis": Essays in Honor of Rupert T. Pickens,* ed. Keith Busby, Bernard Guidot, and Logan E. Whalen, 415–30. Amsterdam: Rodopi, 2005.

McClelland, Denise. *Le vocabulaire dans les Lais de Marie de France.* Ottawa: Éditions de l'Université d'Ottawa, 1977.

McKenzie, Kenneth, and William A. Oldfather, eds. *Ysopet-Avionnet: The Latin and French Texts.* Urbana: University of Illinois Press, 1919.

Ménard, Philippe. *Les lais de Marie de France.* Paris: Presses Universitaires de France, 1979.

Merceron, Jacques. *Le message et sa fiction: La communication par messager dans la littérature française des XIIe et XIIIe siècles.* Berkeley and Los Angeles: University of California Press, 1998.

Mickel, Emanuel J., Jr. *Marie de France.* New York: Twayne, 1974.

Murphy, James. *Rhetoric in the Middle Ages.* Berkeley and Los Angeles: University of California Press, 1974.

Naïs, Hélène. *Index des Lais de Marie de France.* Cahiers du CRAL, 1ère série, no. 34. Nancy: Centre de Recherches et d'Applications Linguistiques de l'Université de Nancy II, 1979.

Osborne, June. *Stained Glass in England.* London: Frederick Muller, 1981.

Owen, D. D. R. *The Vision of Hell: Infernal Journeys in Medieval French Literature.* Edinburgh: Scottish Academic Press, 1970.

Bibliography

Pächt, Otto. *The Rise of Pictorial Narrative in Twelfth-Century England.* Oxford: Clarendon Press, 1962.

Paris, Gaston. *Histoire poétique de Charlemagne.* Paris: A. Lainé & J. Harvard, 1865. Reprint, Geneva: Slatkine Reprints, 1974.

Payne, Robert. *The Key to Remembrance: A Study of Chaucer's Poetics.* New Haven: Yale University Press, 1963.

Pickens, Rupert T. "Thematic Structure in Marie de France's *Guigemar.*" *Romania* 95, nos. 378–79 (1974): 328–41.

———. "La poétique de Marie de France d'après les prologues des *Lais.*" *Lettres Romanes* 32, no. 4 (1978): 367–84.

———. "Poétique et sexualité chez Marie de France: L'exemple de *Fresne.*" In *Et c'est la fin pour quoy sommes ensemble: Hommage à Jean Dufournet,* ed. J.-C. Aubailly et al., 3 vols., 3:1119–31. Paris: Champion, 1993.

———. "Marie de France and the Body Poetic." In *Gender and Text in the Later Middle Ages,* ed. Jane Chance, 135–71. Gainesville: University Press of Florida, 1996.

———. "Marie de France: Translatrix." *Le Cygne: Journal of the International Marie de France Society,* n.s., 1 (fall 2002): 7–24.

———. "*En bien parler* and *mesparler:* Fecundity and Sterility in the Works of Marie de France." *Le Cygne: Journal of the International Marie de France Society,* n.s., 3 (Fall 2005): 7–20.

Pontfarcy, Yolande de. "La souveraineté: Du mythe au lai de *Guigemar.*" *Acta Litteraria Academiae Scientiarum Hungaricae* 32, nos. 1–2 (1990): 153–59.

Priscian. *Institutiones grammaticae.* In *Grammatici Latini,* 8 vols., ed. Heinrich Keil, 2:1–2. Leipzig, 1855–80.

———. *Praeexercitamina.* In *Grammatici Latini,* 8 vols., ed. Heinrich Keil, 3:436–39. Leipzig, 1855–80.

Quintilian. *The Institutio Oratoria of Quintilian.* Trans. H. E. Butler. 4 vols. Cambridge, Mass.: Harvard University Press, 1920–22.

Richards, Earl Jeffrey. "Les rapports entre le *Lai de Guigemar* and le *Roman d'Eneas:* Considérations génériques." In *Le récit bref au moyen âge: Actes du colloque des 27, 28, et 29 avril 1979,* ed. Danielle Buschinger, 45–56. Paris: Champion, 1980.

Rigolot, François. "*Ekphrasis* and the Fantastic: Genesis of an Aberration." *Comparative Literature* 49, no. 2 (1997): 97–112.

Ringger, Kurt. "Die altfranzösischen Verspurgatorien." *Zeitschrift für romanische Philologie* 88, nos. 4–6 (1972): 389–402.

———. "Prolégomènes à l'iconographie des œuvres de Marie de France." In *Orbis Mediævalis,* ed. Georges Guntert et al., 329–42. Bern: Francke, 1978.

Bibliography

Robertson, D.W., Jr. "Marie de France, *Lais*, Prologue, 13–16." *Modern Language Notes* 64, no. 5 (1949): 336–38.

Le roman d'Eneas. Ed. J.-J. Salverda De Grave. 2 vols. Classiques Français du Moyen Age 44, 62. Paris: Champion, 1925–29.

Rothschild, Judith Rice. *Narrative Technique in the Lais of Marie de France: Themes and Variations.* Vol. 1. Chapel Hill: University of North Carolina, Department of Romance Languages, 1974.

———. "Description and Visualizable Movement in Marie de France's *Lais*." In *L'imaginaire courtois et son double: Actes du VIe Congrès Triennal de la Société Internationale de Littérature Courtoise (ICLS), Fisciano (Salerno), 24–28 juillet 1989,* ed. Giovanna Angeli and Luciano Formisano, 409–19. Naples: Edizione Scientifiche Italiane, 1989.

Runte, Hans R. "'Alfred's Book,' Marie de France, and the Matron of Ephesus." *Romance Philology* 36, no. 4 (1983): 556–71.

———. "Marie de France, traite et retraite." *ALFA: Actes de Langue Française et de Linguistique: Symposium on French Language and Linguistics* 3–4 (1990–91): 229–35.

———. "Marie de France dans ses *Fables*." In *In Search of Marie de France: A Twelfth-Century Poet,* ed. Chantal Maréchal, 28–44. Lewiston, Maine: Edwin Mellen, 1992.

———. "Fable (Isopet)." In *Medieval France: An Encyclopedia,* ed. William W. Kibler and Grover A. Zinn, 331–32. New York: Garland, 1995.

Rychner, Jean. *La chanson de geste: Essai sur l'art épique des jongleurs.* Geneva: Droz, 1955.

Schmolke-Hasselmann, Beate. *Der arthurische Versroman von Chrestien bis Froissart.* Tübingen: Niemeyer, 1980.

Spitzer, Leo. "The Prologue to the *Lais* of Marie de France and Medieval Poetics." *Modern Philology* 41, no. 2 (1943–44): 96–102.

Stefenelli, Arnulf. *Der Synonymenreichtum der altfranzösischen Dichtersprache.* Vienna: Hermann Böhlau, 1967.

Tobin, Prudence Mary O'Hara, ed. *Les lais anonymes des XIIe et XIIIe siècles.* Publications Romanes et Françaises 143. Geneva: Droz, 1976.

Tobler, Adolf, and Erhard Lommatzsch, eds. *Altfranzösisches Wörterbuch.* 11 vols. Wiesbaden: F. Steiner, 1956–1973.

Van Vleck, Amelia. "Textiles as Testimony in Marie de France and *Philomena*." *Medievalia et Humanistica* 22, no. 1 (1995): 31–60.

Vielliard, Françoise. "Sur la tradition manuscrite des *Fables* de Marie de France." *Bibliothèque de l'École des Chartes* 147 (1989): 371–97.

Vitz, Evelyn Birge, Nancy Freeman Regalado, and Marilyn Lawrence, eds. *Performing Medieval Narrative.* Cambridge: D. S. Brewer, 2005.

Ward, Susan L. "Fables for the Court: Illustrations of Marie de France's

Bibliography

Fables in Paris, BN, MS Arsenal 3142." In *Women and the Book: Assessing the Visual Evidence,* ed. Lesley Smith and Jane H. M. Taylor, 190–203. Toronto: University of Toronto Press, 1997.

Warnke, Karl. "Die Quellen des *Esope* der Marie de France." In *Forschungen zur romanischen Philologie: Festgabe für Hermann Suchier,* 161–284. Halle: Niemeyer, 1900.

Whalen, Logan E. "A Medieval Book-Burning: *Objet d'art* as Narrative Device in the *Lai* of *Guigemar.*" *Neophilologus* 80, no. 2 (1996): 205–11.

———. "Marie de France and the Ancients." In *"De sens rassis": Essays in Honor of Rupert T. Pickens,* ed. Keith Busby, Bernard Guidot, and Logan E. Whalen, 719–28. Amsterdam: Rodopi, 2005.

———. "*Ex libris Mariae:* Courtly Book Iconography in the Illuminated Manuscripts of Marie de France." In *Courtly Arts and the Art of Courtliness,* ed. Keith Busby and Christopher Kleinhenz, 745–53. Woodbridge, UK: Boydell & Brewer, 2006.

Yates, Frances A. *The Art of Memory.* Chicago: University of Chicago Press, 1966.

Zanoni, Mary-Louise. "'Ceo Testimoine Precïens': Priscian and the Prologue to the *Lais* of Marie de France." *Traditio: Studies in Ancient and Medieval History, Thought, and Religion* 36 (1980): 407–15.

Zarnecki, George. *English Romanesque Sculpture: 1066–1140.* London: Alec Tiranti, 1951.

Zumthor, Paul. *Essai de poétique médiévale.* Paris: Seuil, 1972.

Index

Acta sanctorum, 138n1
ad Herennium. *See* Rhetoric ad Herennium
adventure (*aventure*), 27, 38, 48, 51, 54–56, 62, 71–72, 83, 87–89, 93, 117, 120, 140, 144–45, 149, 169, 172–73
Aeneid, 3n3, 25, 146. *See also* Virgil
Ætheldrede. *See* Audree
aide-mémoire, 101, 130
Albertus Magnus, 22, 176
Alcuin, 15
Alexander, J. J., 125
Alfred, King, 42, 66, 105, 115n25
Amer, Sahar, 33, 105, 107–8n13, 116–17, 119
amplification (*amplificatio*), 2, 46, 51, 62, 168
anaphora, 24, 74–75
ancients, 10, 15, 21–22, 41, 43–46, 59, 101, 108, 125
antiquity, 1, 3–4, 10, 13–14, 20–21, 38, 40, 63, 125, 146, 175
Aquinas, Saint Thomas, 22
Aristotle, 7, 22, 64. *See also* De anima; De memoria
arrangement. *See* dispositio
Ars amatoria, 98n68. *See also* Ovid
ars dicaminis. *See* Seneca
ars memorativa, 4–5, 7, 22–23, 87, 134, 176
ars poetica, 10, 49; of Horace, 14. *See also* arts of poetry and prose
Ars versificatoria. See Matthew of Vendôme
Arthur, King, 149

arts, liberal, 1, 3n3, 9, 13, 21n31. *See also* Quadrivium; Trivium
arts of poetry and prose, 1–2, 6, 9–10, 13, 16, 18, 38, 47, 49, 63, 93, 139, 142, 149, 163, 165, 168, 173, 175–76
auctoritas, 44n14, 60, 101, 164
audience, 2–4, 13, 18, 23, 28, 36–39, 50–51, 54, 56, 59–60, 62, 65, 72–78, 80–81, 86–87, 92–93, 96–99, 101–3, 112, 121, 124, 126–27, 132, 134, 137, 143–47, 149, 151–52, 154, 158–59, 165, 168–73, 175–77, 179; courtly, 2, 7, 26, 176; lay, 139, 143, 144–46, 152, 156, 158, 169, 173
auditor, 24, 97
Audree, Seinte, 138n1, 162, 165–66, 168–72
author, 1–3, 6–7, 9–13, 15–17, 23–25, 29, 32, 37–39, 42–45, 52, 63–64, 81, 98, 101, 103, 105–8, 122–23, 130–34, 137, 139, 145–46, 149, 158–61, 163, 165, 168–73, 175–76, 179
authorities, 1, 4, 42, 50, 52n37, 101, 108, 175
authorship, 27n42, 30, 130n46, 159–61
Avalon, 92

background (rhetoric), 12, 73
Barbarismus. See Donatus
Baum, Richard, 36n2, 160–61
Bayeux Tapestry, 68–69
Beatrice, 178
Bédier, Joseph, 20
Beer, Jeanette M. A., 144n14
bees, 40
Benedeit. *See* Benoît de Saint-Maure

Index

Benoît de Sainte-Maure, 9, 146
Bernard of Clairvaux, 144
Béroul, 40
Bertrand de Born, 179
Bestiaires d'amours, 7, 48. See also Richard de Fournival
bestiary, 5, 7, 22, 32, 48, 113, 121–22, 126, 143, 158. See also Philippe de Thaon
Bibliotheca Apostolica Vaticana (Vatican City): Ottob. Lat. 3064, 127, 129, 133, 184–85
Bibliothèque de l'Arsenal (Paris): Arsenal 3142, 104, 122n36, 130, 132, 163n45, 184–85
Bibliothèque Nationale de France (Paris): BNF, fr. 1446, 122n36, 131, 163n45, 184–85; BNF, fr. 1593, 104, 184–85; BNF, fr. 1594, 132–33; BNF, fr. 1822, 126, 184–85; BNF, fr. 2168, 104, 120n34, 127, 131, 184–85; BNF, fr. 2173, 32n50, 122n36–23n37, 129, 131–32, 163n45, 184–85; BNF, fr. 4939, 109, 127, 184–85; BNF, fr. 12603, 126, 184–85; BNF, fr. 19152, 111n19, 184–85; BNF, fr. 24310, 109, 184–85; BNF, fr. 24428, 127–29, 184–85; BNF, fr. 25407, 139
birds, 27, 87–90; hawk, 87, 101; nightingale, 85n53, 87–90, 170; swan, 82, 87
Blanton, Virginia, 162, 172
Blanton-Whetsell, Virginia. See Blanton, Virginia
Bloch, R. Howard, 106, 160
Bodleian Library (Oxford): Douce 132, 126–27, 184–85
Bodmer Library (Switzerland): Cologny, Bodmer 113, 32n50, 123n37, 184–85
Boldrick, Stacy, 69
book (as memory), 5, 29, 30, 40–41, 53, 58–59, 66, 96–99, 101, 109, 113–14, 122n36, 131–34, 143, 147, 162, 167, 178

Book of Hours, 66
Bradwardine, Thomas, 22, 176
Bretons, 16, 42, 55, 57, 72
British Library (London): BL, Add. 70513, 161, 163; BL, Cotton, Domitian A xv, 138n1; BL, Cotton Nero A. v., 113; BL, Harley 978, 35, 54, 61, 81, 104, 109n14, 111n19, 120n34, 123n37, 184–85; BL, Harley 3846, 142
Brittany, 62
Brucker, Charles, 106–7, 109–11, 114, 116
Bruckner, Matilda Tomaryn, 63n8
Burgess, Glyn S., 18n21, 52n36, 55n45, 67n18, 73n29, 75n32, 160n33
Busby, Keith, 52n36, 55n45, 67n18, 73n29, 77, 80–82, 95n66, 122n36

Calkins, Robert, 64–66
Calogrenant, 149
cantilènes, 20
captatio benevolentiae, 17, 36, 55, 60, 164, 175
caritas, 175
Carruthers, Mary, 5–7, 15, 20, 22–23, 26, 33, 40, 113, 177
Carthage, 25
cathedrals, 68, 162, 176; Angoulême, 70; Canterbury, 70; Chartres, 70; Ely, 162; York, 70
causa scribendi, 36, 44n14, 57, 60, 166
chanson de geste, 20–21, 145n16
Chanson de Roland, 70
Char, René, 121
Charlemagne Window (Chartres), 70
chasse, 90
chastity, 172. See also virginity
Chaucer, Geoffrey, 118n31, 124, 147, 177, 179
Chrétien de Troyes, 2–3, 6, 9, 15, 17, 25, 40, 63–64, 89n55, 91, 94n64, 144–45n16, 149, 160, 179. See also individual works by title

Index

Cicero, 1, 5, 10, 11–12, 13n10, 15, 21–22, 47–48, 175. *See also De inventione*
Clemence of Barking, 167
cleric, 20
Cligès, 25
Codex Avianus, 131
collatio, 3
colligo, 47–48n26
color, 66–67, 126–29
commentaries, 13, 22, 57, 59, 68
composition, 11, 15–16, 29, 35, 47, 62, 63n8, 120n34, 122–23, 139n3; Latin, 29; literary, 1, 9, 14, 16–17, 21, 32, 36, 40, 42, 49, 52n37, 148–49, 167, 173, 175, 179; meditational, 3
conception, 7, 15–16, 24, 38, 137, 141, 148–49, 173
conjointure, 2, 63
conte, 149; *d'aventure*, 144–45, 169
crozier, 162
Curley, Michael, 141, 144–45, 161, 169
curriculum, 40, 42
Cuthbert, Saint, 170–71

Dante, 5, 147, 178–79. *See also Divina Commedia*; *Vita nuova*
De anima, 22. *See also* Aristotle
De descriptione, 47, 182. *See also* Priscian
De inventione, 10, 11, 13, 47. *See also* Cicero
De laude, 49, 182. *See also* Priscian
delivery (rhetoric). *See pronuntiatio*
De memoria, 7, 22. *See also* Aristotle
deposition, 65
De purgatorio Sancti Patricii, 29, 53, 138, 140–42, 144, 146, 152, 159, 168. *See also* H. of Saltrey
descriptio, 24, 28, 30, 47, 51, 76, 97, 106, 122, 145, 165, 168, 175; art of, 3, 7, 18, 100. *See also* description
description, 3–5, 18, 24–29, 42, 46–49, 51–52, 70n26, 76–77, 81–83, 87, 89–95, 99, 101, 106, 130, 137, 146, 152–56, 158, 170–73, 177, 179; architecture of, 122; art of, 24, 52n37, 60, 134; detailed, 25, 28, 39, 49, 62, 91, 93–94, 106–7, 110–13, 115, 120–22, 137, 158, 178; developed, 26, 29; elaborate, 92; of events, 3, 7, 23–26, 28, 64, 77, 101, 137, 156, 158, 171, 177; literary, 93n61; marvelous, 4, 154; narrative, 25, 33, 39, 61, 63, 121, 176–78; of objects, 3–4, 7, 13, 19, 24–28, 49, 64, 76–77, 81, 90, 93–94, 100, 103, 106, 110, 115, 137, 153, 158, 170–71; of people, 3, 7, 24, 26, 28, 64, 77, 91, 94, 137, 152, 156, 171; of places, 3, 7, 22, 24, 26, 28, 64, 77, 137, 171; strategic, 4, 106; textual, 62, 177; visual, 4, 176; vivid, 3, 7, 48, 76–77, 91, 94, 175, 179. *See also descriptio*
De secunda translatione, 138. *See also Vie seinte Audree*
Deuteronomy, 19
Dewilde, Peter, 140
Dialogues. *See* Gregory the Great
discourse, 13, 27, 35, 39, 50n32, 83, 86, 90, 99–100, 106, 110, 132, 145, 165, 169, 173
dispositio, 10–11
Divina Commedia, 5, 178; *Inferno*, 178–79; *Purgatorio*, 179n6
diz, 58, 125, 134
Donatus, 14
Donner à voir. *See* Eluard, Paul
Donovan, Mortimer, 45–46
Durham, 170

edification, 59, 125–26, 143, 147
education, 20, 113
Egfrid, King, 172
Ekphrasis, 93
Eleanor of Aquitaine, 1
Eliot, T. S., 81. *See also* objective correlative
elocutio, 10–11, 183. *See also* style
Eluard, Paul, 122
elucidation, 24, 36
embellishment, 25, 112, 152

201

Index

energeia, 94
England, 1, 49–50, 62, 64–66, 68–70, 105, 138, 144, 160, 176
epilogue, 6, 23, 36n2, 51, 53, 59, 61, 165–67, 173; to the *Audree*, 28, 53–54, 161, 165–66; to *Eliduc*, 167; to the *Espurgatoire*, 28, 31, 53, 141, 146–47, 158, 161, 165, 169; to the *Fables*, 28–29, 53, 57–58, 105, 123–24, 131–32, 161, 165, 184–85
Erec et Enide, 2, 25; Erec's coronation robe, 3, 25
eros, 171
escïence, 17–18, 37–38, 166. See also knowledge
Espurgatoire seint Patriz (the *Espurgatoire*), 27–32, 53, 55, 57, 137–39, 143–46, 149, 152, 155, 158, 159, 161, 163–65, 167–69, 171–73, 177, 179
essample, 108, 121, 125, 127–28, 131, 134, 151
estoire, 6, 48, 142, 148–49, 164–65, 168–69. See also *historia*
Etheldreda (Ethelthryth), Saint. See Audree
exemplar, 138n1, 141–42, 149, 155
exornationes, 11, 16

fable, 3, 25, 28–29, 32, 58–59, 66, 68, 103–12, 114–35, 138, 143, 151, 175, 184–85; Aesopic, 28, 57–58, 103, 105, 131, 134; Phadrean, 103. See also *Romulus Nilantii*; and individual fables by title
fables, Latin: *De agno et lupo*, 111; *De contentione habita inter hominem et leonem*, 115; *De Gallinacio, qui . . . invenit margaritam*, 109; *De mure, qui . . . a rana petivit auxilium*, 112; *De mure rurali*, 114
Fables, of Marie de France, 7, 27–29, 32, 36n2, 42, 53, 55, 57, 59, 103–4, 106–8, 112, 114, 122–24, 129, 137–39, 142, 146, 161, 163, 179, 184–85; *De l'arunde e del lin*, 115; *De la femme ki fist pendre sun mari*, 115; *De la suriz de vile e de la suriz de boiz*, 114; *De la suriz e de la reine*, 111; *Del l'asne ki volt jüer a sun seignur*, 111; *Del chien e de la brebiz*, 111; *Del cok e de la gemme*, 109, 126; *Del corbel e del gupil*, 111, 115; *Del fevre e de la cuinee*, 103–04; *Del lëun e del vilein*, 115, 129, 151; *Del lu e de l'aignel*, 104n6, 110; *Del sengler e de l'asne*, 127; *Del teissun e des pors*, 127. See also Isopet
fabliau, 103, 115n25, 126
fairy mistress, 91
Faral, Edmond, 10n3, 49
figura, 16–17, 26, 149. See also *exortationes*; figure
figure (rhetoric), 11–12, 16, 26, 40. See also *exortationes*; *figura*
fin'amors, 98, 101
flower, 17, 39–41, 57
formulae (rhetoric), 20–21
Foulet, Lucien, 76
France, 6, 9, 20, 49–50, 53, 69, 124, 159–60, 177
Francesca (and Paolo), 179
frescoes, 69, 176
Fresne, 86–87

genre, 2–3, 20, 25, 32, 36n2, 61–63, 76, 103–4, 106–8n13, 121, 125, 140, 154, 176
Geoffrey of Monmouth, 31
Geoffrey of Vinsauf, 47
geography, 24, 30, 62, 72–73, 93, 96
gloss, 41, 43
glossator, 10, 45n17
Graelent, 76–77
grammar, 1, 3n3, 9–10, 13–16, 32, 39, 42, 46, 49–50, 60, 63, 175
grammarian, 10, 15, 42–43, 46, 48
grammatica, 13–14, 181–82
Gratian, 144
Gregory the Great, Pope, 146

Index

Guigemar, 4, 75, 92, 96, 99–100
Guillaume de Lorris, 177–79

H. of Saltrey, 29, 53, 66, 138–40, 142–46, 148, 152, 158, 168, 179. *See also De purgatorio Sancti Patricii*
hagiography, 9, 28, 31, 54, 139, 140, 143, 149, 167–68, 175
hazel branch, 7, 27, 78–81
Henry Plantagenet (Henri II, king), 1, 66, 160
Hermogenes of Tarsus, 46, 50
historia, 148, 168. *See also estoire*
historiography, 9
Holy Writ, 23
Homer, 140
honeysuckle, 79–81
Horace, 14. *See also ars poetica*
House of Fame. See Chaucer, Geoffrey
Huchet, Jean-Charles, 161
Hugh of St. Victor, 144
Hunt, Tony, 42n10, 45

iconography, 65, 66n13, 69, 70–71, 87, 122–23, 132, 162
illumination, 7, 64–65, 67, 71, 122n36, 129–34, 162–63, 176, 184–85
illuminator, 7, 26, 29, 32n50, 123, 125, 129–30, 132, 134–35, 163
image, 3–4, 7, 12–13, 16, 18, 22–23, 26, 47, 62, 64–65, 66, 68, 71–72, 79–81, 91–92, 95n66, 99–101, 106, 110, 116–17, 119, 121–23, 128–31, 133–35, 144, 152, 158, 162–63, 176–79, 184–85; mental, 7, 106, 113; visual, 6–7, 23, 26, 63–64, 68–69, 177
imagination, 2–4, 7, 16, 18, 38, 47, 73, 109, 115, 117, 137–38, 153, 158, 177
imagines rerum, 113
Inferno. See Divina Commedia
ingenium, 2, 16–17, 25, 38, 124, 175
initials, 125–29, 162; flourished, 126, 128; historiated, 126, 131–32
Institutio oratoria. See Quintilian

Institutiones grammaticae, 14, 42–43, 46–47, 50, 181. *See also* Priscian
instruction, 2, 9–10, 14–15, 42, 47, 49, 113, 123, 133, 163, 175–76. *See also* training
inventio, 2, 7, 10–11, 15–16, 18, 22n35, 25, 28, 37–40, 54, 56, 59–61, 63, 123, 141–42, 148–49, 163, 165, 168, 173, 175. *See also* invention
invention, 11–12, 15–16, 23–24, 46; medieval literary topical, 10, 15–16, 18, 23–24, 28, 32–33, 36, 38, 47, 50–51, 53, 60n48, 137, 148, 175. *See also inventio*
Ireland, 62, 139
Irvine, Martine, 13
Iseut, 7, 56, 78, 80–82
Isopet, 27, 32, 68n21, 103, 109, 115n17, 122, 132, 143, 160, 163n45, 165, 173, 184–85. *See also* fable; *Fables*, of Marie de France
Isopet-Avionnet, 132

Jambeck, Karen, 33, 184–85
Jenkins, Thomas A., 141
John of Garland, 22
Joie de la Cort, 145n16
jongleur, 21, 75
journey, purgatorial, 137, 139–40, 146, 149–52, 153, 157–58, 178. *See also* voyage

Kalilah wa Dimnah, 105n8
Kelly, Douglas, 6, 9, 15–16, 24, 33, 38, 45–46, 48, 50, 52, 80, 149
Kibler, William W., 21
Knapton, Antoinette, 66–67
Knight's Tale. See Chaucer, Geoffrey
knowledge, 1, 5–6, 13, 17–20, 36–37, 43, 46, 48, 50, 63n8, 68, 80, 95, 98, 124, 142, 147n24, 166, 168, 175. *See also escience*

La Fontaine, 105
lai, 2–3, 6, 25, 28, 35–36n2, 44, 51–52,

Index

lai, (cont.)
  54–57, 59, 61–63, 71–77, 81–84, 86–87, 91–97, 99, 101, 106, 123n37, 154, 175; *anonyme*, 32, 63, 76–77, 176; Arthurian, 62; Breton, 38, 176
Lais, of Marie de France, 5, 16–18, 27–29, 35, 42, 44–45, 48, 53–54, 56–58, 61, 63–64, 66, 68, 71, 76–77, 81, 84, 87, 90–93, 104, 106, 108, 112, 114, 122, 137–39, 142–43, 145–46, 153–54, 158, 160–61, 165–67, 173, 179; *Bisclavret*, 55–57, 101; *Chaitivel*, 56, 77; *Chievrefoil*, 27–28, 56, 62, 77–78, 81; *Deus Amanz*, 24, 71, 74n31; *Eliduc*, 28, 56, 62, 101, 145n16, 167; *Equitan*, 55, 101; *Fresne*, 27, 84, 86–87; *Guigemar*, 2, 4, 13, 22n35, 27–28, 35–36, 53–54, 61, 63n8, 69, 77, 92–93, 96, 98–101, 115, 121, 154, 157, 167, 177, 179n6; *Lanval*, 24, 74–75, 91–92; *Laüstic*, 27, 87–89, 170–71; *Milun*, 82–85, 87; *Yonec*, 67, 84–85, 87, 101
laisses similaires, 20–21
langue d'oïl, 1
Lanval, 24, 74–75, 77, 91–92, 145n16
Legend of Good Women, The. See Chaucer, Geoffrey
lessons, 7, 13, 23, 101, 124, 127–28, 135; moral, 19, 23, 25, 29–30, 103, 106, 113, 124, 130. *See also* moral; *moralité*
letters, 78, 127. *See also* initials
letters (correspondence), 40, 82–83, 84
listener, 24, 45, 106, 137, 169
literature, 7; courtly, 154, 173; French, 1, 38n6, 141n10, 146n23; medieval, 179; secular, 172; vernacular, 1, 4, 6, 9–10, 13–14, 21, 24, 33, 38–39, 48–49, 54, 107, 109, 139, 143, 145, 147–48, 153–54, 156, 164, 168–69, 171–73, 179
locus (loci), 4, 28, 40, 96; *molestus*, 100
Lombard, Peter, 144

Lommatzsch, Erhard, 30–31, 98, 120n34, 158
Lough Derg, 139
Louis VII (king), 1

Macrobius, 3n3
maniple, 170
manuscript, 1, 5, 7, 14, 22, 26, 28–29, 32, 35, 42n10, 46, 48, 53n39, 61, 66–67, 69, 71, 81, 87, 95n66, 103–4, 108–9, 111n19, 113, 115n27, 120n34, 122–23, 125–35, 138–42, 149, 159, 161–63, 165n48, 176, 184–85; illuminated, 65n10–67, 69, 128–29. *See also specific manuscripts by repository and title*
Maréchal, Chantal, 125–26, 131
markers, 12; mnemonic, 29; moral, 128–29, 184–85
marvel (marvelous), 153–54. *See also merveille*
matere (matire), 157, 164–65, 168–69. *See also materia; material; matière*
materia, 10n4, 15–16, 23–24, 26, 148–49, 175. *See also matere; material; matière*
material, 2–3, 5, 7, 11–12, 15, 17–18, 21, 23, 36n2, 38, 40–42, 47–48, 51–52, 63, 90, 109, 123–24, 137–38, 141, 143, 147–49, 157, 164, 167–68, 173, 175–76, 179. *See also matere; materia; matière*
matière, 50, 149; *de Bretagne*, 1; *de France*, 1; *de Rome*, 1. *See also matere; materia; material*
Matthew of Vendôme, 47, 49
McCash, June Hall, 33, 182, 159–61, 163, 167–68
McClelland, Denise, 54
meditation, monastic, 3, 21
membrer, 31, 76n37, 165. *See also remembrer*
memoire, 6, 30–31, 51, 53, 54, 59, 63, 82, 101, 143, 145–46, 148, 150, 164–65, 168–70. *See also artes memorativa; memoria*; memory

Index

memoria, 5, 7, 10–12, 13n11, 15, 18, 20, 28, 148, 164–65, 167, 175. *See also artes memorativa*; *memoire*; memory

memory, 2, 4–7, 10–13, 16, 18–19, 21–26, 28–31, 33, 37–42, 44, 47–48, 51–57, 59–65, 70–71, 73, 76, 82, 84, 86–87, 90–93, 101, 106, 108, 110, 113, 116, 118, 122–24, 130–32, 134, 137, 143, 145–52, 158–60, 163–71, 173, 175–79; architecture of, 4, 22–23, 25, 30, 61, 175; art of, 4–5, 22–23, 29, 32, 152, 176; artificial, 12, 22, 38; faculty of, 4, 20, 22, 30, 40, 59, 78, 81, 101, 134, 147, 158, 165, 167, 175, 177–79; *loci* of, 4, 40; natural, 12, 38; poetics of, 6–7, 101, 137, 159, 163, 173, 179; storehouse of, 2, 15, 18–19, 23, 31, 87, 117, 134–35, 158; treatises on, 5–6. *See also artes memorativa*; *memoire*; *memoria*

merveille (*merveilleux*), 13, 62, 72, 137, 152–58, 170–73. *See also* marvel; *mirabilis*

Metamorphoses, 146. *See also* Ovid

metaphor, 5, 39–40, 74, 80, 99, 178

mezuzah, 19

Mickel, Emanuel J., Jr., 140, 142, 145, 161

Middle Ages, 2–3, 5, 10, 13–15, 19, 21–24, 29n44, 32, 39–40, 42, 46, 64–66, 113, 140–41, 144, 146, 149, 159, 175, 178

Milun, 82, 84–85n53

mind (related to memory), 4, 6–7, 12, 17, 23, 26, 38, 47, 50, 73–74, 76–77, 80–81, 90–91, 93, 97, 107, 113, 121–22, 124, 147, 157, 176–77; mind's eye, 23, 29, 38–39, 48, 71, 81, 106, 118, 130, 147, 175

miniatures, 29, 64–65, 129–33, 162, 184–85

mirabilis, 154, 158. *See also* marvel; *merveille*

Miracula, 138. *See also Vie seinte Audree*

mise-en-abyme, 96–97, 117, 130. *See also* specularity

mise-en-page, 29, 123, 126, 135

mnemonic: architectural, 4, 22, 26, 60, 63, 106, 122, 176; Ciceronian, 22

model, 16, 19, 24, 156, 168, 172

monastery, 139–41

moral, 59, 107, 120–22, 124–30, 134, 151, 184–85. *See also* lessons; *moralité*

moralité, 29, 58, 107, 124–28, 130. *See also* lessons; moral

mouvance, 44

Muldumarec, 145n16

Murphy, James, 11, 14, 32

narrative, 3–7, 13–14, 18, 20, 23, 25–30, 36, 39, 49–51, 57, 60–61, 63–66, 68n21, 70–71, 73, 77n41, 82, 86, 91, 93, 95n66–97, 99, 105–6, 111–12, 119, 122, 130, 134, 137, 139–40, 145, 151, 156, 158–59, 163, 165, 168, 171–73, 175–76, 179; pictorial, 64–66, 68–69

narrator, 7, 96, 177–78

Nottingham University Library: Mi Lm 6, 32n50, 104, 123n37, 184–85

object, 3–4, 7, 12–13, 19, 24–26, 28, 49, 64, 67, 76–78, 80–84, 86–88, 90–91, 93–94, 100, 103, 106, 110, 115, 130–31, 133, 137, 153, 158, 170–71; nonverbal, 27, 77, 84, 86, 93–94; quasi-verbal, 27, 76–77, 93–94; verbal, 27, 77, 81–82, 86, 88, 90, 93

objective correlative, 81, 106

objet d'art, 96–97, 99–101

ogam alphabet, 80

orality, 10, 19–21, 39, 63, 73, 76, 85n53, 89–90, 101, 130–31, 138, 176

ordo, 11n5, 148–49, 168, 175. *See also ordre*

ordre, 148–49. *See also ordo*

ornatus, 16

Other World, 91, 140

Index

Ovid, 27, 66, 89, 94n64, 96–99, 101, 146. *See also individual works by title*
Owein, 140, 144–45, 149–53, 155, 157–58, 169
Owen, D. D. R., 144n15, 147n24

Pächt, Otto, 65, 71
pain, 30, 146, 155
painter, 7
painting, 5, 7, 22, 28, 63, 66, 69, 94, 96–97, 99–101, 114–15, 117–18, 120–21, 130, 151; wall, 4, 27, 69, 71, 94, 96–97, 99–100, 117, 154, 177–79
painture, 177–78
Paolo (and Francesca), 179
parable, 37; of the talents, 36
paradigm, 37, 44, 51, 59n48, 106, 148–49, 163; grammatical and rhetorical, 10, 15
paradise, 140, 146, 153, 157, 179n7
Paris, Gaston, 20
parole, 48, 56–57, 76n36, 82, 177
Patrick, Saint, 30, 139–40, 158. *See also* Purgatory
patronage, 1, 58, 133–34, 138n1, 161–62
pavilion, 91–92
Payne, Robert, 124
peine, 30, 57, 146–47. *See also* pain
Pentateuch, 19
Perceval, 25; *See also* Chrétien de Troyes
performance, 19, 123, 135
Petit livre de moralité en prose, Le, 126
phylacteries. *See tefillin*
Philippe de Thaon, 113, 158. *See also* bestiary
Philomela, 89
Pickens, Rupert T., 26, 33, 36, 44, 77, 89, 159
picture, 3, 26, 65, 67, 111, 113, 121, 158, 177; mental, 114, 121
pieds de mouche, 127
poetics, 6–7, 9–10, 16, 18, 24, 26, 33, 37, 44, 46, 57, 100–101, 137, 158–59, 163, 173, 179
Poetria nova. *See* Geoffrey of Vinsauf

poetry, 4, 21, 30, 39–40, 46n21, 95n66, 121–22. *See also* arts of poetry and prose
Pontfarcy, Yolande de, 53n39, 138n1, 140–41
portrait, 12, 162–63; of author, 122n36, 130–31, 163
posterity, 23, 29–31, 47, 52–53, 55, 124, 168, 175
Praeexercitamina, 46–50, 181–83. *See also* Priscian
preservation, 13, 51, 55, 106, 175–76
Priscian, 1, 14, 41–52, 60, 66, 175, 181–83. *See also Institutiones grammaticae*; *Praeexercitamina*
Progymnasmata. *See* Hermogenes of Tarsus
prologue, 6, 23, 28, 53, 59, 61, 138, 147, 165; to the *Audree*, 53, 165; to *Equitan*, 55; to the *Espurgatoire*, 30, 53, 141, 145–48, 158, 165; to the *Fables*, 29, 53, 57–58, 105, 108, 123–26, 131, 134, 165 184–85; General Prologue to the *Lais*, 14, 17–18, 35–39, 41, 43–44, 48, 50–54, 57, 59, 61, 108, 142, 166–67; to *Guigemar*, 35–36n2, 53–55, 61, 167
pronuntiatio, 10–11
proverb, 58–59, 125, 131
Psalter, 64, 66; St. Albans, 65–66
Purgatorio (Dante). *See Divina Commedia*
Purgatory, 30, 53, 139–40, 143–45, 150–53, 157–58, 179n6; Saint Patrick's, 29, 139–40, 158. *See also Espurgatoire seint Patriz*; *De purgatorio Sancti Patricii*

Quadrivium, 3n3. *See also* liberal arts
qualitas, 16, 183
Quintilian, 14n13

reader, 3, 24, 29, 37n4, 40, 43, 65n10, 92, 94, 96–97, 106–7, 113, 118n31, 123, 125–28, 130, 132, 134, 137, 161, 169, 177

Index

recall, 4, 12, 23, 30–31, 38, 74, 76, 124, 135, 147, 175
recollection, 25–26, 29–31, 75
record, 30, 38–39, 53, 58, 124, 143, 164
recorder, 31, 54, 76n37, 164–64, 169
recordor, 31n48, 54n40
Remedia amoris, 98–99. *See also* Ovid
remembering, 6, 28, 61, 76, 83–84, 124, 146–47, 152, 158, 169–70, 173, 175, 179
remembrance, 6, 30–31, 36, 44, 51–56, 59, 63, 76n37, 82, 106, 113, 123–24, 145–46, 148, 164–65, 170, 177–78
remembrer, 31, 44, 52, 54, 56, 58–59, 76n37, 82, 123–24, 134, 164–65, 169. *See also membrer*
repetition, 23, 36n2, 71, 74, 86, 158
representation, 4, 64–65, 69, 71, 93, 98n68, 118, 129, 131, 133, 177, 179; authorial, 132; descriptive 64; iconographical, 115n27; literary, 146; pictorial, 66n13; secular, 70; symbolic, 84; visual, 26, 65, 69
reproduction, 29, 70n25, 122n36, 162n44
retention, 24, 30, 77, 90, 134
rhetoric, 1–3, 5–6, 9–18, 21–24, 28, 32, 36–37, 40–42, 46, 49–50, 60, 63, 106, 142, 148–49, 163–66, 168, 170, 175–76
Rhetorica ad Herennium, 1, 11–12, 13, 15–16, 22, 38, 47, 175
rhetorician, 10, 15, 42, 46
Richard de Fournival, 7, 48, 177, 179. *See also Bestiaires d'amours*
Rigolot, François, 94
ring, 27, 67n18, 82–87
Robertson, D. W., 45
Roman de Brut, 31
Roman d'Eneas, 25, 63n8–64
Roman de la Rose, 178
Roman de Thèbes, 64, 91n57
Roman de Troie, 31
romance, 2, 6, 9–10, 25, 40, 48, 62–63, 126, 145n16, 154, 168; *romans d'antiquité*, 3, 25, 126. *See also* individual romances by title
Romulus, 103, 108
Romulus Nilantii, 105, 107, 109–11, 114–15, 117–19, 138, 143
rubric, 5, 31, 128, 131
rubricator, 128
Rychner, Jean, 21, 99

St. Mary's, Holmecultram, 114
samite, 27, 89, 170
san, 51. *See also sen*
Schmolke-Hasselmann, Beate, 62
scribe, 7, 26, 29, 111n19, 123, 125, 127–29, 132–33, 134–35, 163
sculpture, 69–70
sen, 149. *See also san*
Seneca, 40
Serments de Strasbourg, 1
Sermon de la croix en vers, 126
Sermones de voragine en prose, 126
ship, 4, 27, 92, 94, 154
Södergård, Östen, 161
source, 2, 3n3, 6, 9, 23, 29, 38, 40, 42, 48, 50n32, 52, 56, 63–64, 66, 68n21, 73, 91n57, 103n1, 105, 107–8, 109, 111, 113–15, 117, 137–39, 141–42, 144–45, 148, 156, 164, 168, 172, 175–76; Breton, 63; Eastern (Arabic), 107n12; Latin, 20, 53n39, 110, 112, 116–18, 148n25, 151, 169; oral, 138; written, 5, 131–34
souvenir (sovenir), 31, 54, 76n37, 165–66
specularity, 96n67, 117, 130. *See also mise-en-abyme*
speech, 11, 14, 39, 47–48
Spiegel, Harriet, 33, 104n3, 109n16, 121n34, 137
Spitzer, Leo, 45
stained glass, 70, 176
Stefenelli, Arnulf, 31, 146n20
stole, 170
storehouse (memory), 2, 12, 15, 18–19, 23, 31, 37, 87, 117, 123, 132, 134–35, 158, 179

Index

style, 10, 15, 18, 49–50, 61, 100, 110, 112, 115. *See also* elocutio
suffering, 146, 150, 152, 155. *See also* pain
synecdoche, 77, 80
synonyms, 30–31

tales, 2, 7, 18, 29, 57, 62, 72–74, 76, 87, 90, 104, 114–15, 122, 134, 140–42, 144–45, 148; Breton, 101; hagiographic, 175
tally stick, 80
tefillin, 19
textiles, 27, 68–69, 71, 89n55
Thomas d'Angleterre, 40
titles (in manuscripts), 104n, 109n17, 115, 128–29
Tobin, Prudence Mary O'Hara, 62, 76
Tobler, Adolf, 30–31, 98, 120n34, 158
topos (*topoi*), 41, 44n14, 50, 101, 105
torment, 139, 147n24, 149, 151–52, 155–58. *See also* pain; suffering
tradition, 9, 14, 19, 64–66n13, 103, 122, 175: Aesopic, 28, 57; Arab, 105n8; classical, 9, 14; iconographic, 131; Latin, 107; manuscript, 28n43–29, 32, 115n27, 122, 126, 142n11; oral, 10, 20, 176; Phaedrean, 103, 134; Purgatory, 140; Roman, 2; scholastic, 9; textual, 2; of *translatio studii*, 37, 142; written, 13, 122
training, 9–10, 12, 16, 18, 21n31, 23, 38, 42, 47, 50, 52n37, 63, 113, 139, 145, 168, 173, 175–76. *See also* instruction
translatio: *imperii*, 168; *memoriae*, 159; *studii*, 1, 25, 36–37, 44n14, 50, 55, 60, 85n53, 108n13, 116, 139, 142, 168, 173, 175–76
translation, 29, 31, 53, 107, 134, 138–39, 141–42, 148: of body, 162; Latin, 7, 22, 46, 50
transmission, 10, 20–21, 42, 44n14, 51, 86–87, 100, 106, 179; of knowledge, 19, 36–37

Tristan, 7, 27, 56, 77–82
Trivium, 3n3, 13–14. *See also* liberal arts
trope, 11n7, 16, 24, 40
trover, 58, 60n48, 123

ut pictura poesis, 97

Venus, 27, 69, 96–100, 115, 154, 177
vernacular, 1, 9, 33, 39n7, 54, 107, 109, 143, 154, 164, 169, 173
Vie d'Edouard le Confesseur, 168
Vie seinte Audree (the *Audree*), 27–28, 31–33, 53–55, 137–39, 159–61, 163–71, 173, 177, 179
Vie de seinte Catherine d'Alexandrie. *See* Clemence of Barking
Virgil, 3n4, 25, 140, 146, 182. *See also* Aeneid
virginity, 171–72. *See also* chastity
Vision of Saint Paul, 146
Vita nuova, 5, 147, 178
Vita sancte Ætheldrede, 138. *See also* Vie seinte Audree
vocabulary, 6, 28, 32, 53, 64, 71, 75–76, 137, 142, 148, 153, 169–70, 172–73
voyage, purgatorial, 146. *See also* journey
Voyage of Saint Brendan. *See* Benoît de Saint Maure

Wace, 9, 31
Warnke, Karl, 24, 42, 141
William, Count, 58
Wolfram von Eschenbach, 144
writing, 11, 14–15, 22n33, 26, 30, 39–40, 44, 50–51, 57, 59, 64, 81, 82, 90, 93, 98, 124, 131–32, 146, 176; monastic, 3, 145

Yates, Francis, 21n32–22, 33
Yvain, 25, 149

Zanoni, Mary-Louise, 43–44, 46–47, 50n32

208